INFINITY IN YOUR HAND

A guide for the spiritually curious

William H. Houff

Second Edition
Skinner House Books
Boston

Copyright © 1990, 1994 William H. Houff.
Cover art copyright © 1989 Don Greene.
Book design by Sheryl Stewart.
Typesetting by Spokane Imagesetting, Spokane, Washington.

Published by Skinner House Books, an imprint of the Unitarian Universalist Association, 25 Beacon Street, Boston, MA 02108-2800.
First edition published in 1989 by Melior Publications.

Skinner House edition 1-55896-311-1
Printed in the U.S.A.

10 9 8 7 6 5
99 98 97 96 95

Houff, William H., 1928-
     Infinity in your hand.
Bibliography: p.
     1. Spiritual life. 2. Houff, William H., 1928-
I. title.
BL624.H69   1988   248.4   88-13701

INFINITY IN YOUR HAND

To Peggy —
Try to remember!
who you really are!
Fond regards,
Bill Houff

To see a world in a grain of sand
And a Heaven in a wild flower,
Hold Infinity in the palm of your hand
And Eternity in an hour.

—William Blake (1757–1827)

Table of Contents

Acknowledgements

Upon finishing *The Adventures of Huckleberry Finn*, Mark Twain's young narrator said, ". . . and so there ain't nothing more to write about, and I am rotten glad of it, because if I'd knowed what a trouble it is to make a book I wouldn't a tackled it and I ain't agoing to no more."

Initially, I assumed that Twain was indulging in his usual grumpy hyperbole. For me, the composition of the manuscript for this book was one of the more satisfying things I've ever done. Again and again, I got so charged up that I kept right on working after going to bed. It played hell with my sleep for weeks.

And, when I did sleep, I had that exhilarating experience of waking up in the morning awash with ideas I didn't know were in me. (Perhaps they weren't!) Thus, it's something of a mistake to say I've written a book; the book actually wrote me.

But, as both my publisher and lawyer warned when I appeared before them with manuscript in hand, there's a considerable difference between a writer and an author. I've been a writer for years. In the form of sermons and similar works, I've turned out the equivalent of fifty or sixty books. But a writer doesn't become an author until he/she has gone through all of the essential tedium of researching references, securing permissions to quote copyrighted material, revising and proofreading, proofreading, proofreading. That's when I began taking Mark Twain seriously!

Now that it's nearly over, however, my equanimity returns. And, while I'll not likely ever again underrate what it takes to "make a book," neither will I regret the attempt. In its myriad ambiguities, writing and publishing a book may qualify as a spiritual discipline.

One of the more sublime gifts in all of this is the recognition of how many people have made it happen.

I think first of all of the congregation of the Unitarian Church of Spokane, Washington, and its encouragement, support, and friendship. With gratitude and affection, I remember the hundreds who listened and responded to sermons, took part in workshops on spiritual growth and meditation, joined in countless discussion groups and, in general, made my own spiritual growth possible.

Next comes the board of Eliot Institute and its 1983–84 presidents, Beverly Sensiba and Don Morgan, as well as the two hundred or so conferees. They made possible the lectures, "Through the Eye of the Needle: Toward Oneness," that served as the conference theme and which later became the corpus of this book. I remember especially four wise "old" women—Mary Scriver, Sallirae Henderson, Billie Severtsen and Jennie

Fallein—who heeded my call and came to the conference to share their skills as journal-writer, spiritual guide, meditation teacher, and yoga instructor/chanter.

My thanks go also to the Program Committee of the Unitarian Universalist Ministers Association, who in 1986 invited me to conduct workshops on spiritual growth for liberal ministers. There it was that I could test and enlarge my thoughts and intuitions in concert with some of the warmest yet sharpest thinking I've encountered.

Almost none of this would have come to pass without my colleague and bosom buddy, Sam Wright, who engaged me in many a stimulating conversation around innumerable campfires over a span of twenty-five years and during wilderness adventures that covered a thousand miles.

In one way or another, every sentence and idea in this book was born through the patient feedback of my spouse and perennial sermon critic, Patty. She listened to many a dissertation and dared to suggest that some of my most cherished concepts deserved a better hearing than my initial composition efforts allowed.

To Susan Whaley, graphic artist, I am thankful for her skillful rendering of two dung beetles at work.

To David Roberts, attorney and friend, I am most appreciative for much support and good advice on the legal intricacies of producing a book.

To Larry Shook, journalist and convivial companion in nuclear issues, I give thanks for many ideas.

For their loving and tireless labors in promoting a wide distribution of this book among Spokane-area Unitarian Universalists, I am indebted to Katherine Gellhorn and Bud Cox.

To Lila Girvin, good friend and artist, I give thanks for her reading every word and offering many helpful suggestions.

To John Shideler, a good friend in the publishing business, I am grateful for encouragement and friendly guidance. Also garnering my appreciation are Barbara Greene Chamberlain and Sheryl Stewart who, it seemed to me, put more than an ordinary amount of caring and creativity into this project.

To Don Greene, many thanks for the striking cover illustration.

Most especially, my deep appreciation goes to my competent and encouraging editor and producer, Judy Laddon, who is a skilled writer and an experienced publisher. Judy's enthusiasm was infectious. Over and over, I found myself responding to her suggestions like a house cat to stroking.

— W.H.

"Nothing happens next. This is it."

Drawing by Gahan Wilson; © 1980 The New Yorker Magazine, Inc. Used by permission.

Introduction

Although I have often read and appreciated his written works, the only time I ever heard Gregory Bateson speak was at a 1980 lecture series in the San Francisco Unitarian Church. Already in the midst of his epic battle with cancer, the great anthropologist and philosopher hobbled slowly to the pulpit and towered there like an unsteady giant who might topple over at any moment. It added considerable suspense to the drama of what he was saying.

Listening to Bateson was one of the more fascinating experiences of my life. I was confounded, then intrigued and finally amazed by the way the man's mind seemed to work. Initially, I had only the vaguest notion of what he was doing as he offered a series of anecdotes and concepts, all fascinating but none bearing any discernible connection to the other. By the time he was two-thirds done, I had been considerably entertained by his meandering discourse, but I still had only a scant sense as to where he was headed.

Then, near the end, he told a single anecdote and made an observation about it. Immediately, all the pieces of his speech began falling into place. Like a masonry arch being constructed by workers, the structure Bateson was building only stood alone when the keystone was added. Unexpectedly, I laughed aloud in my own relief and at the speaker's audacity. My "enlightenment" came as sheer delight.

That's the way spiritual growth usually works. The pilgrim travels about, going this way and that, sometimes with a plan, other times with no discernible intention but necessarily, I think, with a certain attentiveness that allows glimpses of the route and destination. Then comes an "aha!"— an insight great or small which changes everything within an instant. After that? More meandering.

In his *Speeches*, Friedrich Schleiermacher wrote, "Religion must be some intuition of the infinite in the finite." This, I think, defines the task of the serious spiritual pilgrim. All of our theological systems, religious institutions, and spiritual practices are attempts—sometimes productive, too often otherwise—to facilitate that search.

That search is the focus of this book.

* * *

Jiddu Krishnamurti used to say, "Truth is a pathless land," by which he meant that there is no one way to get there.

While it certainly has its communal aspects, spiritual growth is an intensely personal undertaking. To me that means we can only talk with confidence and credibility about our own pilgrimages. Not that we cannot learn a great deal from hearing about the journeys of others, but when we share news of the path we have traveled, we reveal something of who we are.

That sounds like the proper place to begin.

I was born and raised on a farm in the Shenandoah Valley of Virginia. My mother was a Southern Methodist, my father was a Dunkard—both austere and joyless religious perspectives that often left me quaking in fear and mired in guilt.

By the time I went off to the College of William and Mary (on a chemistry scholarship), I vowed to give up churchgoing "forever." After earning three degrees in organic chemistry, including a Ph.D. from Michigan State, I set out to become a scientist. For a year I conducted research for the Ag Chem Department at Michigan State, and then I yielded to the lure of a higher salary by selling my talents to the chemical industry.

Moving east, I became a Unitarian almost by accident. On a near whim, I attended a worship service at the First Unitarian Society of Albany, New York, and, astonished by the gospel coming from that pulpit, was "born again" on the spot.

My yearning to live in California took me to the San Francisco Bay area to become a chemical research group leader for a large oil and chemical firm. I also entered deeply into the life of a suburban Unitarian fellowship in Walnut Creek and was the president of the board of trustees when that congregation called its first minister.

By all external parameters, my profession was going well. Having published over a dozen papers and secured a similar number of patents as the result of a broad array of research projects, I enjoyed chemical research and was rising in the company hierarchy. But my dislike for the politics and ethics of large corporations was reaching such toxic proportions that, had I stayed there and taken advantage of my career opportunities, I would, I'm convinced, be dead by now of some psychosomatically caused illness.

Fortunately I had come to love church work and began searching for a way to do it full time. With the encouragement of two ministers, James Madison Barr and Aron Gilmartin, I decided to make a career change by enrolling in Starr King School for the Ministry, a pedagogically liberated Unitarian Universalist seminary on Berkeley's Holy Hill. Following graduation in 1964, I served congregations in Redwood City, California, and Seattle, Washington. Then, in 1973, I was called to be the minister of the Unitarian Church in Spokane—one of the denomination's strongholds of religious humanism.

Over the span of a fifteen-year ministry in Spokane, and encouraged by my own intuitions and the publication of such books as Lawrence LeShan's *The Medium, The Mystic and The Physicist* and Fritjof Capra's *The Tao of Physics*, I changed, leaving a belief in scientific humanism for a larger view which I would call mysticism.

By 1980 I was back in Berkeley on sabbatical, attending classes at the Graduate Theological Union and teaching a course in New Age thought.

From then on, my spiritual urgings were nearly relentless. I preached to a receptive and growing congregation on spiritual growth and mysticism, all the while taking an active stance on several controversial social and political issues. I led many discussion groups on spiritual subjects, taught meditation, learned T'ai-chi, and rejoiced over what I saw as a convergence of the advancing front of science and the purest of the great religious traditions.

Something of a breakthrough came when I was invited to be the theme speaker at a week-long Unitarian Universalist family conference, called Eliot Institute, which was held in July 1984 at Seabeck on Washington's Hood Canal. My topic was spiritual growth. My title was "Through the Eye of the Needle: Toward Oneness." It was a pivotal week.

Thrilled by the response and cross-fertilization of some two hundred religious liberals from the Pacific Northwest, I began tinkering with the idea of someday writing this book. In that ambition, I was not so much attracted by the hope for fame and riches (books on spirituality seldom lead there) as by the prospect that the effort would cause me to expand and sharpen my own understanding.

But the project languished while I took out three years to help found and lead a grassroots nuclear concern group called the Hanford Education Action League (HEAL). Then, as a result of being enlisted as a spirituality workshop leader in a continuing education program for liberal ministers, I was able to test my thoughts, theories, and practice with my colleagues. It was at the first of these workshops, at a ministers' conference in Southern California, that the following episode took place:

"How does it happen, Bill, that you, a former scientist and the current occupant of John Dietrich's pulpit in Spokane, are leading workshops on spirituality?" The questioner said the latter word as though it were slightly tainted. "What would Dietrich think?"

He was referring to the ministry of John Hassler Dietrich, a Pennsylvania Dutch Reformed minister expelled for heresy, who switched his affiliation to the Unitarians and moved to Spokane. There, between 1911 and 1916, he brilliantly preached the religious humanism that would establish him as one of the pioneers of this then-outrageous religious philosophy which made humans rather than God the measure of all things.

So effective was Dietrich in the pulpit that the Sunday services were held in a downtown theatre in order to accommodate crowds of one thousand to twelve hundred. His sermons were printed in full in each Monday morning paper! Dietrich's rhetoric and example have been cited ever since by those arguing for the superiority of a scientific or religious humanist theology.

My California colleague's challenge was logical. It arose from the historical belief that there is some necessary antagonism between humanism and theism and even between humanism and mysticism. But, unknown to many of those who honor him today, Dietrich himself recognized this artificial conflict.

Retired in Berkeley, Dietrich explained in a 1958 essay: "I realize now how my utter reliance upon science and reason and my contempt for any intuitive insights and intangible values which are the very essence of art and religion, was a great mistake; and the way in which I cut mankind off from all cosmic relationship, denying or ignoring every influence outside of humanity itself, was very short-sighted and arrogant."

Like Dietrich, I more and more recognized that humanism is fine as far as it goes. But it does not go far enough. Scientific humanism, like science, is a powerful perspective for dealing with the physical world. Like science, though, it simply ignores a vast and important area of human experience which cannot be dealt with analytically.

In my own theological metamorphosis, I did not so much abandon humanism as expand it. I am no less a scientist today than I was a quarter of a century ago. But I now know there is more: a whole realm where linear thought and language must yield to other modes of understanding and communicating. This is the unknown and the mysterious. Those who learn how to listen to their inner wisdom come to a new and expansive appreciation of the Old Testament command, "Be still and know that I am God."

Whether, as Einstein fervently wanted to believe, the universe is friendly, I do not know. But I do find it logically consistent and experientially congruent that the universe is nourishing, and, as a phrase in Max Ehrmann's "Desiderata" said, it is "unfolding as it should."

The treatise that follows is founded on prose that was meant to be spoken and heard. In reworking it for this book, much of the pulpit style has remained intact. Also retained is a certain redundancy in the presentation of basic ideas, because this allows the reader (and me!) a better opportunity both to examine concepts and impressions, as well as to make our own new interpretations and syntheses.

We are like hawks soaring round and round over the same territory, looking for tasty morsels of understanding. Even though we circle above the same panorama, we continually see it from different angles. In doing this, we spot things we have not previously noticed. This is the way that "spiritual knowing" evolves.

Next, since spiritual truth is essentially personal, I am using the quotations of others not so much for their authority as because my own experience and intuition resonates to their observations and thoughts. Through my experience and the shared experience of these others, it is my primary intention to invite the reader to take courage and set forth on his or her personal quest for Self-becoming.

Finally, between the chapters, I have included some short essays, stories, longer quotations, and even a cartoon or two. These at first may seem only loosely related to the surrounding chapters and overall theme. Some of these are offered because they make or emphasize crucial points not sufficiently covered in the chapters. Others are put in for their aesthetic qualities and practical wisdom, or simply to provide a break.

* * *

One of the presuppositions of this book is that we can find much of value within the current spiritual traditions. But a radical willingness to retrace and reinterpret the original meaning of terms and concepts is essential.

When I use the word "spirituality," for example, I mean something quite different from what that term popularly denotes.

In today's world, spirituality and sentimentality get hopelessly confused. Of course, a mature spirituality may contain sentimental feelings and even passion. Yet I believe spirituality is far more than nostalgia or warm, fuzzy emotions, or even piety.

To me spirituality has to do with the special kind of connectedness implied in Schleiermacher's "intuition of the infinite in the finite." I would say that spirituality points toward the interface of the finite and the Infinite. Or to use the Reverend Jacob Trapp's phrase, spirituality is where "the window of the moment open[s] to the sky of the eternal." This isn't restricted to some otherworldly realm. As every mathematician knows, the finite is, by definition, included within infinity. Thus, the interconnectedness implied in my idea of spirituality takes in all types of relatedness.

"Spiritualism" is quite different. It refers to ephemeral entities called spirits and to various esoteric modes for contacting or relating to those entities. Spirituality and spiritualism have about the same relationship as do mysticism and magic. The latter is not the focus of this book.

One more comment on spirituality: it is not necessarily related to institutional religion, although one would hope that spiritual growth would be the main concern of churches. Martin Buber's entire thought revolved around what he called I-It relationships and I-Thou relationships. The I-It is secular, utilitarian, and impersonal. The I-Thou rises above objective distinctions and all duality. Whether it involves the self and a dapple gray horse or the self and whatever one might mean by the Eternal Thou (Buber's term for God), an I-Thou relationship is always essentially spiritual.

* * *

It is important, I think, for those reading a book on spiritual growth and mysticism to have some inkling of the author's theological perspective or cosmology at the outset.

Within the limitations of linear language, the following paradigm comes as close as I am able to come in describing how I currently make sense of the cosmos.

Imagine a vast ocean—formless, infinite, eternal. Mighty surges of energy stir the depths and sweep the surface of this cosmic ocean, expelling myriad droplets of water—each unique, finite, and transitory.

The ocean, being infinite, is all there is. That being the case, it cannot be described as matter or mind, since the infinite includes them both. We call this ocean by many names—God, Allah, Tao, Brahman, Buddha, Cosmic Consciousness, Supreme Identity, Ground of Being, the Infinite.

Although distinct, those transitory droplets of water are also part of the infinite ocean. But separated as they are—finite and unique—we call them life, matter, stuff, existence.

To the degree that these droplets acknowledge one another's being, they focus upon separateness and, except for a forlorn longing for relationship, they miss seeing the cosmic connections.

This means that they also "forget" where they came from—who they really are. They may have intimations (religious experiences or mystical intuitions) of who they are, but the "ego" keeps getting in the way by insisting that it is the primal ground of the individual.

As finite fragments of the infinite Whole, the droplets can never comprehend the Whole, except upon enlightenment. Still there is longing, intuition, and finally, returning. With the return, the previously perceived finite multiplicity is revealed as illusion. It is, in the words of the mystic, "Not two. . . . Not two."

1

What's Real?

Quantum theory, walking on fire and telekinesis

We shall not cease from exploration
And the end of all our exploring
Will be to arrive where we started
And know the place for the first time.

—T. S. Eliot

Why are we here? The question has no objective answer. But that we will (and must!) ask it is clear in every spiritual tradition.

T. S. Eliot is correct: the premier purpose of life is to discover what has been in our possession all along. "Knowing" this, however, confronts us with Lao-Tzu's legendary warning: "All the great truths are paradoxical."

It occurs to me that, as we take our first deliberate steps on the spiritual journey, we are rather like one of those tiny Mexican dogs, the chihuahua, addressing the task of eating a dead elephant. The "elephant" is impossibly large and we are tiny—at least, that is how we perceive ourselves. The way a chihuahua goes about eating a dead elephant is to take a bite and be very present with that bite. In spiritual growth, the definitive act is to take one step and let tomorrow's step take care of itself!

When we go in search of ultimate reality, we immediately encounter the upsetting fact that the world as ordinarily perceived is not the real world at all.

One September I was walking around the barn of our Pend Oreille County "farm," preparing the place for an eastern Washington winter. There were garden tools to be cleaned, bee supplies to be organized, fertilizers and chemicals to be sorted, and the antifreeze in the tractor to be checked. In the course of my rounds, I glanced into a five-gallon plastic pail. There in the bottom was a large hairy black spider, scuttling around, unable to climb the slippery sides.

At first I passed on by, my mind focused on my tasks. But autumn usually puts me into a reflective frame of mind. Abruptly, as a wave of creaturely identification swept over me, I returned to gaze at the spider. "That poor critter will starve or freeze in there," I mused. And I picked up the pail, carried it outside, and emptied its occupant onto the grass.

Later as I went about my chores, I pondered the nature of the spider's experience. Probably it had been in the bucket for days. It may have given up hope of release. Then the miraculous happened and, all at once, it was free. "What sense," I asked myself, "did the spider make of it all?"

Well, of course, it couldn't really know what had taken place. Its perceptive and cognitive skills were too limited. It lacked the understanding of the real world that I had. And then, a humbling reflection swam into my awareness: "What assurance do I have that I'm significantly closer than that spider to knowing what reality is?"

Later, as I was replacing the oil in the Rototiller,™ an old joke came to mind. Two goldfish were having a theological argument. Finally, one challenged the other. "Okay! If there's no God, who changes the water?"

The possibility that the world as perceived is not the real world is no mere metaphysical speculation. It may well be the most basic spiritual fact. Not only is it a spiritual fact, but it is also a scientific fact.

I spent many years as a research chemist and teacher, and I remember how confidently I drew the usual formulae and equations on the blackboard, explaining the properties and permutations of matter. In those days, when I drew the formula for some compound, I had little doubt that there was something real out there that conformed to that description. Thus, when I drew water—H_2O—I knew there was all sorts of scientific evidence showing how two spherical atoms of hydrogen are bonded to one spherical atom of oxygen, with the connecting bonds being a certain minuscule length and at a certain established angle to one another. We occasionally used Tinker Toy–like models to demonstrate these mysteries to students.

Make no mistake about it—the drawings and models worked! But they were not true in any absolute sense. They worked because they conformed to the experience of all scientists; they allowed us to make sense of our observations. But what I now know is that they were only approximations pointing in the general direction of a truth. Those drawings and those models were useful, but they were not actual, true-to-life pictures of anything.

Such images are like myths. They allow people to talk about their experience, but they should not be taken literally. There is a poem entitled "The Great Wound" by Robinson Jeffers, who began as a medical doctor and ended as a poet, which makes the point precisely.

The mathematicians and physics men
Have their mythology; they work alongside the truth,
Never touching it; their equations are false
But the things *work*. Or, when gross error appears
They invent new ones; they drop the theory of waves in
    universal ether and imagine curved space.
Nevertheless their equations bombed Hiroshima.
The terrible things *worked*.

Whenever I read this poem, both the scientist and theologian in me smile humbly. I remember the days when my fellow religious liberals and I were quite confident that we would, via the scientific method, establish a myth-free religion. It was not possible, of course. As we discovered the fallacies of the old myths and gleefully debunked the legends of our superstitious forebears, we inevitably installed new ones. Jeffers knew this. He knew it for the poets and religionists, as well as for the scientists.

The poet also
Has his mythology. He tells you the moon arose
Out of the Pacific basin. He tells you that Troy was burnt for a
    vagrant
Beautiful woman, whose face launched a thousand ships.
It is unlikely; it might be true; but church and state
Depend on more peculiarly impossibly myths:
That all men are born free and equal. Consider that!
And that a wandering Hebrew poet named Jesus
Is the God of the universe. Consider that!

Actually, there is lots of evidence that the world out there does not look and work the way we ordinarily suppose it does. As J. S. B. Haldane, the British biochemist, said, "The universe is not only queerer than we imagine, it's queerer than we *can* imagine."

Some years ago while reading one of Charles Darwin's journals, I was intrigued to learn that, when his ship, the *Beagle*, first dropped anchor off Patagonia, the natives on shore could "see" the long boats as they were rowed to the beach but steadfastly denied being able to see the much larger mother ship. Apparently, the ship was simply too far beyond their reality framework to be acknowledged.

In a similar example, when a group of Bedouins was shown pictures of camels, they were unable to recognize these very familiar beasts. They had never learned to "see" two-dimensional photos. So, too, jungle-dwelling African pygmies, upon first seeing a human being at a distance in open country, were quite perturbed. Not being accustomed to seeing anything far away, they thought that the distant human had somehow been shrunk.

Admittedly, such perceptual distortions are rationally explainable by us sophisticates. We call them aberrations of the mind and let them go at that.

But normality and strangeness are not always so readily sorted out. A couple of personal friends, who spent half a dozen years living an isolated existence in the Brooks Range of Alaska, were initially skeptical when told that the inland Eskimos could tell when migrating caribou were close to the village. Gradually, my friends realized that somehow the native people not only knew when caribou were nearby but when grizzly bears were, too. After they had lived in the wilds for a few years themselves, my friends developed parallel "feelings," which they insisted had nothing to do with the five senses.

We have all heard the old stories about times of the full moon being particularly restless periods for emotionally "sensitive" people. The word lunacy comes from an ancient belief that the moon and madness are somehow related. At one time there was even a legal distinction made between those committing crimes at full moon and those doing their misdeeds at other times.

More recently, such notions were dismissed as superstitious. Now, however, the American Institute of Climatology has published a statistical study showing an unmistakable correlation between such crimes as arson, kleptomania, and homicidal alcoholism, and the full moon.

I could go on and on describing such "impossible" phenomena. There are the studies of plants responding favorably to kind words, gentle thoughts, and classical music, and poorly to harsh language, violent thoughts, and raucous or dissonant music. There is one haunting Russian study concluding that female rabbits separated by great distances from their young reacted violently at the instant the babies were killed.

In evaluating the work of J. B. Rhine and others in extrasensory perception and psychokinesis, much of the scientific community simply ignores or ridicules the findings that, indeed, some people have uncommon powers of perception and action. Many skeptics attack Rhine's credibility or methods. The president of the American Institute of Mathematical

Statistics, however, said, "If the Rhine investigation is to be fairly attacked, it must be on other than mathematical grounds."

To be sure, there are many tricksters in such fields of endeavor. Uri Geller, famous for his spoon bending, is often cited as an exposed fraud. Yet, when two Stanford Research Institute scientists, Russell Targ and Harold Puthoff, brought Geller into their lab under controlled conditions, he was apparently able to affect consciously the performance of scientific instruments located in another room.

In one experiment, Targ and Puthoff instructed Geller to "move" a steel ball bearing resting under a bell jar on a heavy, smooth bench. Geller began to focus his attention and energy, but nothing happened. Finally, in a fit of temper, he threw his hands into the air and shouted, "Dear God! Help me move this shit!" And the ball bearing rolled to the side of the bell jar!

Lawrence LeShan, a clinical psychologist with a strong humanist orientation, has investigated many "paranormal" happenings and concluded that, to the degree they do occur, the person displaying such powers is in an altered state of consciousness and working in a reality framework where the usual laws of existence do not apply.

As a scientist, I am both very interested in and very careful around all such phenomena. I don't believe them. Nor do I disbelieve them. I hold my evaluation in abeyance. I am all too familiar with those numerous episodes where the most renowned and skeptical of scientists were abysmally wrong in some narrow-minded conclusion.

I recall my surprise and delight some thirty-five years ago when I first glimpsed how tenuous scientific truth really is. I was in graduate school taking a course in advanced organic chemistry. A name that cropped up repeatedly was that of Hermann Kolbe, a giant in nineteenth century organic chemistry. One of the subjects we studied was stereoisomerism, the phenomenon by which complex chemical compounds having precisely the same chemical groupings nonetheless end up with different properties because of one subtle variation in structure. This variation is explained by the fact that such compounds are somewhat like a pair of gloves—they are identical in all respects except that one is a mirror image of the other and, of course, one will fit only the right hand and one only the left.

The possibility that organic compounds might be thought of in a similar way hit the scientific world like a thunderbolt. Two young chemists named van't Hoff and Le Bel *separately* proposed it. As the controversy reached a crescendo, the renowned Kolbe entered the fray. In one of the most prestigious German chemical journals, he published a paper which is almost unique in the history of scientific journalism.

After tediously denouncing—chapter, line, and verse—van't Hoff's and Le Bel's experimental evidence, Kolbe drew himself to his full professorial eminence and referred to the "fanciful nonsense" and "supernatural explanations" of these two "unknown" chemists. Finally, Herr Doktor Hermann Kolbe concluded with the judgment that offering such a theory to the scientific fraternity was like taking a well-rouged prostitute off the streets of Berlin, dressing her up in suitable finery, and trying to pass her off as the city's most respectable lady!

But the evidence supporting van't Hoff's and Le Bel's hypothesis mounted, Kolbe died, and today the principles of stereoisomerism constitute some of the most respectable and useful theories in organic chemistry. And the two young and unknown chemists are honored for their brilliance and courage.

What all of the foregoing teaches us is the essential roles of openness, doubt, and humility when we come face to face with the strange or the unknown. I have long "known" that, under the right circumstances, the impossible happens. My knowledge took a considerable jump a few years ago when I personally did something that, until then, I'd only heard about: I walked on fire.

Now, I've charcoal broiled steaks. I know that fire cooks meat, whether dead or alive. But I've also heard about fire-walking, and I've accepted that it happens, especially since the famous *National Geographic* article some years ago with pictures of fire-walkers in Ceylon, including someone with a pyrometer measuring the temperature of the fire.

I had not, however, had any direct experience with fire-walking. In the fall of 1983, Tolly Burkan came to Spokane conducting fire-walking workshops. For fifty bucks of your money and four hours of your time, Burkan would teach you to walk on red-hot coals, or at least let you see other people do it. I would have gone to the event, I'm sure, but an out-of-town business trip made it impossible. Several people whom I knew did go to the workshop, and they walked barefooted across the coals without so much as a blister. A journalist was present and reported the event in the newspaper.

In May 1984 Burkan was back. I tinkered with the idea of going, but I hesitated under the impression that I was too busy. Then, a woman I knew called to say that she and her husband would like to give me paid admission to the fire-walking class.

I drove to a location out in the country which was the home of an Eastern Washington University professor. The first thing I did was sign the required legal waiver. Seated around the living room were twenty-five to thirty persons, mostly younger than I and more women than men.

Tolly Burkan began by taking up his guitar and leading us in singing such old favorites as, "I got shoes, you got shoes, all God's children got shoes." The line about "putting on my shoes and walking all over God's heaven" did not escape our humorous notice.

Then Burkan began his pitch. "The world is divided into two groups of people," he said, "those who walk on fire and those who do not walk on fire." He said he had taught about seven thousand people to become members of the first group.

Burkan was good—a real talker and an outstanding motivator. His emphasis, well-punctuated with laughs, admonitions and several magic stunts, was: reality is not what we ordinarily think it to be, and we can overcome fears and limitations. He used terms like "stepping through the membrane of fear" and described how fears are more in our heads than "out there." He said he'd used visual imagery to cure himself of cancer.

After an hour, we all filed outside silently and cooperated in the construction of a huge pile of firewood. Using a half-gallon of kerosene, Burkan ignited the stack while we stood in a circle, hands joined, and chanted "Om."

Leaving the blazing inferno, we trooped back inside for more instructions, especially the importance of "paying attention and being in the here and now." Burkan repeatedly stressed that the decision to walk on the fire must be personal and voluntary. Although often humorous, he never underplayed the risks. He occasionally used the daunting term "charred stumps" and admitted that three of his students had been burned badly enough to require weeks of hospitalization. He pointed out that the surface of the fire had been measured at 1300 degrees Fahrenheit, and that aluminum melts at 1100 degrees. "Fire-walking isn't something to play with," he cautioned. "People can and do get hurt if they're not in the proper frame of mind. So don't go to a barbecue this summer and say, 'Move the ribs, Uncle Harry, I'm gonna walk!' "

But mostly Burkan was encouraging. Two hours later we were back outside, again silently but this time with our shoes off and our trouser legs rolled up (for safety). I flinched at the sharpness of the driveway gravel, correlating that modest discomfort with the prospect of walking on a 1300-degree fire.

We stood and chanted while Burkan methodically raked a fifteen-foot "runway" through the foot-deep heap of red-hot embers. Near the exit end of the fire, someone with a garden hose was creating a mushy puddle in the grass. Tolly finished the raking and stuck the metal end of the utensil into the water. It hissed, and a cloud of steam rose. I had already pretty much decided I wouldn't walk, but my attention was thoroughly focused!

Without further ado, Burkan tramped through the fire. The incandescent coals crowded up the sides of his feet, and glowing sparks fell off as he unhurriedly stepped into the puddle. Several other persons, including a local psychiatrist I knew, quickly followed. Over the next few minutes, more went singly. Everyone emerged calmly and looked comfortable. "One more minute!" called Burkan, meaning that he was about to extinguish the fire with the hose. Another half dozen surged forward and came through without apparent harm.

I crossed the circle to the starting point and hesitated. Something inside said, "It's okay," and I stepped forward. At that instant, the coals shifted in my perception to crimson cobblestones. There was little sensation of heat. It felt like walking through popcorn. Five steps and I was through and into the water.

A few seconds later, spray from the hose hit the fire and a cheer went up from the circle. We returned to the house for debriefing. Again, the sharp gravel tortured my feet. A warm, exuberant feeling welled up inside me.

Foot inspection time. Two or three persons had small blisters. Not I. Everyone, including those who had chosen not to fire-walk, was smiling a lot and chattering softly. I was home by eleven. After sitting for my meditation, I washed a gray deposit of ash off my feet and went to bed. There was a quiet contentment.

What I learned firsthand from all of this was something I've often preached: reality is largely in our heads. I don't want to leave the impression there is no reality whatever "out there." I'm not a solipsist. I don't believe the world disappears if there's nobody around to think about it. I appreciate the wisdom of the limerick that goes:

There was a young man who said: "God,
I find it exceedingly odd
    That a tree, as a tree,
    Simply ceases to be
When there's no one around in the quad."

"Young man, your astonishment's odd;
I am always around in the quad.
    So the tree, as a tree,
    Continues to be
Since observed by yours faithfully, God."

I now know what the ancient Hindus taught: reality as perceived is illusory. What we know is not out there but a picture in our heads, and we can change what is in our heads. That's a very important practical and spiritual fact!

Significantly, this idea is also gaining scientific credibility. Fritjof Capra's *The Tao of Physics*, Gary Zukav's *The Dancing Wu Li Masters*, and especially Peter Russell's *The Global Brain* all suggest that scientific evidence points to a dynamic, interconnected cosmos which is more conscious than material, much as ancient mystics speculated. I think we need to be careful in our comparisons of science and mysticism, though; the two start from totally different points and serve totally different purposes. Some of the claims made by Capra, Zukav, and others have been substantially challenged by scientists, philosophers, and metaphysicians. The new physics does not "prove" that ancient mystics were correct. But then, the mystics never needed any proof beyond their own experience. To my way of thinking, proof is not the issue.

In his book *Quantum Questions: The Mystical Writings of the World's Great Physicists*, philosopher Ken Wilber questions whether modern physics offers any significant support to ancient mysticism. He calls "trivial" the evidence of Capra and others correlating the two. But he also notes that all of the pioneering physicists were mystics as well—surely more than coincidence!

I think Wilber's label "trivial" is too severe. I agree that, as knowledge, mysticism is several levels above physics. Mysticism "knows" what physics can never get close to. But the descriptive similarities offered in *The Tao of Physics* and half a dozen other books are important, simply because we have been living in a world where multitudes have believed that physics and the other hard sciences disprove mysticism.

Perhaps this analogy will help. As knowledge (pure knowing), mysticism is at the top of the mountain. Physics is near the bottom (where most people are, which encourages them to accord physics a higher authority than mysticism). Thus, when in its searching and theory making the new physics inadvertently glimpses the top of the mountain, it is apt to make some true observations. Admittedly, because of the distance, these observations will not be very profound. But they are useful, at least in establishing that the mountaintop exists!

Let's trace the so-called convergence of science and mysticism a bit. The shift in scientific perspective began in the early part of this century with Einstein's two theories of relativity and with the elucidation of quantum theory. Einstein's work established the equivalence of matter and energy (making the atomic bomb feasible) and the fact that time is another dimension like the original three. People began talking about space-time. Quantum theory cast doubt on the nature and behavior of matter itself. Werner Heisenberg's famous uncertainty principle not only suggested that there is no way of measuring the location and speed of a subatomic particle simultaneously, but also that the very consciousness of the scientist has an impact on the results of the investigation.

The old scientific paradigm of a solid, mechanistic, inorganic world separate from the live, organic world began breaking down. And a scientific controversy arose which continues today but now more and more favors a dynamic, holistic cosmos in which there is no matter as we have understood it, and in which consciousness is an essential component, if not in fact the fundamental fact of existence.

"There is no stuff out there—just interconnected events," asserts Fritjof Capra.

Bell's Theorem suggests that subatomic particles somehow communicate with one another at speeds greater than the velocity of light. Astronomer James Jeans has said that the cosmos is more like a great thought than a great machine. And his professional colleague, Sir Arthur Eddington, argues: "The stuff of the universe is mind-stuff." Small wonder that physicist and Nobel Laureate Eugene Wigner now bluntly tells his audiences, "We goofed! We physicists tried to explain the world in strictly material terms! Until we include consciousness, we will never understand."

One of the best scientific illustrations of the idea of some sort of pervasive consciousness is contained in the work of Rupert Sheldrake, a British plant physiologist. Sheldrake does not use the word "consciousness." Instead he talks about "fields," of the same class of phenomena as electrical fields, magnetic fields, and gravitational fields. Now, please appreciate that when scientists talk about fields, they are describing their experience. Nobody knows what a field is, we just know how it acts. And what it does is exert a force—that is, have an effect—over distance without any apparent connection between the source of the field and whatever the field acts upon.

Rupert Sheldrake's fields are on the outer edge of scientific credibility. He calls them morphogenetic fields. And what he says is that, once an event happens for the first time, the likelihood of it happening again is increased. In other words, once something takes place, it is as though the whole universe has been modestly but significantly changed.

For a very long time, scientists have talked about instinct. Nobody really knows what it is. The one-year-old Baltimore oriole, even though it has never seen it done before, instinctively knows how to build those marvelous hanging nests. Sheldrake says that the oriole knows because the information, as a morphogenetic field, is already "out there" in the universe, put there by the millions of other Baltimore orioles who have built nests.

A parallel sort of thing happens in chemistry. Every organic chemist knows how hard it is to crystallize a newly synthesized compound. But once the first crystallization has been accomplished, subsequent crystallizations are much easier. Traditionally, we have explained that this is because seed crystals of the first preparation are floating around the laboratory, and these serve as patterns for subsequent crystallizations, but this does not satisfactorily explain why it is that, when a second chemist in a laboratory halfway around the world prepares the same compound, he or she does not have the first chemist's difficulty. Scientists have suggested that seed crystals somehow migrate halfway around the world to assist the second chemist.

Rupert Sheldrake is not convinced. There are simply too many similar occurrences, involving both inorganic and organic systems, where the explanation isn't believable. Sheldrake believes that, with the first crystallization of the new compound, a new field is established which everywhere assists in future crystallizations. In other words, even scientific fact shifts as things happen. And scientific "laws" may really be more like habits than like immutable truths which have always existed! Consciousness, in this sense, constantly evolves—a possibility which is very important in thinking about spiritual growth.

Another scientific theory related in its metaphysical utility to Rupert Sheldrake's morphogenetic theory is actually older and has to do with the hologram. Most people know the hologram as a three-dimensional image contained on a two-dimensional film surface. But a much more startling property of the hologram is that all of the information contained as an image on the film is distributed throughout the hologram.

The significance of this can be seen by comparing what happens when an ordinary photographic negative is cut into pieces with what happens when a hologram is cut into pieces. Let us say we have an ordinary transparency of a person. Were we to cut that transparency in two and project each half, the images on the screen would also be halved—head in one, feet in the other. If the same were done to a holographic film of the same person, the image on the screen would be complete—head, feet, every part of the person—in both projected halves. The only loss in either half would be some decrease in clarity, in definition. Even if the hologram were cut into many pieces, each piece would still contain the same original image; only clarity or precision would be lost.

Because of this peculiar holism, the hologram has become a metaphor or model for consciousness, including even Cosmic Consciousness. Karl Pribram, a Stanford University neuropsychiatrist, has suggested that the cosmos works like a great hologram and that the human mind works as though it were a fragment of that cosmic hologram. Translating the metaphor into conventional metaphysical language, one might imagine the cosmos as the mind of God and each of our minds as being less well-defined projections of that cosmic mind. Might not the one-year-old Baltimore oriole have a minute holographic image fixed in its mind, "put there" through the bird's connection to the cosmic hologram? Is that what instinct is?

Whether accurate or not, the holographic model of the cosmos is uniquely useful in terms of our continuing discussion about the interplay between the whole and its parts as well as between the finite and the Infinite which, according to theologian Friedrich Schleiermacher, is what spirituality is about.

Science is filled with such intriguing possibilities. Again and again I am awed by the creative genius represented in the best of science. Equally, I am rendered humble by the fact that even the most innovative discoveries will soon be found wanting and tossed aside into the dustbins of history. Most of all, I am delighted that the classic void between science (at its best) and religion (at its best) is more apparent than real. The quest for wholeness is unending!

The responsibility in all of this is awesome, however. At the same time the search for truth goes on, we are warned to hold lightly the truth we find. It is ever incumbent upon us to maintain the essential balance between commitment and humility. For, whether we ask scientific questions or theological questions, it's serious business, often too serious. And the only prudent response may be a chuckle.

One of the maddening marvels about truth is that, where it is questioned persistently enough, we finally come to the point where we can explain no further. There is no closure. Unless we have a sense of humor! And so I love The Turtle Story:

A university professor has just finished a learned lecture about the origin and structure of the universe, and a little old lady in tennis shoes stalks up to the podium. "Excuse me, sir, but you've got it all wrong," she charges. "The truth is that the universe is resting on the back of a large turtle." The professor decides to play along. "Oh, really!" he says. "Well, tell me, what is the turtle standing on?" The lady has a quick reply: "Oh, it's standing on another turtle." The professor perseveres. "And what is that turtle standing on?" Without hesitation she answers, "Another turtle." The professor, still game, starts to repeat his question. A look of impatience comes across the woman's face. She holds up her hand, stopping him in mid-sentence. "Save your breath, sonny. It's turtles all the way down."

* * *

What I have been attempting to do so far is establish one important point about reality and introduce a second, at least as important. First, reality as we perceive it is not reality as it is. As the foregoing discussion has shown, I hope, "the facts" of existence are inevitably incomplete and even in error. The problem arises because of limitations in our ability to discern and understand all of what's "out there" and because our biases about reality tend to distort what is actually before our eyes (i.e., we see what we want to see).

Second, as mystics have always known, and as scientists are continually discovering, our notion of the world as made up of separate things is wrong. This error begins with our persistence in seeing our individual selves as separate from everything else—actually, from believing that the boundary represented by my skin is as far as "I" go. Called dualism by philosophers and metaphysicians, the failure to recognize the oneness or interconnectedness of everything is the fundamental concern of all authentic spiritual activity.

In Zen, for example, the purpose of the prolonged sitting meditations (called *zazen*) and the enigmatic koans ("What is the sound of one hand clapping?") is to break the limitations of this dualistic conditioning so that the seeker may experience reality as it is, a seamless whole. The only way to "solve" a koan, for example, is by being with it until one becomes the koan. Intellectual reasoning won't do it, because rational thought is sequential (linear) and fragmenting. Only intuitive "knowing" is holistic and connecting. When we are intellectual, we are standing back from the world; when we are intuitive, we are in harmony with the world. Each mode has its purposes, but, if we would be spiritually whole, we must learn how to "see" reality as it is when we are integral to it.

As John Daido Loori says in his *Mountain Record of Zen Talks*: "When you realize that the bag of skin is the smallest part of who you are and what your life is, then there is nothing restricting you. There are no boundaries. Whether you realize it or not, there are no boundaries, but until you realize it you cannot manifest it. The limitations that each one of us has are defined in the ways we use our minds."

Thus, when we are spiritually enlightened, nothing changes, except the way we perceive, the way we use our minds. This is what the Buddhists mean when they say we are already enlightened, we just don't know it. We shall repeatedly return to this proposition throughout this book.

The Farmer and the Stranger

Once there was a farmer working in the field, when down the road came a stranger.

"I been thinking of moving," said the stranger, "and I wonder what kind of people live around here?"

"Well," replied the farmer, "what kind of people live where you come from?"

"Not very good," answered the stranger. "They're selfish and mean and not at all friendly. I'll be glad to leave them behind!"

"Well," said the farmer, "I expect you'll find the same sort of people around here—selfish and mean and not at all friendly. You probably won't like it here."

The stranger went on.

Shortly afterwards, another stranger came along the same road.

"I been thinking of moving," said the stranger, "and I wonder what kind of people live around here?"

"Well," replied the farmer, "what kind of people live where you come from?"

"Oh, wonderful people!" answered the stranger. "They're generous and kind and very friendly. I'll really be sorry to leave them."

"Well," said the farmer, "I expect you'll find the same sort of people around here—generous and kind and very friendly. I'm sure you'll like it here."

2

Myth-Making and Game-Playing

Mistaking the pointing finger for the moon

One of the encompassing miseries of all spiritual understanding is that language, a most useful human tool, is also limiting; we can experience and know more than we can say. Awareness of this limitation is essential to all communication about spiritual matters. Our words and ideas may point to a truth, but they are not in themselves the Truth. This is what Lao-Tzu, the traditional founder of Taoism, meant when he warned, "Those who know do not speak; those who speak do not know."

When the Zen master asks a novice to meditate on the question, "What is the sound of one hand clapping?" he or she does not expect the novice to answer that paradox in the way one does an ordinary question. What is sought is for the novice to move beyond linear thought, to shut down the cognitive faculties and to open himself or herself up to the cosmic input that we describe as intuitive, transcendental, or holistic.

Fortunately, we are not limited to words and linear thought. Since time immemorial, religious practice has included symbolism, myth, music, ritual (liturgy), movement, poetry, chanting, meditation, and the allied spiritual disciplines.

Keeping in mind the limitations of language, let us now consider religious myth as a tool for spiritual "knowing." I won't go into the theory of myth—for that I recommend the works of Joseph Campbell—but I appreciate that a myth points to a religious truth although it is not generally true itself. Those who argue about the truth or falsity of the Garden of Eden story or the Great Flood or whatever are missing the purpose of myth. They are literalists, and as such they are like the fool who stops and ponders the sign at the boundary of the city instead of traveling into the city itself. A Buddhist would say they mistake the pointing finger for the moon.

In questioning reality, as we did in the last chapter, a couple of questions immediately arise. First, if the perceived world is illusory, largely in our heads, then what is out there? Second, since I depend upon the world out there to tell me who I am, and the world out there is illusory, who, then, am I?

This second question, "Who am I?", is perhaps the core question of spiritual growth. A later chapter is devoted to it. For now, let's use religious myth to approach the first question: "What is out there?"

I am going to use Alan Watts's elaboration of a charming Vedantist sutra as a mythic vehicle. Vedanta is one of the more elevated Hindu sects, and a sutra is a scriptural lesson or teaching. Alan Watts wrote a whole book around the sutra called *Beyond Theology*.

In Hinduism, the Supreme Principle of the Cosmos, the ultimate Ground of Being, is called Brahman. In all persons, unknown to most of them, is an aspect of Brahman called Atman. Thus Atman is the Brahman in us. Most of us live egotistically, out of touch with Atman and, hence, Brahman. This egotistical being is called the self, with a small letter "s". The Atman is also called the Self, but with a capital "S". The Self waits within the self, hoping to be discovered. When the discovery takes place, the self is said to have awakened, to have become enlightened. Because of our divine relationship to Brahman, we may all be said to be Brahman—God.

Now, in everyday Western society, anyone who asserts, "I am God," is apt to receive about the same courtesy as anyone who says, "I am Napoleon Bonaparte." He or she runs a good chance of being carted off to a place where mental disorders are treated. At the very least, there are liable to be questions such as, "If you're God, why aren't you rich?" Or, "How did you create the world in six days?" or "Why don't you eliminate war, and when you're done with that, move on to poverty?" Such queries not only indicate the questioner's skepticism about mortal claims to divinity, they also testify to our prevailing notion that God ought to be a magician or big daddy.

In India, on the other hand, someone announcing, "I am God," would be regarded with about the same concern as someone who said, "I am human." If the listener perceived the speaker to be serious, he or she might well respond, "Congratulations! It's nice you found out."

In the Western religions, gods are almost universally regarded as mysterious and distant entities who have omniscience and omnipotence— who are all-pervasive, all-wise, and all-powerful. It is a very serious business. And God does not have a sense of humor.

Alan Watts writes, "The most remarkable superficial difference between Christianity and Hinduism is in how they each respond to the question, 'Is it serious?'"

Is it serious? Is the universe, existence as we perceive it and conceive of it, serious? The Jew, the Christian, and the Muslim answer, "Yes!" The Hindu says, "No!"

One of the symbolic manifestations of this "No!" is seen in the pictorial and statuary representations of a Hindu deity called Shiva. Shiva is a fearsome, many-armed deity surrounded by flames and unseen terrors, whose cosmic task is to dance the universe. But one hand is always shown upright with the palm turned outward, as though waving. The meaning of the gesture is, "Fear not!"

Fear not! Despite appearances, this is all a big act. It is *maya* and *lila*—illusion and play! Reality is not what it appears to be; neither is the meaning of it all. The solidity of things is an electrical mirage. Space and time are constructs. That which is changeless is constantly changing. It's all a dance—rhythm. All matter, say the physicists, is made up of interdependent rhythms. Wherever we look we see fields of energy in constant harmonic motion. Even life is energetic and rhythmic. George Leonard speaks brilliantly of this sort of thing in his book *The Silent Pulse*.

Rhythm is at the heart of play—the rhythm of running, the timing of strategies, the harmony of team effort, the resonance of what is called concentration, the beat of music and dancing. In the same sense, religious growth depends upon rhythms—chanting, singing, meditation, laughter, rituals, even the cadence of voice and ear resonating to new possibilities in knowing and being. Wherever we look, there are patterns—of the stars, the seas, the seasons, social rituals, and of our own bodies.

There is one characteristic beyond rhythm that play must have—it must not be too intentional. Once the game has begun there must be a certain willingness to let it happen. The outcome must be in doubt if it is to be enjoyed as a game. And so, in the Hindu concepts of *lila* and *maya*—play and illusion—even the gods cannot preordain the outcome of the game without corrupting it.

As noted above, this notion is especially important in Hindu theology because, while most of us are ignorant of the supreme reality called Brahman or the eternal Self, all humans have an essential Self called Atman which is identical with Brahman. In the most enlightened forms of Hinduism, the religious goal is to discover the Atman in oneself, to realize one's unity with Brahman.

A curious aspect of such a concept is its enormous impact on questions about the purpose of existence. Sophisticated Hindus view existence as a great game being played out in the consciousness of the eternal Self. Existence, even for Brahman, is play—*lila*. And the illusion—the *maya*—comes in because Brahman forgets it is a game.

Thus, Brahman is playing a cosmic game of hide-and-seek, and you and I are among the players, unwitting except as we wake up and recognize the Atman in ourselves. Our life stories are the dramas being played out. We are all aspects of the eternal Self acting out our own life scripts and unaware of it, at least until we achieve enlightenment, catch onto the game.

In this way of conceptualizing things, there is no mystery about who is responsible for good and evil or the other ambiguities of life—they are simply part of the game, of the play. Nor is there a mystery about the existential loneliness we all feel nor in the often faltering ways we reach out for love. We are indeed lost in a cosmic game of hide-and-seek, one in which the eternal Self is as intensely involved as we are. It is lonely. The theological term is estrangement.

One way to get closer to this idea of existence as the eternal Self playing a great game of hide-and-seek is to imagine what you would do if you had the ability to dream anything you wished. Imagine, too, that these dreams were as vivid as the most compelling reality. What would you dream?

How, in other words, would you like to live?

In the beginning most of us, I suspect, would spend a good deal of time fulfilling our more obvious fantasies. Might there not be fabulous mansions and magnificent banquets and gloriously convivial gatherings, exquisite finery in clothing and appointments, lavish entertainments and lovemaking bouts, expansive vistas of seasides and mountains? And then, when these had been exhausted of much satisfaction, might not one spend time in the company of sages and celebrities, among great works of art and in traveling to faraway places, including interstellar space, the past and the future? At some point danger—risk—would probably come into our fantasies: climbing mountains, hang-gliding, racing fast horses or vehicles, facing deadly beasts, entering the arena, going off to wars, experiencing all the natural disasters to which we are subject. Too, there would be great creative bursts—constructing, composing, performing, inventing, learning, governing, maybe even creating the world in six days!

Surely, if we could maximize our dreams for our own excitement, they would become longer and more involved, until they lasted a lifetime and included myriad experiences. Inevitably, we would start dreaming multiple lifetimes—sequential and simultaneous reincarnations. Our fantasies would lead us through entire civilizations with all the parts, individually and collectively, experienced in detail and in every conceivable combination. Might we not, at some point in our dreaming, reach the place where our dreams would include great suffering and loss—disease, torture, hunger, imprisonment, disgrace, desertion, the death of loved ones—all the miseries to which humans are subjected on this ambiguous ball called Earth? Naturally, too, our dreams would permit escape from or triumph over such misfortune and unhappiness, for those moments of relief and release are among the most delicious we have.

Our dream game would, of course, include mystery, the unknown and the unknowable. To sweeten it all, there would be secret insights through which we could penetrate the fog and glimpse possibilities and promises lying beyond, as well as still more confounding mysteries. In the one case, we would know the joy of enlightenment, in the other, the multiplication of doubt and despair would be our lot.

Only one thing would be required to keep the dream interesting and make it real. Only one thing. We would have to forget it was a dream, a game of hide-and-seek for our true selves. We would even need to forget our previous dreams, except as they added to the reality of our unfolding game. The moment the dream seemed like only a game, it would be over.

The dream, the game, would have to extend up to the very moment of death. To the end. In fact, death itself would add a poignant and fearful meaning to the process, because death as we know it appears to negate the whole game.

And yet even this view is a human perception, a construct or illusion, *maya* multiplied by *maya*.

Imagine, now, that all of this—your magnificent cosmic dream—the complex game of hide-and-seek, is what the eternal Self is doing, through you, and me, and all of our fellows! Such a vision is entirely consistent with the Hindu doctrine of *tat tvam asi* ("Thou art that"), a doctrine which asserts the identity of oneself with the Godhead. At a mythic level, Hinduism posits that all experience whatsoever is God's—Brahman's—and that God is the one and only knower and seer because *there is nothing else* except, of course, you.

That's a far cry from the dualistic theology of the religions we know, with their separate and capricious deity who rules over his kingdom and his subjects like one of the later Roman emperors. In these religions, life is characterized by whimsical chances and arbitrary suffering. Death, in such a lonely existence, becomes the greatest of potential tragedies. Even the anointed or saved show no great eagerness to receive their reward.

In Hinduism, the only tragedy in human life lies in not becoming aware of one's divine connection and identity, in not sharing the ultimate bliss of the eternal Self in the game being played.

We Westerners inevitably have trouble with all of this. Convinced that our ego and its scanty bag of possessions are all we have in an enormous, complex, alien, and fundamentally unknowable cosmos, we shiver in unnecessary terror—unnecessary because the happier alternative to such a self-defeating dualism is to join up with that which we see as our adversary.

Mystics, of course, know this. Even Western mystics know it. They know that our sense of separation is the greatest illusion of all. Because they do not share our prevailing "bad news theology," such mystics are branded unrealistic, impractical, even heretical.

Many Westerners fear that the notion of God as the eternal Self will be used as a rationalization for deliberate wickedness. The vision of the tyrannical, quick-to-anger father or emperor seems essential as long as humans view themselves as willful, selfish, and undisciplined children. The fact that such a notion has done nothing to discourage childish behavior but has often been enlisted to justify the most unthinkable collective wickedness seems to escape us. Perhaps the time has come to examine the possibility that we are wicked, not because of our innate sinfulness but because we have imagined and described ourselves erroneously.

Certainly the time has come to challenge any theological concept that allows a separate and perfect God to create an imperfect world out of nothing and then condemn its frail creatures for acting imperfectly. There have been such challenges. Some have come via the installation of a nineteenth century scientism which sees the universe as mechanical and indifferent but one wherein human beings will, if they act analytically and rationally, move toward perfection on their own. That hasn't worked either, mostly because it ignores those human qualities and needs which are nonlinear, poetic, intuitive, ecstatic, and relational. Now that twentieth century physics and ancient mystical wisdom are coming together in a convergent but pluralistic holism, there is a promise for people who are seeking the best of the possibilities.

No, I do not literally believe that I am God playing a game called Bill Houff. To believe that literally I would have to be convinced that I have happened upon some sort of final truth. I am more interested in what helps me make sense of the existence I am in than in trying to establish final truths, especially when final truths seem thoroughly elusive.

Also, I am not trying to establish the overall superiority of Hinduism over the Western religions. While it is evident to me that the Hindu doctrine *tat tvam asi* ("Thou art that"), being non-dualistic, overcomes some critical theological problems, there are other features of Hinduism that I don't care for at all. (As a matter of fact, of the Eastern religions, I resonate most to Taoism.)

But I do believe that I am—that all of us are—part and parcel of a creative transcendent principle which can be called by many names. I am persuaded that the religious task is to recognize and come into harmony with our own divinity. As such, the idea of a cosmic game of hide-and-seek involving us and the creative, transcendent principle is a useful and fascinating model. It has mythic possibilities.

Besides, it relieves some of the deadly seriousness with which we are wont to surround ultimate things like religion. Even Dante, we need to remind ourselves, could back off from his grim theologizing long enough to equate the praise sung by the angels in heaven to the laughter of the universe.

The Baby Squirrel:
Leaping the abyss

Black squirrels (half the size of the gray ones) are the only squirrels on our farm. While they make themselves obvious in the warmer months by scurrying about and denouncing all intruders, they are seldom seen in winter.

One of my favorite recollections about the squirrels dates from one summer when one of them set up housekeeping in a birdhouse mounted on a steel-pipe pole and proceeded to raise a family of three. As the summer went on, the house gave evidence of its growing occupants by swaying about and yielding thumping sounds. The babies were frolicking.

By August they were vying for a vantage point at the entry. Nudged by its siblings, one or another would peer at the strange world beyond. Rather quickly they took to hanging precariously halfway outside, jostled meanwhile by the two inside who wanted to hang out, too.

One afternoon Patty and I were sitting on the deck observing the contest when suddenly the youngster hanging out lost its grip and plummeted to the ground. Seizing the dog, who had suddenly become very interested, we sat back to watch further developments.

Figuratively shaking its head, the fallen baby squirrel picked itself up, looked about, and tentatively made its way over to the metal pole holding the squirrel house eight feet up. Addressing a problem almost totally foreign to ordinary infant squirrels, it reached out, put its front paws on opposite sides of the pipe, and began inching its way up.

Arriving at the house, it then faced the challenge of the wooden sides extending two or three inches all around. The baby arched its head, stretched and craned and seemed about to give up. And then, with a tiny, shrill squeak, it lunged with its front feet for the vertical side, and made it!

Now, back on familiar wood, the furry little critter scurried to safety. Once more the house swayed and thumped. And the whole world seemed to give a sigh of relief.

3

The Perennial Philosophy

A lump of salt, a pan of water

The objective world of separate objects is an illusion. This is an idea that religion at its best has always expressed. Mysticism, in fact, is often defined as an awareness and practice of the harmonious and organic unity of all things. And science, especially theoretical physics and ecology, appears more and more to point toward a dynamic wholeness in which the idea of the cosmos as a great machine is being replaced by the idea of the cosmos as a great thought. Consciousness, not matter, is the fundamental stuff.

Although the evidence for this view is both ancient and modern, it is not easily talked about because of its paradox. In the Mundaka Upanishad, a Hindu scripture, this paradox is expressed clearly:

It is not outer awareness,
It is not inner awareness,
Nor is it suspension of awareness.
It is not knowing,
It is not unknowing,
Nor is it knowingness itself.
It can neither be seen nor understood,
It cannot be given boundaries.
It is ineffable and beyond thought.
It is indefinable.
It is known only through becoming it.

In a parallel way, the Tao-Te-Ching discusses the absolute nature of the fundamental unity called Tao by saying, "The Tao that can be named is not the eternal Tao."

And when we come up to modern times, we find T. S. Eliot saying:

> At the still point of the turning world. Neither flesh nor
>   fleshless;
> Neither from nor towards; at the still point, there the dance is,
> But neither arrest nor movement. And do not call it fixity,
> Where past and future are gathered. Neither movement from
>   nor towards,
> Neither ascent nor decline. Except for the point, the still point,
> There would be no dance, and there is only the dance.

One of the crucial characteristics about these kinds of statements is that they do not yield their meaning in the same way that discursive statements do. The key question is not, "What is that supposed to mean?" The key question is, "What does it stimulate in me?" As such, these examples are mystical (or devotional) literature. They take time, lingering time, and openness. Impatient persons inevitably have a hell of a time with such writings.

The central mystical fact is that everything is connected to everything else. Francis Thompson, the mystical poet, put it well in his little verse:

> All things by immortal power near or far,
> Hiddenly to each other linked are
> That thou canst not stir a flower
> Without the troubling of a star.

This is an awareness reaching back into antiquity. Chuang-Tzu, a Taoist sage writing three hundred or four hundred years before the birth of Jesus, said, "I and all things in the universe are one."

Plotinus, a third century Egyptian philosopher of the neo-Platonic school, wrote in some dismay, "Man as he now is has ceased to be the All. But when he ceases to be an individual, he raises himself again and penetrates the whole world."

And Meister Eckhart, my favorite among the Christian mystics, put it this way: "All that man has here externally in multiplicity is intrinsically One. Here all blades of grass, wood and stone, all things are One. This is the deepest depth."

Finally, Henry Suso, a German Dominican, wrote: "All creatures . . . are the same life, the same essence, the same power, the same one and nothing less."

The realization of our essential unity: that is the purpose of spiritual growth. Nor is this unity merely the oneness of all existing things. Religion, remember, has to do with wholeness, and it is a wholeness in which the Divine reaches out and encompasses everything.

When we examine the popular manifestations of the major religions, we are struck by their diversity. But when we examine the core teachings of these religions, we are struck by their similarity.

How the bewildering diversity arises may be illustrated by considering what happens when we take a written page and make a copy on a duplicating machine, and then copy the copy, and then copy that copy, and on and on. As we all know, such a process will in short order yield a document which is quite unrecognizable. So it is when human beings and their institutions go to work on religious teachings.

Compare, for example, the sublime teachings of Jesus's Sermon on the Mount with the operant religion of most Christians. How many live like the lilies of the field and the birds of the air? How many use the Beatitudes as a life guide? How many love their enemies?

So it goes. The popular expressions of every great religion bear little or no resemblance to the original teachings. A few years ago, a six-hour film titled "Tibet" came to Spokane. I asked the members of our spiritual growth groups to go see it, because I expected they would appreciate the contrast between the simple teachings of the Buddha and the elaborate theology and ritual of Tibetan Buddhism. As it turned out, the film was an exhausting and bewildering marathon of chanting, marching, horn-blowing and drum-beating. Few lasted all the way through. As I endured the final tedious ritual with its complex appeals to one deity or another, I reflected that the Buddha must be spinning in his grave. I recalled and appreciated his deathbed appeal to his disciples that they should forget him.

And yet, behind the elaborations or corruptions of the great religions, we find not only deep wisdom but a convergence of viewpoints. This convergence is what the German philosopher Leibnitz called the Perennial Philosophy. Aldous Huxley wrote an entire book by that title (which every serious student of spiritual growth should study). According to Huxley, "The Perennial Philosophy is primarily concerned with the one, divine Reality substantial to the manifold world of things and lives and minds." What this says is, the world is not what it appears to be. Behind appearances is an encompassing reality which is both more fundamental and more worthy of human attention. The names applied to this encompassing reality are many: God, Yahweh, Brahman, Tao, Allah, the Cosmic Consciousness, the Ground of Being, and dozens of others.

Many people, including quite a few religious liberals, will hear such a statement and reply that they do not believe in a supreme being. Asserting that they have no objective evidence for the existence of a God, they find the whole idea irrelevant, or worse.

But this objection misses the whole point. The Perennial Philosophy is not claiming that there is a God out there, or in here, or anyplace. Rather it is saying that there is a reality which is fundamental to everything else, a reality which has been called many different names.

Such a notion would be no more than an exercise in semantics, were it not for something else central to the Perennial Philosophy and hence to all the higher religions. Huxley puts it this way: " . . . the ultimate reason for human existence is the unitive knowledge of the divine Ground." In other words, the fundamental task for each human being is the discovery that God is everywhere and, especially, that he or she is God. Note carefully that what is required is not a belief that there is a God. That is a conceptual confusion, born of the refusal or inability to see the wholeness of things. It reduces the ultimate to the status of a mere thing. We are all God; we just don't know it!

The duty we all have is to rise above our ignorance, to discover who we really are—to awaken, as the Eastern religions would put it. That duty carries with it a whole assortment of requirements which stand at the center of all true religious concern and which go on to make up the practical substance of the Perennial Philosophy.

In the Hindu Upanishads, there is a series of stories about a boy named Svetakatu. As the son of a priest, Svetakatu is sent forth to a wise teacher to learn about Brahman (God). After several years, the lad returns filled with pride over his knowledge. But the father is dismayed that the boy still does not understand the concept of Brahman. So he directs his son to dissolve a lump of salt in a pan of water and then explain where the salt is. Being in solution, it is everywhere. The boy recognizes this, whereupon the father exclaims, "Like the salt hidden in the water, so is Brahman hidden in all the world. Brahman is spirit. Brahman is all that which is really, really true. Brahman is you, my son."

Within these four sentences we have the essence of the Perennial Philosophy. And it is a message as Christian as it is Hindu, as Jewish as it is Buddhist, as Islamic as it is Taoist.

Now all of us having any substantial knowledge of either Judaism or Christianity will recognize immediately that what I have just said about the identity of God and the individual is foreign to both religions as popularly taught. In fact, it is even regarded as a grievous and damnable heresy. Human beings have been stoned or burned for less. And even today any person claiming his or her identity with God is apt to be scorned or considered a candidate for the booby hatch.

It is also painfully apparent in today's world that very few people live as though they were one being, brothers and sisters, alike in flesh and essence. But that fact does not negate the Perennial Philosophy. Rather it shows what happens when humans refuse to attend to the primary business of life, which is awakening to their mutual divinity.

Let's take some time to examine just a few fragments of the evidence that the Perennial Philosophy really is what it claims to be.

In Hinduism, for example, the Sanskrit saying *tat tvam asi* expressed the belief that the Absolute Principle of all existence, called Brahman, and the essence of every human being, called Atman, are one. Furthermore, the duty of every person is to realize over this, to know that he or she is God.

Thus, Shankara, a ninth century commentator on the Hindu scripture Bhagavad-Gita, wrote, "The wise person is one who understands that the essence of Brahman and of Atman is Pure Consciousness, and who realizes their absolute identity. The identity of Brahman and Atman is affirmed in hundreds of sacred texts. . . . "

A parallel teaching pervades Taoism. Thus the Book of Chuang-Tzu, which dates from the third or fourth century before the birth of Jesus, states, "Do not ask whether the Tao is in this or that; it is in all things."

The same central idea shows up in Mahayana Buddhism and was carried over into Zen. Yung-Chia Ta-shih, the founder of Zen Buddhism, wrote, "One Nature, perfect and pervading, circulates in all natures. One Reality, all-comprehensive, contains within itself all realities."

Well and good, the skeptic may say, but these are religions of the Far East, noted for their esoteric mysteries and ego-negating philosophies. What about Christianity or Judaism?

Jesus is supposed to have said, "The Father and I are one." And Christians of the orthodox mainstream have seized upon such utterances to claim that Jesus bore a special relationship to God, one not shared by plain mortals. But what if Jesus were speaking as a plain mortal?

Such conjecture can continue ad infinitum. Yet it is significant that through the centuries, some of the greatest minds of Christendom have suggested the same.

"The Ground of God and the Ground of the Soul are one and the same," wrote Meister Eckhart, the medieval Christian mystic. And at another place he said, "God and I, we are one knowledge." Obviously, if God is all-knowing (as Eckhart believed), then the only way the individual can be all-knowing is by being one with God. Finally, on a different occasion Eckhart asserted, "The eye with which I see God is the same eye with which God sees me."

Although Eckhart often tried the patience of the Catholic hierarchy, he was not alone in such claims. Saint Catherine of Siena wrote, "My Me is God, nor do I recognize any other Me except my God Himself." In other words, "I am God, and that's all that I am." And Saint Bernard said, "In those respects in which the soul is unlike God, it is also unlike itself."

When we turn our attention to Judaism, a religion that is even more dualistic than Christianity, we are hard pressed to find statements suggesting the unity of human beings and God. Some Biblical scholars insist that there are none in the Old Testament, that the void between Yahweh and the individual human being is absolute and uncrossable. But I am not so sure. In the Book of Psalms is that marvelous declaration, "Be still and know that I am God." Consider those words for a moment. Who is speaking? Traditionally, we have assumed that it is God. Perhaps I take liberties with the text. Yet I do know that by meditating, by being still, I do come closer to that awareness that I am God.

Regardless of how the ancient Hebrews regarded the matter, we do, at the beginning of the Christian era, have the great rabbi Hillel speaking in Yahweh's name, "If I am here, everyone is here. If I am not here, no one is here."

And let us not forget that Jesus was a Jew. His teachings about love— love of God, love of neighbor, love of self, love even of enemies—were not sentimental doctrines having to do with mere affection or respect. When Jesus spoke of love, he meant oneness. He was talking about knowing who we are. He called us to recognize not our solitary condition, which we may transcend by some sort of weak-kneed and ephemeral emotion, but the fact that we are of one being. "Inasmuch as you have done it unto one of the least of these my brothers, you have done it unto me," he said. And I will dare say that he was not speaking metaphorically!

Finally we come to Islam, a religion in its contemporary manifestations which seems even more dualistic and separated than do popular Christianity and Judaism. But, believe it or not, Islam has more than its share of mystics, and they are as congruent with the Perennial Philosophy as the mystics of any other faith.

Most Islamic mystics called themselves Sufis—a reference to the wool garments many of them wore. Sufism holds that individual things exist only because of the divine power within them. They have no other reality than this divine consciousness. Therefore God is all. Not only is there no god but Allah, there is no being but Allah. Each soul is God, and the faithful Sufi shamelessly asserts, as did Abu Yezid around A.D. 900, "Verily I am God, there is no God but me; worship me."

Needless to say, ordinary Moslems were as intolerant of such heresy as were the Hebrew Sanhedrin and Catholicism's Grand Inquisitor. When Husein al-Hallaj said, "I am He whom I love . . . I am the truth," he was arrested, scourged a thousand stripes, and burned alive. Religious authorities have never taken well to those claiming a direct relationship to or identity with the Ground of Being. It dilutes their power and cuts back on the revenues.

His terrible fate notwithstanding, al-Hallaj's disciples were not in the least deterred by their teacher's violent death. Like the followers of Jesus, they claimed to have seen and talked with al-Hallaj following his execution.

Some of the most beautiful mystical poetry has been composed by Sufis, especially by a twelfth century Arab named Rumi. This Sufi mystic was the equal of Saint Francis of Assisi in the lines, "O God, I never listen to the cry of the animals, or the quivering of the trees, or the murmur of water, or the song of the birds, or the rustling wind, or the crashing thunder, without feeling them to be an evidence of Thy unity."

This may seem as far from liberal theology as if it had happened in the further reaches of the Andromeda galaxy. But wait! Ralph Waldo Emerson and his fellow Transcendentalists were filled with an unbridled enthusiasm for natural beauty, as evidence that the Oversoul (Emerson's word for God) encompasses everything.

Emerson, who is as close as anyone to being the patron saint of the liberal faiths, was often given to utterances such as, "Within man is the soul of the whole, the wise silence, the universal beauty, to which part and particle is equally related, the eternal One." On another occasion, the Sage of Concord simply exclaimed, "I am part and parcel of God."

For many religious liberals, Emerson has a cherished poetic authority which, however, is less convincing than the authority of modern science. Let us linger briefly over this latter authority. For here, too—among scientists—we find the Perennial Philosophy.

Many of the world's pioneering physicists were mystics. Einstein, Heisenberg, Schrödinger, de Broglie, Jeans, Planck, Pauli, Eddington— these are the names associated with modern theoretical physics. And every one of them wrote of his mystical proclivities.

In a lovely utterance Erwin Schrödinger, the discoverer of wave mechanics (which is one of the principle ideas in quantum theory), asks the reader to imagine:

> . . . sitting on a bench beside a path in high mountain country. There are grassy slopes all around, with rocks thrusting through them. On the opposite slope of the valley there is a stretch of scree with a low growth of alder bushes. Woods climb steeply on both sides of the valley, up to the line of treeless pasture. Facing you, soaring up from the depths of the valley, is the mighty, glacier-tipped peak, its smooth snowfields and hard-edged rock faces

touched at this moment with soft rose color by the last rays of the departing sun, all marvelously sharp against the clear, pale, transparent blue of the sky.

According to our usual way of looking at it, everything that you are seeing has, apart from small changes, been there for thousands of years before you. After a while—not long—you will no longer exist, and the woods and rocks and sky will continue, unchanged, for thousands of years after you.

What is it that has called you so suddenly out of nothingness to enjoy for a brief while a spectacle which remains quite indifferent to you? The conditions for your existence are almost as old as the rocks. For thousands of years men have striven and suffered and begotten and women have brought forth in pain. A hundred years ago, perhaps, another man sat on this spot; like you, he gazed with awe and yearning in his heart at the dying light on the glaciers. Like you, he was begotten of man and born of woman. He felt pain and brief joy as you do. Was he someone else? Was it not you yourself? What is this Self of yours? What was the necessary condition for making the thing conceived this time into you, just you, and not someone else? What clearly intelligible scientific meaning can this "someone else" really have? If she who is now your mother had cohabited with someone else and had a son by him, and your father had done likewise, would you have come to be? Or were you living in them, and in your father's father, thousands of years ago? And even if this is so, why are you not your brother, why is your brother not you, why are you not one of your distant cousins? What justifies you in obstinately discovering this difference—the difference between you and someone else—when objectively what is there is the same?

Erwin Schrödinger goes on to cite the basic mystic principle in Vedantist Hinduism: *tat tvam asi* (Thou art that!). Or as one Vedantist passage says, "I am in the east and in the west, I am below and above, *I am this whole world.*"

"Thus," concludes the renowned physicist, "you can throw yourself flat on the ground, stretched out upon Mother Earth, with the certain conviction that you are one with her and she with you. You are as firmly established, as invulnerable, as she—indeed a thousand times firmer and more invulnerable. As surely as she will engulf you tomorrow, so surely will she bring you forth anew to new striving and suffering. And not merely 'someday': now, today, every day she is bringing you forth, not once, but thousands upon thousands of times, just as every day she engulfs you a thousand times over. For eternally and always there is only now, one and the same now; the present is the only thing that has no end."

Fantastic! Erwin Schrödinger sounds rather like Ralph Waldo Emerson.

All of this rhetoric may seem to have only theoretical implications, no practical purpose or consequences. But please be patient!

Huxley states forcefully, "It is because we don't know Who we are, because we are unaware that the Kingdom of Heaven is within us, that we behave in the generally silly, the often insane, the sometimes criminal ways that are so characteristically human. We are saved, we are liberated and enlightened, by perceiving the hitherto unperceived good that is already within us, by returning to our eternal Ground and remaining where, without knowing it, we have always been."

Huxley reiterates that, because we are estranged from our own divine nature, we fail to cooperate with the Tao or the Logos or whatever term one may use in referring to the ultimate harmony. Instead, "We try to dominate and exploit, we waste the earth's mineral resources, ruin its soil, ravage its forests, pour filth into its rivers and poisonous fumes into its air."

When we realize that Huxley said this in 1944, we must acknowledge his standing as an environmental prophet alongside his talents as a philosopher. Nor is this the only upshot of our predominating view of ourselves and the cosmic principle. I share Huxley's belief that because we embrace an alienating theology, we also embrace inhumane purposes that all too readily tempt us into the use of propaganda, repression, and violence upon one another.

Can it be, perhaps, that herein we have a clue to the puzzle that, while Judaism, Christianity, and Islam have fomented innumerable wars and atrocities in the name of one holy ideology or another, Hinduism, Buddhism, and Taoism "have never been persecuting faiths, have preached almost no holy wars and have refrained from . . . religious imperialism"?

Although I have spent most of my time arguing an intellectual acceptance of the Perennial Philosophy, that is but the bare beginning of what is required to live according to its teachings. The Way is indeed narrow and steep. Jesus was being neither trivial nor obtuse when he said, "It is easier for a camel to pass through the eye of the needle than it is for a rich man to enter the Kingdom of Heaven." (Some Biblical scholars suggest "The Eye of the Needle" was the colloquial name of a gate in the walls of Jerusalem which was too narrow for a loaded camel to pass through.)

The reason he singled out the rich man was not that there is something inherently evil about being rich. Rather, the teaching refers to the fact that becoming and staying rich is a distraction. Those who have their attention fixed on temporal concerns are quite unlikely to be interested in "unitive knowledge of the divine Ground," much less to undertake the effort and suffering that go with achieving such enlightenment.

It is no happenstance that all of the great religious traditions preach against the dangers of selfishness, or attachment, or egoism, or desire. The Buddha warns that the cause of all suffering is desire. The apostle Paul condemns sins of the flesh (causing the erroneous impression that he is talking about sex when his concern is much broader). And Hinduism declares that the world most of us call real is an illusion and is not to be trusted. Taoism teaches that we should all pass through life like water flowing down the side of a hill, following the line of least resistance, conforming to where we find ourselves, and having no grand plans about what we want to do next.

Formulations such as these receive a nearly violent reaction from most of us. Imbued as we are with expressing ourselves, with being unique and significant, with accumulating experience and knowledge, with exercising power, and with making progress in the world, we heatedly reject such "life-negating" philosophies. Self-righteously, we point to the anonymity, uncaringness, and misery of the Eastern cultures. We declare that only when people have individual dignity and freedom is life worth living.

What then of the preoccupation with nonattachment that, without exception, characterizes every version of the Perennial Philosophy?

It is, quite simply, the crux—the winnowing ground—of every vow to grow spiritually. For it is indeed wholly impossible to make progress toward enlightenment, salvation, satori, union with the Divine, or whatever, while dragging around an assortment of "indispensable" possessions. Even life itself must be finally surrendered. That is what Jesus undoubtedly meant when he commented that those who would keep their lives shall lose them and those who give up their lives willingly shall find them.

What an awesome demand this places upon us Westerners! With our obsessive focus on money, energy, power, sex, knowledge, and youth, how shall any of us ever grow spiritually? Maybe there is an answer here as to why so few of us do. Maybe, too, there is a commentary on our popularized religions which, at the same time they trumpet the teachings of Jesus, manage to find within those teachings permission to commit the most regrettable of acts.

This is all as ironic as it is unfortunate. For in our efforts to garner some possessions, fame, power, and prestige, and in our struggle to hang onto the past, including our appearance, sexiness, and particular biases, we engage the whole cosmos in an unwinnable battle. Yet by relaxing and letting go we can "have it all" by "becoming it all"!

Practically all of us have intimations of this truth. Each one of us has had moments when we have forgotten ourselves and our wants, and reached out to others, to something larger than ourselves, and for a while experienced a sublime sense of belonging and purpose and worthiness. Then the moment passes. We return to our bondage, once more deafened to the still, small voice that urges us toward wholeness.

There is a special relevance in all of this for religious liberals, *if* we have the perseverance, courage, and openness for which we celebrate ourselves. We should be heartened by the dawning of interest in spiritual growth among us. This shows, not that we are discarding our rationality or our humane concerns, but that we are enlarging what it meant to be religious fully human, fully alive. Spiritually, we are growing up!

Today, we have a mounting interest in worship and liturgy. Many of us practice spiritual disciplines. We have long stressed right action as essential to religious concern. We have avoided the grosser forms of literalism and idolatry. We have acknowledged the worth of all of the world's great religions. We claim an openness to truth wherever it may be found, and we honor change and growth as both desirable and essential. These are all to our credit.

But we also have some debits. These include an overemphasis on rationalism and a corresponding distrust or misunderstanding of mysticism. Many of us believe almost exclusively in the power of cognitive thought as the only safe path to religious maturity. There have been times when we have rejected intuitive knowledge, symbolism, ritual, and sacrament. Many of us have sought to reduce the real and relevant to only that which is available to the five senses—to what Hindus have warned is, in actuality, illusory.

We have also embraced a militant form of individualism which, as egoism or selfness, must almost inevitably bar us from the unitive knowledge of the whole that is the ultimate purpose of the Perennial Philosophy. And as creatures of our culture, we have been enamored of the same evil of attachment that, along with egoism, is the most formidable obstacle to wholeness. We are, in short, very proud of *our* knowledge, *our* power, *our* aesthetic achievements, and *our* own individual dignity.

It is not that these qualities are in themselves sinful, but that in clutching at them too desperately or pridefully, we isolate ourselves from the endpoint of human existence. We need to remind ourselves that the word "sin" is singular, not plural. It refers not to an assortment of wrongful acts but rather to a condition—to the condition of being separated from God, of not even recognizing that we are God. Humility and simplicity are words that we could bring more creatively into our attitudes about religion and life.

Yet, having aired these criticisms, I am nonetheless heartened by our new and growing interest in spiritual growth, an interest especially difficult to pursue in these times. There are so many distractions—temptations, one might say. And there are so many dubious or false paths, easy or flamboyant practices which are really thinly disguised ego trips.

Yet, even as real growth involves a willingness to suffer, so there is also required of us a gentleness. Those who are fanatical about their growth are also guilty of attachment. "Do not push the river," goes a Buddhist aphorism.

In the end, I think of Christmas Humphreys's admonition, "It is not important how fast you go; it is important that you do not stop."

The Fruits of Victory

In some Zen Buddhist orders, it is part of the discipline to engage in aggressive and often loud arguments about the finer points of the practice. Usually the admission of wandering monks to a temple depends upon the stranger's winning such a dispute.

Two brother monks dwelt together in a temple in northern Japan. The elder brother was learned, but the younger one was dull and had but one eye. One day a wandering monk came to the door and asked for lodging. Being tired, the elder brother sent the other to meet the visitor and engage him in argument. Knowing that his brother was not quick with words, the elder directed: "Request the dialogue in silence."

The young monk and the stranger went to the shrine and began their silent disputation. But it was not long before the stranger rushed up to the elder brother and exclaimed: "Your younger brother has defeated me utterly. I shall go."

The elder monk was astonished: "Tell me the dialogue."

"Well," explained the visitor, "first I held up one finger, representing the Buddha. So he held up two fingers, signifying the Buddha and his teaching. I replied with three fingers, representing the Buddha, his teaching, and his disciples living the harmonious life. Then he shook his fist in my face, signifying that all three come from a single realization. Thus, he won, and I must go." And he walked out the door.

Suddenly the younger monk ran up. "Where is that fellow?"

"He said you won the dialogue and left."

"Won nothing! He insulted me, and I'm going to beat him up."

"Please tell me the subject of the dialogue," asked the elder monk.

"Well, the very minute he saw me he held up one finger, insulting me for having but one eye. Since he was a visitor, I tried to be polite and held up two fingers, congratulating him for having two eyes. But then he held up three fingers, indicating that between us we have only three eyes. So I got mad and challenged him to a fistfight. That's when he ran out."

4

Mystical Experience

And Brahman on the elephant's neck

Spiritual growth is not easy. If it were, we would all shortly be enlightened, and that might well end the purpose of human existence.

Paradoxically, as Aldous Huxley and numerous other students of mysticism are quick to point out, we all are already enlightened. But we don't know it. In *The Atman Project*, Ken Wilber, one of our brightest and most innovative metaphysicians, says, "It is not that an individual is first an ego and then may become a Buddha [enlightened one]—it is that he was first Buddha and then became an ego."

In other words, our human beingness is a finite expression of the infinite Great Being which manifests itself in the countless realms of creation with an endless diversity of forms and events.

And the nature of the Great Being is suggested in a Buddhist teaching: "All the Buddhas and all sentient beings are nothing but One Mind, beside which nothing exists." One Mind, beyond space and time: that is the basis of everything, outside of which there is nothing. And through our finite interconnectedness we are all related to this infinite One Mind.

We do not know, however, of this vast interconnectedness until we "awaken," as the Vedantists would put it. Until then, we feel and act unenlightened, egotistical, alienated, attached, fearful of loss, away from home, and subject to all the private and public ills of existence.

Besides attachment and egoism, there are other associated roadblocks standing in the way of our recognizing the Atman within and knowing that we are part and parcel of Brahman. The possibilities for misinterpretation and abuse are almost unlimited, especially for the naive and devious. An important mitigating factor is that, for those who are disciplined and sincere, possibilities for growth are also almost unlimited.

Some persons, upon first hearing of the "I am God" idea, come to the facile conclusion: "That being the case, why bother? I'll just lie back and enjoy my exalted position. If I'm God, I can do whatever I please."

Ramakrishna, a well-known Hindu mystic, had a favorite fable that reveals the fallacy in that line of thinking:

A young spiritual novice has just been taught by his guru that he is identical in essence with the power of the universe. He walks away in a state of ecstatic absorption, and as he is going down the road leading out of the village, he beholds, coming in his direction, a huge elephant bearing a howdah on its back with the driver riding on the beast's neck. Striding along, the young candidate for sainthood is meditating on the proposition, "I am Brahman; all things are Brahman." When he sees the huge elephant coming toward him, he thinks, "The elephant, too, is Brahman. We are all one."

Meanwhile, the elephant, with its bells jingling to the rhythm of its stately approach, is bearing down upon the novice who, in his ecstasy, is maintaining his course in the middle of the road. And the driver, seeing this, becomes alarmed and starts shouting, "Clear the way! Clear the way, you idiot! Clear the way!" But the youth, caught up in his rapture, is thinking, "I am Brahman; the elephant is Brahman," and when he hears the shouts of the driver, he adds, "Should Brahman be afraid of Brahman? Should Brahman clear the way for Brahman?"

The distance rapidly closes. The driver keeps shouting; the elephant lumbers on; the youth, continuing his meditation, holds the center of the road. Suddenly, as a collision is about to take place, the elephant reaches out with its trunk, picks up the novice, and hurls him into the bushes.

Physically shocked and spiritually stunned, the youth recovers his senses enough to stand up, dust off his clothes, and return to the guru for further instructions.

Somewhat indignant, he blurts out an account of his experience with the elephant and continues, "You told me that I was Brahman."

"Yes," answered the guru, "and so you are."

"You told me that all things are Brahman."

"Yes," responded the guru, "all things are indeed Brahman."

"That elephant, then, was Brahman, too?" asked the youth, his voice edging toward hysteria.

"So it was," replied the guru. "That elephant was Brahman. But why didn't you pay attention to the voice of Brahman, shouting from the elephant's neck, and get out of the way?"

I would like to explore now why mystical experience is so important to spiritual growth. But first a definition or two.

As a mystic is one who is actively interested in coming into harmony with the Divine Principle (God, Brahman, One Mind, Cosmic Consciousness, Eternal Thou, Whomever), so a mystical experience is an unexpected yet unforgettable result of making progress on this ultimate spiritual task. To begin our consideration of mystical (or religious) experience, let me share something that happened to me almost a quarter of a century ago.

It had been a long day. My friend Sam Wright and I were midway on a backpacking trip along the John Muir Trail in California's Sierra Nevada. The weather was changeable. It had started out sunny as we made our way along the South Fork of the San Joaquin River and came into the lower end of Evolution Valley. Of all the lush meadows of the High Sierra, Evolution is perhaps the most memorable. The hiker ascends through a succession of stepped plateaus, each a little greener and fresher than the previous one.

We paused along the creek in Colby Meadow to eat lunch and wash our clothes, stretching the jeans and shirts, socks and underwear on warm, flat granite rocks to dry in the sunshine. Already thunderheads were boiling up over the mountains to the west. Up ahead, peaks with names like Darwin and Wallace and Huxley were being brushed by fast-moving clouds. An afternoon rain seemed likely.

The clothing dried quickly and we collected our gear. We moved a bit more urgently than usual. The trail now rose rapidly, skirting the jumbled granite shoulder of the Hermit and leading onward toward Evolution Lake at nearly eleven thousand feet. Coming in from the southwest, the rain swept in like a curtain driven by the wind, stinging our faces as we trudged on under our ponchos. A mile or two later we arrived at the lake which, under such adverse conditions, was a wild and lyrical place.

We pitched our camp some thirty or forty feet above the troubled waters on a narrow peninsula projecting into the lake. Gradually the rain slackened and we assembled our fly rods, intending to have trout for supper. Under still menacing skies we caught four goldens and took them back to our campsite to embellish our powdered soup, instant potatoes, and coffee.

And then it happened.

Sundown was only minutes away. Far to the west, over the valley we had just traversed, the sun broke through the blue-gray storm clouds. The whole world flamed crimson. The mountain slopes behind us flowed with an undulating luminescence, and the water below reflected the aura of incandescent clouds.

Startled, delighted, we were transformed. Whooping our joy, we dashed up the mountainside striving for new vistas and reveling in the chromatic explosion that surrounded us. For fifteen or twenty minutes it continued while we, now thoroughly pagan creatures, alternately ran around and stood still, eyes ablaze, jaws slack, arms waving in wonderment and praise.

As the color abated, we made our way, separately and without words, back to our modest camp above the lake. When only a dull scarlet triangle remained of the recent glory, we looked at one another and wept unashamed tears. Then, spontaneously, we made a pact and shook on it. Whoever lived the longer agreed to bring the other's ashes to Evolution Lake for consignment. Again without words, we undressed and climbed into our sleeping bags as droplets of rain began drumming on the taut canvas over our heads. Even as I drifted off to sleep, I knew that death had forever lost some of its sting.

This is the sort of occurrence that William James called a "religious experience." Abraham Maslow named it a "peak experience." And James Joyce used the word "epiphany."

An epiphany is "a sudden, intuitive perception of or insight into the reality or essential meaning of something, usually initiated by some simple, homely, or commonplace experience," reports the Random House dictionary. The Greek source, *epiphaneia*, was a happening during which the gods revealed divine secrets to human beings.

William James wrote an entire and classical book on religious experience. Abraham Maslow more recently did likewise, drawing upon an exhaustive study of the subject. Maslow pointed out that peak experiences are far more common than most of us admit, even to ourselves.

Since the experience is an emotional one, usually nonrational, the compulsively objective person either avoids epiphanies from the beginning or minimizes their significance. Maslow calls such people nonpeakers. And he includes us religious liberals among the nonpeakers. But a lot has changed for religious liberals in the quarter century since Maslow wrote his book. We are now much more accepting, and even welcoming, of peak experiences than we were then.

Curiously, among the orthodox, mysticism or religious experience has had a bad name for quite a different reason. Such an experience, being personal and not easily mediated or moderated by the powers-that-be, is threatening to institutional hierarchies. When the faithful look to their own intuitions instead of the directives of leaders, the leaders are apt to lose their power. That is why the Gnostics, one of the more fascinating and enlightened of early Christian sects, were bitterly and violently opposed by the church fathers.

In his book *The Bond of Power* Joseph Chilton Pearce comments pungently on this. In a chapter titled "The Great Vaccination," Pearce asserts that most contemporary churches play it safe by inoculating their members with just enough religion that there's little danger they'll catch the real thing and slip the leash of ecclesiastical control.

When we look at the early histories of most religious movements and at the biographies of their founders, we are struck by the centrality of religious experience. As Abraham Maslow says, "The very beginning, the intrinsic core, the essence, the universal nucleus of every known high religion has been the private, lonely, personal illumination, revelation, or ecstasy of some acutely sensitive prophet or seer."

Buddha, Lao-Tzu, Zoroaster, Jesus, and Mohammed were all such prophets. In each case, a religious institution sprang up to promulgate and enlarge upon the original vision. In essence, what these institutions sought to do, at least in their beginnings, was to communicate the prophet's peak experience to the world of nonpeakers. Then comes an ironic institutional development. The churches fall into the hands of nonpeakers, and the original vision is lost or corrupted, even though the institutions themselves go on. Partly because they lack the skill or stomach for administration, the mystics get shoved to one side. It seems clear, for example, that had it not been for the apostle Paul, a real organizer, the mystical insights of Jesus would have been lost altogether.

Religious experiences—epiphanies—are the signals that tell us of significant spiritual growth. That is their real meaning. The situations that yield such growth, causing the signal, are many and varied. Gautama Buddha is said to have spent six years fasting and mortifying his flesh without finding the answers to the questions about death and suffering that troubled him. Only when he gave up ascetic practices and sat down under the Bo tree did the long-sought enlightenment flash into his mind. His response was a faint half-smile of knowing followed by forty-five years of traveling and teaching which changed the world.

A woman I know described the birth of her first child as a peak experience. She apprehended not only the miracle of life but the mystical union of all living creatures. Most of all, she knew in a fundamentally different way her own participation in the creative web of things. Years later, she still could not describe the experience without shedding tears of joy over the depth of her recognition.

Most of us have, I suspect, spent time with another human being which was so rich and so affirming in terms of the communication achieved that forever afterwards the wholeness of existence seemed more real and practical.

I remember a peace march in San Francisco during the Vietnam War. There were an estimated sixty thousand people in the march itself, and standing along the curbs were many thousands more, some signaling support, others waving fists and shouting obscenities. Suddenly, our section of the procession reached the crest of a high hill, from which we could see a multitude of people sidewalk-to-sidewalk stretching down into the valley and disappearing over the next hill. Instantly, my despair and fatigue about the war evaporated, and I was exhilarated to realize how many others shared my concerns. My feelings, which I would describe as oceanic, even extended to include the hecklers on the sidewalk whom I no longer hated but recognized as fellows and as an aspect of my own doubt and frustration.

Once I heard a young woman tell of nearly drowning when she was a child. So close to death was she that her terror gave way to resignation and then to the perception of soft, lilting music and misty, colored lights. When she was revived, her first reaction was enormous regret at having been called back from something so beautiful and promising. As she told her story to a gathering, she suddenly stopped and choked up. Finally she said, "I've never told this story before, and now I realize how lonely I've been."

Finally, I recall the death of a man in one of my congregations. An ex-seaman, he had true joie de vivre. He was diagnosed as having an incurable cancer. But instead of retreating into the desperation of his condition, he redoubled his usual activities as one bringing humor and sanity into the lives of others. His family (a wife and three nearly grown children) was the particular focus of his caring and courage. His death, when it came, was the most assertive affirmation of life I've ever witnessed. Following the memorial service, in a true celebration of life, we all gathered at his home for an uproarious wake that rivaled any the Irish have ever given.

Not every religious experience is mind-blowing. Most, in fact, if we are paying attention, come as nudges and sparks, as subtle awarenesses and after-the-fact recognitions. We wake up one morning and recognize that we are different from the persons we were five years ago. We are surprised and pleased.

Sometimes the intellectual content of an epiphany is so whimsical or even trivial that the experience does not receive the respect it deserves. I once had such an episode.

Shortly after the U.S. Olympic hockey team beat the Russians in 1984, a sports writer turned out a newspaper column on upsets. The greatest upset of all, suggested the columnist, was a particular horse race. I'm not enamored with horse races, but I read on. The contest took place many years ago at Saratoga, New York. Before the race, it had been a foregone conclusion among the experts that either Gallant Fox or Whichone would win. The other entrants were too undistinguished to merit mention. But then the race began and, as one commentator told it, "A total stranger came pounding down the Saratoga horse track late this afternoon, flinging huge muddy divots into the countenance of the aristocratic Gallant Fox. A chestnut colt by the name of Jim Dandy won the Travers by six lengths, at odds of 100 to one."

As I read those words, I practically came unglued right there over my morning coffee. There was something about an underdog winning that touched a glorious responsive chord in me. Tears came to my eyes. Even now, a lump rises in my throat.

Some epiphanies don't get classified as such. I think of creative insights. This is a whole subject in itself, but my readings on creativity, my conversations with creative people, and my own personal experience persuade me that authentically creative episodes are of the same essence as religious experience.

Generally, there is a period of preparation during which one is undergoing the work or discipline necessary to acquire a potentially creative skill—learning to paint, play music, write, gain proficiency in a scientific field, whatever. Then comes a time of focus and effort, often marked by fatigue and discouragement. Finally comes the creative burst, the discovery or insight or artistic achievement. Like a peak experience, this comes unbidden; it cannot be ordered up on command. It has a different source than does linear thought or activity. It comes "whole," so to speak. Frequently, the creative burst only comes after one backs off, moves away from the task or concern. As almost all of us know, the insight, when it hits us, is surprising, pleasing, and transforming.

The one essential common characteristic of all epiphanies, I'm sure, is that they do in their own way signal a nonreversible change in human lives. We are not, in other words, the same persons that we were before the epiphany happened.

The feelings—the signals—include excitement, exuberance and ecstasy, delight, bliss and aliveness, wholeness, absorption and involvement, simplicity, uniqueness, acceptance, gratitude, elation, and affection for the nature of things. More often than not, authentic religious experiences will lie at least partially beyond the reach of language. Words may be inadequate, but there is an encompassing feeling of connection, an awareness of belonging, a sense of being part of a nourishing and creative cosmos.

Ralph Waldo Emerson was no doubt reporting a peak experience when he wrote in his *Journal*, "We walked this afternoon to Edmund Hosmer's and Walden Pond. The south wind blew and filled with bland and warm light the dry and sunny woods. The last year's leaves blew like birds through the air. As I sat on the bank of the Drop, or God's Pond, and saw the amplitude of the little water, what space, what verge, the little scudding fleets of ripples found to scatter and spread from side to side and take so much time to cross the pond, and saw how the water seemed made for the wind and the wind for the water, dear playfellows for each other, I said to my companion, I declare this world is so beautiful I can hardly believe it exists."

Inevitably when I reflect upon religious or mystical experience, T. S. Eliot's lines from "Little Gidding" come to mind:

> We shall not cease from exploration
> And the end of all our exploring
> Will be to arrive where we started
> And know the place for the first time.

Thus, to me, religious experience always has a "coming home" aspect to it. And you wonder why you ever left. . . .

Women and Spirituality

At a workshop I was doing recently on spiritual growth, a middle-aged woman came up at break time. There was a smile on her lips, but there was challenge in her eyes. "How can a man teach women about spiritual growth? You haven't had our experience!"

"That's a good question," I admitted awkwardly, all the while thinking rapidly. "Naturally, every spiritual path is a personal one. We can only move in terms of who we are and our personal experience. We're all different, and our stories vary enormously. We can, however, learn from one another."

"But all of your theologies are patriarchal," she insisted. "And women haven't had an equal opportunity to develop their own identities or to tell their own stories."

"I disagree that all theologies are patriarchal; some have said for thousands of years what feminism now claims to have discovered. But I agree that women have been discounted and that the Western theologies especially are patriarchal, and I hope that the new feminine consciousness is going to correct that. You know, the problem isn't peculiar to women. All oppressed persons need to get out from under the burdens of poor self-image and dehumanizing theologies before they can make substantial progress on their own spiritual journeys."

"But women are different from men! Carol Gilligan says. . . ."

It was a familiar conversation. And it's a relevant conversation. Aside from the social justice issues involved, it points toward the fact that women, like any other group (whether defined by theology, culture, or gender), must be free to choose their own paths if they're going to get very far as spiritual pilgrims. Indeed, the individual members of any such group will probably vary as much in their needs as will the groups themselves.

I envision spiritual growth as being like climbing a mountain. (If you don't like the hierarchical implications of that image, choose a different metaphor, like descending into a valley or passing through a wilderness.) The mountain has a single peak; the final goal of spiritual concern is the same for everyone. (If that isn't a valid assumption, then the entire ideal of spiritual growth as a movement toward wholeness, reconciliation of the finite with the Infinite, or whatever, is fatally flawed. And Ultimate Reality is worse than dualistic.)

In climbing the mountain of enlightenment, we naturally start from different places, and we inevitably follow different routes. Many of these routes are equivalent. Some, however, are inferior or are even misleading. Especially for women, a route that uses the trail map of a patriarchal theology is going to result in tough going and may quickly lead to an unscalable cliff or an active avalanche area. (Actually, such a route won't work very well for men either, and they'll be even less likely to notice.)

But for those climbers who get past the lower slopes, the trails followed become more and more similar; even though the peak is seen from different directions, it is the same peak. And for those pilgrims who make it to the top, it doesn't make any difference what color they are, what stories they have to tell, what theologies they commenced with, or whether their genitals are male or female.

As even that old male chauvinist the apostle Paul admitted, "In Christ there is neither male nor female."

5

Methods in the Paths of
Discipline and Knowledge

Like the Zen archer: taking aim in the dark

When we start examining the hows, the techniques, of promoting spiritual growth, we enter fascinating and confusing territories. First of all, let me be clear that mystical practice is not like baking a cake. Just putting the ingredients together correctly and baking it in an oven at the proper temperature for the specified period of time does not insure a successful result. Enlightenment comes on its own schedule. All we can do is put ourselves in a good place for it to happen.

Obviously there are many paths. Jiddu Krishnamurti spoke of following a path in a pathless land. He also noted that a guru, a teacher, is unnecessary—that we must do it ourselves. Yet even into his eighties he taught, lecturing brilliantly to large audiences about spiritual subjects.

Krishnamurti also questioned the value of meditation as a spiritual discipline, and yet almost all other spiritual teachers believe meditation or one of the allied disciplines to be essential to progressing spiritually. I am much inclined to agree with the latter.

I cite Krishnamurti because his example advises caution about getting too rigid in our approach. I regard him as one of the wiser and more enlightened among a large crowd of contemporary spiritual figures. Through a mysterious process which seems closely related to psychic channeling, he effortlessly came up with erudite and moving insights.

It does seem clear that from among the many possible paths one needs to select two or three and stay with them awhile. As Christmas Humphreys says, "You cannot tramp off after one guru after another and grow."

A few years ago there was a flap in some Eastern schools over the introduction of Transcendental Meditation into the educational system. Critics claimed that TM constituted the teaching of sectarian religion. This is not true, of course. Spiritual practices are creedless and beyond theologies. Thus, in theory, the holding of prayers in public schools should pose no real problem. The catch, however, is that our society is predominantly Christian, and prayers are generally regarded as Christian practices. The temptation to introduce Christian doctrine into allegedly nonsectarian school prayers would, in most cases, be too great to resist.

During the school prayer controversy, there was a marvelous newspaper cartoon. In the first frame, the teacher introduces a distinguished-looking classroom visitor: "Children, this is Senator Helms. Senator Helms is here today to observe how we practice nonsectarian praying." And in the next frame: "Donald, would you offer our nonsectarian prayer today?" In the third frame, the teacher and senator are piously bowing their heads as a voice comes from among the students: "Oh Lord Buddha, Master of the Universe. . . ." By the last frame, Senator Helms's head is no longer bowed. There is a scowl on his face and he's shouting, "Hold it!"

So spiritual practices can get co-opted by particular theologies. Curiously, authentic mystics of different spiritual traditions have few such problems. "All mystics," said Saint Martin, "speak the same language, for they come from the same country." It has been said that there is more agreement between the mystics of variant religions than there is between the mystics and nonmystics within any one religion.

I do not mean that a theological perspective is unimportant in spiritual living. Just as language is crucial to the discussion of spiritual activity, so a perspective which envisions the supreme reality and one's place in it is crucial to orienting oneself in one's growth.

Spiritual growth is a highly personal undertaking. This does not mean that religious community is inconsequential. Anyone who has attended a silent meeting of Quakers knows the reinforcing power of a gathered meeting; one can sense the energy and encouragement. I have noticed the same thing in teaching meditation classes.

Religious liberals tend to discount the worth of contemplative or monastic communities—monasteries and nunneries. I would call attention to the writings of Thomas Merton and David Steindl-Rast, both Catholic contemplatives. Steindl-Rast has written a lovely book titled *A Listening Heart* in which he says, "The monastery is a controlled environment for the professional pursuit of cultivating man's contemplative dimension." It is a place where people have the time and support to simply listen.

But why, asks the skeptic, is a community necessary to such a solitary pursuit? The response: because it is not solely solitary. In an explanation applicable to every religious community, Steindl-Rast explains:

> Community is always poised between two poles: solitude and togetherness. Without togetherness community disperses; without solitude community collapses into a mass, a crowd. But solitude and togetherness are not mutually antagonistic; on the contrary, they make each other possible.

> Solitude without togetherness deteriorates into loneliness. . . . Togetherness without solitude is not truly togetherness, but rather side-by-sideness. To live merely side by side is alienation. We need time and space to be alone, to find ourselves in solitude, before we can give ourselves to one another in true togetherness. . . .

> A human being cannot survive without community.

Obviously, permanent life in a contemplative community is possible and suitable only to a few. But I believe that every person serious about spiritual growth can profitably spend some time in a retreat setting such as a Trappist monastery (Merton's choice), a Zen center, Buddhist abbey, and so on. An excellent way to study such a possibility would be to read any one of a number of personal accounts, such as Merton's *The Seven-Storey Mountain* or John Daido Loori's *Mountain Record of Zen Talks*. (Parenthetically, let me also recommend Loori's book for anyone seriously interested in Zen theory and practice.)

All of the great religious systems recommend procedures by which their adherents may grow spiritually. These procedures can be conceptualized in various ways, but in general they are organized into four paths: (1) The path of spiritual discipline; (2) The path of knowledge; (3) The path of celebration or devotion; and (4) The path of witness and action.

Let's note that no single path is complete or sufficient. Just as people differ in the deliberateness and intensity with which they progress, so they will tend to focus on one or two paths for a period of time, to the relative neglect of the others. Eventually, however, the possibilities and challenges of all four paths will command the attention of those who are serious about achieving religious wholeness.

The Path of Spiritual Discipline

The path of spiritual discipline is the one path that should, at all times, be followed. Almost all mystics and spiritual teachers agree on this. The

path of spiritual discipline (often simply called the path of discipline) includes a whole array of strategies by which one may focus one's attention
and energies upon the innate impulse toward spiritual maturity.

All spiritual disciplines are, in some sense, methods of indirection.
Growth comes as we are "ready" for it and not as a direct, predictable result
of the particular discipline chosen. Patience, perseverance, and humility
are essential. The following is a brief description of a number of spiritual
disciplines.

The queen of the disciplines is meditation. By that I do not mean that
all the other disciplines are inferior. I mean rather that meditation is so
multi-faceted and so widespread that it is clearly preferred by the majority
of pilgrims. But there are many other disciplines, such as prayer, contemplation, mindfulness, yoga, chanting, the Zen arts, T'ai-chi and other stylized
movements, Sufi dancing, fasting, repetitious rituals, and journal-keeping.

While some disciplines work better for some people than others, and
some shopping around is advisable, it is essential to pick a discipline or two
and stay with it. Those who go in for something different every few months
are experience junkies rather than serious seekers after oneness.

If no teacher is available, one may carefully study and follow the directions of a good manual such as Lawrence LeShan's *How To Meditate*. Other
contemporary books on meditation worth consulting are Patricia
Carrington's *Freedom in Meditation* and Willard Johnson's *Riding the Ox
Home*.

The function of meditation is the quieting of the mind so that one can
hear what is already there. Most meditations do this via a repetitive mental exercise which, with practice, ties up the noisy cognitive chatter that
routinely drowns out what the Quakers call "the quiet still voice within,"
or what Bradford Smith calls "the good news that flows out of silence."

One of the more common, easily learned and least hazardous meditative procedures involves sitting in a quiet place and counting one's own
breaths: one, two, three, four, one, two, three, four. . . . It isn't advisable to
continue the sequential count past four or six, because the meditator will
be tempted to keep track of the numbers: "I got to 280 yesterday! I've got
only 20 more to go and I'm done." That's not meditating; that's thinking!

Many novice meditators have the idea that they should shortly achieve
some sort of blissed-out state in which the time passes without any cognitive awareness. Such an expectation will certainly yield frustration and
probably failure. Except for extremely advanced practitioners, it is not possible to quiet all extraneous thoughts. In fact, some meditative procedures
simply depend upon watching the extraneous thoughts as they parade by.

You have probably read accounts of Zen adepts and others who have
been wired up to an EEG (electroencephalograph) which produced a

recording of pure alpha waves or theta waves with the tracing uninterrupted even by the periodic ringing of a bell. You won't reach that kind of depth and endurance for a long time. And you shouldn't worry about it! In Eastern mysticism there is a teaching which says that anyone who maintains a pure meditative state for some brief interval (such as six seconds) achieves instant enlightenment.

So be gentle with yourself in your meditation. Persevere, but be gentle! A Sufi tale might be helpful:

There was a king who hated all magicians. Whenever a magician was apprehended in his kingdom, the king had the offender brought before him and, after a brief interrogation, sent him out to be executed.

One day a newly captured magician was hauled before the king. Just as the ruler was about to pronounce the usual sentence, the magician exclaimed, "Wait! If you let me keep my life, I will tell you where you can find a treasure of enormous value."

The king was intrigued. "Speak on!" he said.

"Well, first," said the magician, "you must agree to two conditions."

"I agree," said the king. "What are the conditions?"

"You must dig up the treasure yourself," said the magician.

"I agree," answered the king, growing impatient. "Tell me the second condition, so I can get to the treasure. And you shall go free."

"Second," said the magician. "While you are digging, you must not think of a white bear!"

It is from this Sufi tale that meditation teachers get the term "white bear." All extraneous thoughts and sensations we call white bears. Students are advised to note them as such and gently return to their breath-counting or whatever.

Often enough, novices will experience more elaborate distractions: hallucinations, paranormal impressions and even theological extravaganzas. In Zen, these are called *makyo*, or illusions. Many beginners and even some uninformed veterans think these *makyo*—colored lights, voices, whatever—are the fruits of true meditation. They aren't! They're white bears, and unless they're promptly waved on, they may move in and corrupt spiritual progress.

There is a Zen story of the novice who rushed up to the master exclaiming: "Roshi, Roshi, while sitting in *zazen* I saw the Buddha seated on a thousand-petaled lotus, surrounded by a host of saints and with all the stars of the heavens circling his head!"

"That's very nice," replied the master. "Now return to your breath-counting, and the Buddha will go away."

LeShan's book describes a whole variety of meditations and classifies them according to several useful categories. There simply isn't space or time to go into them all, but I will comment on Transcendental Meditation, since we have all heard of it and hundreds of thousands have taken the instruction. TM depends upon the silent repetition of a custom-designed mantra (usually of two syllables) which costs a fair sum and which is supposed to be kept secret. There has been some controversy about this.

I think that TM has two things going for it. First of all, because of the investment of time and money, beginners are more likely to take it seriously. Second, there is the advantage of group support.

On the other hand, I doubt the absolute necessity of the secret, custom-designed mantra, although this, too, can be an incentive to stay with the discipline. But there are many effective traditional mantras, including "Om" (pronounced Aum) and "Om Manu Padme Hum" and "God is good; God is One" and "Allah Hui." LeShan even suggests that a nonsense mantra may be preferable since it carries no cognitive message and thus cannot be distracting.

Another meditational technique is also based on the silent repetition of a long passage. An East Indian teacher, Eknath Easwaran, describes and recommends this procedure in his book *Meditation*. The meditator chooses and memorizes a spiritual passage, such as the Prayer of Saint Francis, or the Twenty-third Psalm, or one of several possibilities from Oriental scriptures, and simply repeats it silently while sitting in a meditative position. In some ways, Easwaran's technique is as much on the path of devotion as on the path of discipline, but I have known people for whom it was a powerful stimulus to spiritual growth.

Closely related to meditation is contemplation. This involves taking an object—preferably an emotionally neutral one—and simply looking at it. Contemplation means paying attention, really paying attention. As such, it is very hard in the beginning. The novice will make many slips and will have to make many corrections.

Saint Theresa of Avila trained her students in contemplation, saying, "I do not require of you to form great and serious considerations in your thinking. I require of you only to look."

One of the best contemplation objects is the head of a wooden match. I often use the end of a pen and have occasionally reached for my pen and contemplated it for a few minutes as a way of calming and centering myself in a stressful situation. It works! Read LeShan for further instructions.

There is an additional contemplation technique which many people have discovered on their own and which is recommended by some disciplinary schools. This involves listening to the sound of some natural phenomenon, such as that of wind in evergreens, of bees going to and from a hive, of a waterfall, stream, or the surf. There is an ambiguity in these in that, depending upon one's concentration, the sounds may yield attentive inner listening or they may yield a trance state or even sleep. The key is alertness, a continual "hearing" of the sound.

Related to both meditation and contemplation is mindfulness. The Vietnamese Zen Buddhist Thich Nhat Hanh, in his book *The Miracle of Mindfulness*, calls this technique "a miracle." It is not only a spiritual discipline but also a very effective way of living.

Saint Theresa of Avila often spoke of turning her daily life into a meditation. When asked when she did this, she replied, "while drawing water and chopping wood." In other words, she lived in the here and now, an absolute necessity in spiritual living. Whatever she did, she did with full attention. She did not dwell on the memories and regrets of yesterday, nor on the hopes and fears of tomorrow. She lived in the only time available to any of us, the present, the eternal now.

Mindfulness is described in a Buddhist sutra (lesson or teaching) which suggests: "When walking, the practitioner must be conscious that he is walking. When sitting, the practitioner must be conscious that he is sitting. When lying down, the practitioner must be conscious that he is lying down. . . . No matter what position one's body is in, the practitioner must be conscious of that position. Practicing thus, the practitioner lives in direct and constant mindfulness of the body."

Lest you gain the impression that mindfulness is just another esoteric practice not very useful for everyday living, let me offer you an illustration of its usefulness.

Remember all the talk about the "inner game of tennis"? What was being recommended there was concentration, or flow. The inner game player was advised to watch the ball, even to "ride" back and forth with the ball, and to hear the sound as it bounced and was hit. One was not to think about the point just made, or lost, nor be concerned about the outcome of the next point. One was to pay attention to what was happening right now. This is mindfulness. At the height of the tennis craze, there was a TV series on the inner game. In one episode, one of the students was accidentally hit in the mouth by a sharply volleyed tennis ball. The instructor rushed over with the predictable question, "Are you hurt?"

The player answered, "No," fingering her cheek and upper lip, which were already reddening from the impact.

"Now, wait a minute," replied the instructor. "What does it feel like? Is there some pain? If there is, be there—let yourself feel it."

"Well, yes, I guess it does hurt," replied the student a little uncertainly. "As a matter of fact, it hurts quite a bit." She rubbed the impact site, looking reflective.

After a moment the instructor inquired, "How does it feel, now that you recognized and acknowledged the pain?"

Smiling slightly, the student replied, "It's sort of funny. But I don't think it hurts as much."

A small example with a big lesson. Much of the pain of life arises because we avoid living with full attention in the present.

Mindfulness, paying attention, living in the here and now, can not only enrich life but transform it. Again a Zen story:

A monk was walking though the jungle when, suddenly and with a blood-curdling roar, a tiger leapt out at him. Running for his life, the monk shortly came to a cliff over which dangled a vine. Wasting no time, he scrambled down the vine with the tiger towering above him, gnashing its teeth.

Halfway down, the monk suddenly realized that two tigers were lurking below, licking their chops. He looked up. The first tiger was still there, too. But more than that, two mice had appeared out of the side of the cliff and were beginning to gnaw on the vine.

It was then that the monk noticed to one side a wild strawberry plant with one bright red, ripe strawberry growing on it. Reaching over with one hand, he plucked the strawberry and put it into his mouth. It was the most delicious thing he had ever eaten. . . .

One of the more significant and useful of the spiritual disciplines is yoga. Yoga is a Sanskrit word meaning "union." We get our word "yoke" from it. Yoga is a large and complex series of disciplines. It is far more than the physical exercises that it has become known for in the West. Yoga encompasses all four spiritual paths. Raja yoga is the path of discipline; Bhakti yoga is the path of devotion (or love); Jnana yoga is the path of knowledge; Karma yoga is the path of action and selfless service.

Nor are these all. Hatha yoga encompasses all four of the paths and is oriented toward awakening the primal energy or *prana*. It is related to Kundalini yoga, which is a difficult and dangerous practice that should not be attempted without the aid of a competent teacher. Kundalini yoga dabblers have ended up insane or crippled, their circuits blown by the undisciplined power of the mystical force, envisioned as coiled like a serpent at the base of the spine.

This is a good place to reemphasize that not all spiritual disciplines are benign. Some can be dangerous. We need to keep in mind that wherever there is great creative power, there is also the potential for great destructive power. Authentic growth does not occur without risk and suffering.

Of the yogic practices, the one that most tantalizes the untutored imagination is Tantra. Directed toward the use of sexual energy, Tantra suggests to Westerners orgiastic excesses and gross perversions. Images of the Kama Sutra swim luridly into consciousness. These are false impressions. Because of them, Tantra is the most abused of the yogas.

Ask a competent yoga teacher about all this, or buy a copy of a good yoga book such as *Choosing A Path*, a comprehensive explanation by Sri Swami Rama.

The Zen arts are another vast subject surrounded by considerable misunderstanding. The Zen arts include flower arranging, dancing, the tea ceremony, calligraphy, archery, and swordsmanship. Both practical and aesthetic, their real function is training the consciousness—indeed, to bring it into oneness with the Supreme Reality. Technical knowledge is but the beginning. The ultimate goal is the union of the artist and the art. In achieving this, there comes a sense of unity with all things. When the artist reaches this level of spiritual development, he or she has mastered the Zen art of life.

One of the best descriptions of the Zen arts is in *Zen in the Art of Archery*, by Eugen Herrigel. A German philosopher, Herrigel studied exhaustively in Japan and describes the final result in this way:

> In the case of archery, the hitter and the hit are no longer two opposing objects, but are one reality. The archer ceases to be conscious of himself as the one who is engaged in hitting the bull's-eye which confronts him. This state of unconsciousness is realized only when, completely empty and rid of the self, he becomes one with the perfecting of his technical skill, though there is in it something of a quite different order which cannot be attained by any progressive study of the art.

Herrigel goes on to narrate graphically his frustration during months of practice under the severe eye of his master. It did not matter whether he hit the target. What mattered was how he held the bow and released the arrow, or rather, whether the arrow released itself! The correct shot, said the master, must "fall like snow from a bamboo leaf."

One day Herrigel became so frustrated with repeated failure that he challenged his master to shoot blindfolded. "Come to see me this evening," replied the master.

Herrigel arrived after dark. Following tea, he and the master went to the practice hall. Though the hall was brightly lit, the target at the end was lost in gloom. Only a glowing taper stuck in front of the target indicated its approximate location.

Taking up his bow, the master fixed the first arrow to the string and took aim.

> His first arrow shot out of the dazzling brightness into deep night. I knew from the sound that it had hit the target. The second arrow was a hit, too. When I switched on the light in the target-stand, I

discovered to my amazement that the first arrow was lodged full in the middle of the black, while the second arrow had splintered the butt of the first and plowed through the shaft before embedding itself beside it. I did not dare to pull the arrows out separately, but carried them back together with the target. The Master surveyed them critically. "The first shot," he then said, "was no great feat, you will think, because after all these years I am so familiar with the target-stand that I must know even in pitch darkness where the target is. That may be, and I won't try to pretend otherwise. But the second arrow which hit the first—what do you make of that? I at any rate know that it is not 'I' who must be given the credit for this shot. 'It' shot and 'it' made the hit. Let us bow to the goal as before the Buddha!"

T'ai-chi is related to the Zen arts. Next to meditation, it is my preferred spiritual discipline. I do T'ai-chi regularly in the morning when I arrive at work and the phone is not yet ringing. Actually, T'ai-chi is but one of several martial arts having a significant spiritual dimension. To my way of thinking, it is the least suggestive of violence and, therefore, most preferable.

The similarity between T'ai-chi and the Zen arts is demonstrated by the fact that the form is learned for no purpose beyond itself. True, T'ai-chi does testify to its self-defense origins by the fact that all of its postures are stylized parries and blows, and some teachers and practitioners of the art do praise its utility for protecting oneself. For myself, that aspect of the practice is not very important. In a spot of personal danger, I would have more confidence in running for my life and yelling bloody murder or in trying to locate a blunt object quickly.

On the other hand, there is only a modest hyperbole in the promise made in one of the better books on T'ai-chi, Cheng Man-ch'ing and Robert W. Smith's *T'ai-chi:* "Whoever practices T'ai-chi . . . will gain the pliability of a child, the health of a lumberjack, and the peace of mind of a sage."

T'ai-chi is best learned through a skilled teacher. A teacher will not only facilitate the student's learning of numerous subtleties of the various forms, but will also pass on much wisdom that aids in both learning and retaining the discipline.

In essence what happens in learning T'ai-chi is that, via concentration and repetition, the student's body "learns" the exercise—much the way one's body learns to walk downstairs or ride a bicycle. Once that learning has been acquired, the body does the exercise to the student—so much so that pausing to "think" about the movements will just interrupt the rhythm and benefit of the discipline. My own sense is that, in T'ai-chi as in meditation, the rote movements serve to quiet the mind, thereby allowing "the good news that flows out of silence" to be apprehended.

One of my cues that T'ai-chi and meditation serve a useful purpose in my life is that, after an absence from doing either, when I begin practicing again that wonderful sense of "coming home" arrives.

Especially among New Agers, Sufi dancing has become a popular communal celebration and exercise, and is sometimes done to music or drums. But it is more. Related to the marathon dancing of the Whirling Dervishes, Sufi dancing induces an altered state of consciousness through sheer repetition of word and movement. The fact that devoted Sufi dancers also end up exhausted has, I suspect, an added spiritual impact.

Fasting is a practice used by many persons for both health and spiritual reasons. After the first day or so of taking nothing but liquids, fasters report a feeling of physical well-being and mental clarity. I compare fasting to meditation. Just as meditation quiets the activity of the mind, fasting quiets the activity of the body. In view of the mind/body connection, it's reasonable that both cut down on distractions and let us move beyond our finite selves.

Journal-keeping is the most modern and cerebral of the main spiritual disciplines. In some ways it could be appropriately included in the path of knowledge as well as in the path of discipline. What recommends that it be retained among the disciplines is the fact that it takes training and practice and that it draws upon one's inner self for its material.

Although private journals were kept by people ranging from Saint Augustine to Pascal, journal-keeping as we know it today was developed by psychologist Ira Progoff. Thousands have taken part in his Intensive Journal workshops. And there have been several alternative journal-keeping procedures developed.

Using a reflection and feedback process, journal-keeping is much more than recording personal experience. A typical journal is made up of many sections, including long-term and short-term history, encounters with significant events and persons, religious experiences, dreams, and accomplishments. All of these are written down spontaneously and periodically reflected upon. An important technique of Progoff is called "twilight imaging." Somewhat similar to Eugene Gendlin's focusing, twilight imaging takes place in the twilight time between waking and sleeping—a period during which the conscious and unconscious come closer together.

In journal-keeping, both analysis and judgment are avoided. The aim is not to make cognitive decisions nor to turn out a literary masterpiece, but rather to discover patterns and inner sources which clarify and instruct the course of life. Progoff's Intensive Journal even contains a "credo" section in which one may record one's own spiritual insights and truths. Because the procedure requires considerable time, relatively few people stay with intensive journal-keeping, but those who do often become very dedicated and fulfilled.

A procedure somewhat akin to journal-keeping, which is important to the spiritual growth of many people, is dream work. Because it depends upon cognitive analysis as well as intuitive insight, dream work does not fit strictly within the path of discipline. In some respects, since it also facilitates understanding of one's past and of one's current emotions and motivations, dream work is as much a therapy as it is a spiritual discipline. That is not, however, said critically; it has long been apparent to me that all mental health problems have a substantial spiritual dimension.

Modern dream work involves much more than the popular Freudian interpretation of dream symbols. Being substantially derived from Carl Jung's thinking, dream work begins with the immediate and detailed recording of one's dreams in the present tense (i.e. "I am walking along the seashore. . . .") in a journal. These reports are used in one's own private reflections and in group process where the validity of a particular interpretation is signaled by an inner "tingle" or "aha!" in the person who had the dream. Not only is every dream judged to be significant, but all characters are assumed to be aspects of oneself, and all events, however pleasing or discomforting, are believed to contain "a gift" with layers of meaning, which can be successively revealed through the dream work process.

There are several good, practical books on modern dream work, notably those of Ann Faraday (*Dream Power* and *Dream Game*) and Jeremy Taylor (*Dream Work*).

Though brief, this is an overview of the path of discipline. It is my conviction that all persons seriously interested in spiritual growth should have a discipline that is central to their daily life.

The Path of Knowledge

Because it is so familiar to us, the next path, the path of knowledge, takes the least time to discuss. This path is concerned with the search for truth or cognitive understanding. It requires an ongoing encounter with ideas and persons and an openness and honesty with both. By openness and honesty, I do not mean a debate format wherein people struggle with one another to win arguments. Such a dynamic is an egotistical exercise, inimical to spiritual growth.

It is important to this path that one be able to look beyond what appear to be "facts" to what could more accurately be called "tools." Thus symbols, myths, metaphors, stories, and paradigms (models which facilitate understanding) have an essential relevance. Knowledge, we need to remind ourselves, is the raw material and stimulus of intuition and, hence, it is indispensable to all creativity, including spiritual growth.

We do need to recognize the limitations of the path of knowledge. Words and ideas—knowledge—can only take us so far. Beyond a certain point, knowledge and the discussion of knowledge actually get in the way of growth. Consider, for example, how your involvement in hearing a symphony would be affected by an ongoing verbal explanation.

Jiddu Krishnamurti warned us over and over about relying on knowledge. While he lived very much in the here and now, Krishnamurti's memory of past events, place-names, and persons was almost nonexistent. Even though he encouraged the founding of several schools for youngsters, he did not himself appear to make much use of the teachings of others.

In his writing and speaking, Krishnamurti usually referred to himself in the third person. Consider this passage from his *Journal*:

> He . . . discovered . . . recently that there was not a single thought during [his] long walks, in the crowded streets or on the solitary paths. Ever since he was a boy it had been like that, no thought entered his mind. He was watching and listening and nothing else. Thought with its associations never arose. There was no image-making. . . . This is to be alone.

Krishnamurti did acknowledge that, "His brain was active when talking or writing but otherwise it was quiet and . . . without movement."

Moreover, he had little use for theories. "Any explanation is of little significance," he asserted. "All explanations are escapes, avoiding the reality of what is."

As a thinker, a writer, and a talker—as one who does a lot of explaining!—I am both chastened and intrigued by Krishnamurti's low appraisal of explanations and knowledge. For I do regard the man as a rather lofty spiritual being. I am also aware of the apparent contradiction implied in his dozens of published writings and well-attended lectures.

It occurs to me that Krishnamurti largely moved beyond ordinary intellectual activity—that he tapped into some fundamental cosmic source not readily accessible to most of us. Krishnamurti himself acknowledged as much: "There is a tremendous reservoir . . . which if the human mind can touch it, reveals something which no intellectual mythology . . . can ever reveal."

But he also professed puzzlement concerning its nature. "I have often felt it is not my business, that we will never find out. . . . We have come to an impasse. . . . Water can never find out what water is."

From all of this I conclude that, while the path of knowledge is crucial to cognitive understanding and to the communication of spiritual information, it peters out as we venture further into the mystical unknown. One of the best discussions of this limitation is set forth in *Mountain Record of Zen Talks* where John Daido Loori explains the purpose of a koan. "Working on a koan is not like working on a riddle; it's not something you run around in your mind. It is specifically designed to short-circuit the whole intellectual process."

The same could be said for the advanced stages of any spiritual practice. It is not that knowledge has lost all utility, but that, beyond a certain point, other paths will take us further. Nor is it that the enlightened person has no further need for linear thought, but that, as a result of having exceeded the limits of linear thought, there is a greatly expanded capacity for "knowing," including for clear thinking about everyday matters.

At a somewhat more prosaic level, I have an intuitive suspicion that, with our endless elaboration of ideas and theories, all of us are rather like the theoretical physicists. The harder we try cognitively to reach the fundamental stuff, the more it proliferates! Could it be that our very efforts at analysis and understanding continually raise more questions than they answer? It's a notion that has been offered by others. Could it be, as states of mystical awareness suggest, that at its fundamental essence, ultimate reality is startlingly simple, too simple for words and explanations?

One of Alan Watts's favorite haiku comes to mind:

This is all there is:
The path comes to an end
Among the parsley.

The Slow-Moving Neutron:
Dog days of existence

Neut is my dog—part collie, part other breeds not readily identified. Neut is a farm dog, a country boy's pal, if you will. His name is short for Neutron, a large, uncharged, slow-moving subatomic particle—which is an apt description of his usual temperament and behavior.

One thing that Neut does particularly well is grow hair. In fact, he is 97 percent efficient at converting dog food into dog hair. Of course, such a fine production apparatus must have an outlet for its products. Neut deposits most of his hair on the kitchen carpet where it vigorously resists being picked up by anything less than a high-volume vacuum cleaner or a blue suit.

Besides being my steady companion in rural settings, Neut is also good for causing me to take city walks I would not ordinarily take. We have set routes that we patrol in our neighborhood. Especially enjoyable are new houses, which I inspect for the details of construction, Neut for food left behind by untidy workers. We are each diligent in our assigned tasks.

Neut is also a peacemaker. He carries a big stick and pleads for mercy. Upon seeing another dog, he dashes up to introduce himself. Should the other dog prove unfriendly, Neut whines appropriately. Should the other dog attack, Neut yelps in response.

His relationship to humans is congruent to that with his own kind. Everyone is his buddy, even when they don't know it. Once in a while some stranger will inquire, "Does he bite?" And I answer back, "Not unless you're made out of hamburger."

Neut's only evidence of a jungle instinct is with respect to squirrels and night-roaming rodents. Although he gives ferocious chase to squirrels on the ground, he has never come close to catching one. Night-roaming rodents are something else. Often during our evening walks at the farm, Neut will suddenly stop, leap three feet into the air, simultaneously propelling himself forward or sideways, grab at something in the grass, and, after four quick shakes, it's gone—destined to become dog hair. (Neut is not a confirmed vegetarian.)

A being of Neut's sensitivity, vigor, and complexity requires special care. Often he becomes so charged up that depolarization is required. This is best accomplished when Neut is lying on his side. The therapist then must grasp a front foot and a hind foot in separate hands, bringing them together. Immediately, there is a sharp vibration as the electrons flow, bringing Neut back into harmony with himself and the universe. Relieved, he returns to his cosmic function—growing dog hair.

6

The Paths of Devotion and Witness and Action

Praise Allah, and tie your camel to the post!

The path of devotion or love is also known as the path of celebration; it is both ceremonial and devotional. The path of witness and action is sometimes called works.

Path of Devotion

Via celebration we mark and process our beginnings and endings, our passages, our discoveries, our traditions, and our mutuality. We also affirm and enlarge upon the fundamental values of our lives and come to terms with the unknown and the unknowable. The path of devotion includes what is meant by worship—affirmation of that which is true, good, and beautiful, as well as a reckoning with their opposites. It is followed via intuitive, symbolic, and aesthetic motifs at least as much as it is by linear thought and activity. It includes an acceptance of mythology, an appreciation of devotional literature, and the creative use of both.

Twenty-three years ago, when my friend Sam Wright and I hoisted a few carefully chosen possessions onto our backs and headed south along the crest of California's Sierra Nevada, our two-hundred-mile trek was an act of devotion, a spiritual journey. We both loved the Sierra and felt more in church among the granite peaks, windswept pines, and alpine lakes than in any cathedral on earth. Each morning we rose with a song of praise on our lips, and each evening we crawled into our down-filled bags with a prayer of thanksgiving in our thoughts. Traveling in what John Muir called the Range of Light reminded us what we knew beyond every doubt—that the world is beautiful, and it feels good to be here.

Almost a week into our backpack trip, we began the switchback trail up to yet one more pass—this one at 12,500 feet, named Muir Pass in honor of the grand old saint himself. The afternoon was warm, but thunderheads loomed above us. We were grateful to encounter the stone hut dedicated to Muir and erected by doughty Sierra Clubbers some years earlier.

The inside of the hut was rustic and gave evidence of being the permanent abode of an assortment of four-footed and furry wildlife. But it was dry. Plus, there was an aura about the place to which I do not hesitate to apply the term "holy ground." Along one wall was a series of crude shelves upon which were surplus items left by previous visitors: freeze-dried foods, utensils, articles of clothing, and a few paperback books. We sorted through the cache, but only one item interested us—a small Bible, of all things. Opening it, Sam flipped to the nineteenth chapter of the Psalms and read aloud:

> The heavens declare the glory of God; and the firmament
>   sheweth his handywork.
> Day unto day uttereth speech, and night unto night sheweth
>   knowledge.
> There is no speech nor language, where their voice is not heard.
>
> Their line is gone out through all the earth, and their words to
>   the end of the world. In them hath he set a tabernacle for
>   the sun,
> Which is as a bridegroom coming out of his chamber, and
>   rejoiceth as a strong man to run a race.
> His going forth is from the end of the heaven, and his circuit
>   unto the ends of it: and there is nothing hid from the heat
>   thereof.

Sam's reading of that ancient Judaic poem of praise was a devotional act, and it established a celebratory ritual of great meaning to us. Throughout the rest of the trek, at appropriate times, the Bible was retrieved from a pack side-pocket, and the reading began:

> The heavens declare the glory of God; and the firmament
>   sheweth his handywork.
> Day unto day uttereth speech, and night unto night sheweth
>   knowledge.

Looking back, I'm a little surprised that the primitive theology represented in that Bible passage didn't bother us. All I can say is that we were probably far enough from our usual haunts that we could let it be what it was intended to be—an exuberant act of thanksgiving offered in love.

Thus, what we bring to a devotional service is at least as important as what happens there. It is important to bring an awareness of one's needs, but it is also important to bring an openness of mind, spirit, and self. Are we willing to be transformed by what we find? Are we willing to let what happens speak to us, even though its theological perspective may clash with our usual conception? Are we willing to be tolerant as well as to interpret and translate? If so, we are prepared for celebration.

A similar observation should be made about devotional literature. Too often rational types err in approaching such poetry and mythology by dwelling on its factual truth or lack thereof. Religious literalists are guilty of a similar error when they struggle to read their scriptures as historically factual. Both of these approaches are limiting. The primary purpose of devotional literature is not to tell us original and final truths, but to evoke the truth that waits within us. When we read scripture of whatever tradition, we should *listen* to our own inner echoes as much as we should look at the words before us. As was pointed out in chapters one and two, the purpose of myth is not to be true but to point to a truth. In spiritual matters, the most profound and worthwhile truths are intuitive.

Twenty-five years ago Abraham Maslow, in his little book *Religions, Values, and Peak Experiences* had both friendly and harsh words for us religious liberals. Maslow charged that we "make no basic place in [our] systems for the mysterious, the unknown, the unknowable, the dangerous-to-know, or the ineffable." After noting our neglect of mystical experiences, Maslow went on to cite our distrust of "the inexact, the illogical, the metaphorical, the mythic, the symbolic, the contradictory or conflicted, the ambiguous, [and] the ambivalent."

The effect of this selective focus, said the founder of the so-called Third Force in psychology, is that "the liberal religions and semireligious groups exert . . . little influence even though their members are the most intelligent and capable sections of the population. It *must* be so just as long as they base themselves upon a lopsided picture of human nature."

Because we generally admired Maslow's pioneering insights, his stinging criticism of our emotionally cold spirituality was especially hard for Unitarian Universalists and those of similar persuasion to take. But he was essentially correct. We did tend to be, as an old witticism charged, "God's frozen people." And many people who liked our emphasis on freedom, rational thought, and social responsibility simply refused to be deprived of intuitive insights, emotional warmth, and the mystical in their religious thought and celebrations.

Today, in a move that would have cheered one of our nineteenth century patron saints, Ralph Waldo Emerson, we are bringing the head and the heart back into balance. For the first time since the Transcendentalist Revolt, American liberal religion is striving for a harmony of intuition and cognition, while reaching for the creative possibilities in the path of devotion.

In the initial excitement of discovery and with a certain propensity for sentimental motifs, we are not, however, out of the woods. The path of devotion is not a primrose path. It can be narrow and steep, with the blossoms nearly hidden behind thorns and stinging nettles. We can enrich our explorations by studying the older religious traditions, including some of those we may have left behind as outdated or repressive.

In the last chapter when I wrote about yoga as a spiritual discipline, I mentioned that Bhakti yoga is representative of this path at its best and its most demanding. It requires surrender of oneself to the Divine Reality. One loves unconditionally. One serves without expecting a reward. One pledges oneself to the truth, however unfamiliar or upsetting.

Sri Swami Rama, a Hindu teacher, asserts bluntly: "Jesus trod the path of Bhakti, and practical Christianity is the path of Bhakti." Thus, if you wish to know what traveling the path of devotion really means, study the life of Jesus as reported in the Synoptic Gospels. Especially heed the Sermon on the Mount! Pay particular attention to what Jesus called the greatest law of life—the requirement to love God with one's whole mind, heart, and spirit and to love one's neighbor as oneself. Thus, the fundamental requirement for walking the path of devotion is that we must do it united with the whole.

All religions teach the path of devotion. They all direct us to be loving, kind, gentle, truthful. Such a directive leaves no room for sectarian animosities. More than that, it asks us to open ourselves to the possibility of celebration wherever we may be. Keep that in mind next time you happen to be present at an occasion where the theology represented makes you grit your teeth. How will you react? Will you balk at what those words meant to you? Or will you hear the spiritual possibilities behind those words? Will you be stuck in the past, or will you live in the present? Will you be a literalist or will you take what you hear and adapt it to your own needs and growth?

Again, authentic mystical experience is beyond theology. When Jesus reminded us that we must "become as little children," he was not talking about helplessness or gullibility. He was talking about seeing with fresh eyes and hearing with fresh ears. He was talking about freedom—being free from old hang-ups and open to the most creative possibilities of the present, living moment.

Many years ago, in my first church, I drove back and forth to work past a large Catholic church. One evening I was early for an appointment. On an impulse I stopped at the Catholic church and went in. The place was empty of people, but it was not empty of presence. The specific theology represented in the candles and icons and stained glass had no special meaning for me, but the spiritual effect of the place was palpable. I can't name what it was; I don't even need to. I know now that there are sacred places—holy ground. New Agers speak of power points. Thomas Merton, a devout Roman Catholic, was utterly enthralled by the huge reclining Buddhas at Polonnaruwa, Sri Lanka. Later he wrote, "I don't know when in my life I have ever had such a sense of beauty and spiritual validity running together in one aesthetic illumination." Huxley's conclusion that great cathedrals and shrines acquire a sacred aura through the spiritual experiences of their worshipers seems completely credible to me.

Those of us who meditate or pray regularly usually discover that it helps to have a special place. I have long used a particular chair in my office for meditating. Several years ago, I yielded to a long-lurking impulse and bought a Buddha and the other articles of a Buddhist shrine. Using a meditational bench, I now meditate kneeling before that shrine. Silly? Superstitious? Perhaps. But I know that my meditations go better before that shrine. In fact, I now have two of those shrines. One remains at home, where my wife uses it, too. The other stays in my office most of the year but travels to the farm where I spend summer months.

Path of Witness and Action

The last of the four spiritual paths is the path of witness and action. There is a diabolically erroneous opinion in the Western world that spiritually advanced persons are otherworldly and disdain the suffering of the impoverished and persecuted. We've all heard the stories and seen the cartoons of gurus living alone in caves and on mountain tops. These reflect the widespread misconception that spiritual living requires withdrawal from the world. And, while it is true that withdrawal may be temporarily important to spiritual development, so it is also true that return to the world is equally essential. This is the meaning of the perennial story or maxim found in various forms in several spiritual traditions: "If you are deeply into your meditation (or prayers) and hear that someone is suffering or hungry, cease your discipline, go and do what you can for the troubled person, and then return to your meditation (or prayers)."

Let us not forget that one of the essential tasks of the Old Testament prophets was to call their people to justice and mercy and that Jesus preferred the company of the despised and downtrodden to that of the leaders of the religious and political establishment. We should additionally remind ourselves that on the Buddhist Eight-Fold Path, one of the first requirements is right living.

Today, most nominally religious persons accept that spiritual concern includes the practice of social outreach and charity. There is more doubt, however, about the appropriateness of political action. In some modern religious circles, it has become common (almost a virtue, in fact) to say that religion and politics should be kept separate—presumably an update of Jesus's injunction: "Render therefore to Caesar the things that are Caesar's, and to God the things that are God's."

The purpose of most such citations, I suspect, is to avoid conflict over sticky moral issues and the possible corruption of either area of concern by the other. I believe, however, that while the institutions of government and religion should never be in cahoots with each other, they should always maintain a watchful eye over each other. I agree with Mahatma Gandhi: "I can say without the slightest hesitation, and yet in all humility, that those who say that religion has nothing to do with politics do not know what religion means." And from my professional experience, I will also assert that politics has more than a little to do with religion.

The path of witness and action is just as difficult to follow as the others. This is an era of social and political activism. Those of us who feel proud about the stands we take and the evil we oppose need to remind ourselves of Thoreau's pithy comment, "If I heard that a man was coming to help me, I would turn the other way and run as fast as I could."

"Doing good" is risky business, especially for those "done to." The U.S. government, with its political subversion and military intervention, claims it is "doing good" in Central America. Back during the Vietnam era, Sen. William Fulbright told of an Australian coming up to him and saying, "What you Americans don't seem to realize is that the rest of the world doesn't appreciate having you do good *against* them!"

For a few years I was a member of the committee that admitted new students to Starr King, a liberal seminary in Berkeley. We always asked the candidates why they wanted to be in the liberal ministry. We got the usual answers—to work with people, explore religious ideas, help build a better world, promote one's own religious growth. These aims, in moderation, were acceptable. But the candidate who always put our guard up was the one who admitted no personal ambition in the ministry. There is no person so dangerous as the one who claims, "I'm not doing this for myself; I'm doing it for you!"

A few years ago an ex-Buddhist priest with the unlikely name of Jack Kornfield published an article in *New Age Journal* titled, "The Path of Passion—Thoughts on Spiritual Practice and Social Action." At the beginning of the article, Kornfield posed an important question for those contemplating a path of witness and action: "How can we reconcile the question of service and responsibility in the world with the Buddhist concepts of nonattachment, emptiness of self, nonself? First we must learn to distinguish love, compassion, and equanimity from what might be called their 'near-enemies.' "

As Jack Kornfield saw it, "The near-enemy to love is attachment." We have all encountered the person who equates loving with possessing. In my activities as a minister, I often come into contact with people having troubles in their intimate relationships. Again and again, what is clear is that, when most people proclaim their love, what they are really doing is claiming the right to control. And control always compromises love. Even in charitable work, many would-be generous persons put conditions on their offers of help which Ralph Waldo Emerson quite correctly labeled "hooks."

"The near-enemy to compassion is pity." Here is an example of a dynamic that will surface several times in this book: many people do not know the difference between spirituality and sentimentality. Pity, the near-enemy of compassion, rears its ugly head when someone, smitten by another's trouble, exclaims: "Oh, you poor unfortunate thing! I wouldn't want to be in your shoes; here, let me comfort you!" Compassion is a rational response to a need or disharmony; pity is an emotional trip. Compassion sees the other person first; pity thinks of itself first.

"The near-enemy of equanimity is indifference." There is a large difference between the kind of stoicism that accepts that life has suffering and injustice and the attitude that rationalizes uninvolvement because, "Suffering and injustice are inevitable anyway, so why try to do anything about them?" It helps to remember that hatred is not the true opposite of love; indifference is. At least when we hate, we notice a person. When we are indifferent, we ignore that person's existence. Equanimity, in contrast to indifference, does what needs to be done. It acts because it sees and feels responsible for the unity of things.

Seeing and feeling the unity of things! In social action as in all spiritual growth, we risk error when we lose sight of the unity of things. We must include ourselves in what we do. That means that our first project is ourselves. If you want to change the world, begin by changing yourself. Otherwise, forget it! There are too many people out there already imposing their problems onto other people in the name of charity and reform. That's why so many of our well-meaning remedies end up becoming part of our problems.

When we begin from a place of personal centeredness, there are many ways to serve. Jack Kornfield tells of Vimala Thakar, an East Indian woman who spent many years in rural development. Jiddu Krishnamurti asked her to teach in one of his schools, and she became a highly effective and much-loved teacher. Then she cut back on her teaching and returned to rural development work. Kornfield asked her why. In the formal manner of Krishnamurti, Thakat replied, "Sir, I am a lover of life, sir, and I make no distinctions between serving people who are starving and have no dignity in their physical lives and serving people who are fearful and closed and have no dignity in their mental lives. There's no difference to me. I love all of life, and the way that I give is in respond to whatever's presented to me."

"It was a wonderful response!" Kornfield admitted. "There's a Sufi or Islamic phrase that puts it together. It says: 'Praise Allah, and tie your camel to the post.' It's both sides: pray, yes, but also make sure you do what's necessary in the world."

"Doing what's necessary in the world" means all kinds of things. Not all of us can be like Mother Teresa of Calcutta. That's not who we are. But if we pay attention to who we are and to the world around us, if we live mindfully, we will see what we can and should do. The challenge then is to do it!

Perhaps the greatest modern example of someone following the path of witness and action is Mahatma Gandhi. Gandhi recognized that there are two great powers in the world. One is the power to kill others. Most of the world seems to embrace this power in one way or another. But the other power is represented in not being afraid to die. That's the only power that can stop those willing to kill. Gandhi knew that and put it into practice.

Martin Luther King, Jr., practiced this second power. And although King and Gandhi both died at the hands of those willing to kill, still they changed the world. And their power continues.

I have mentioned *The Miracle of Mindfulness* but did not say much about the book's author, Thich Nhat Hanh. During the Vietnam War, he headed the Vietnamese Buddhist Peace Delegation in Paris. He has written several books, including one coauthored with activist priest Daniel Berrigan. He served as a vice-chairman of the Fellowship of Reconciliation, where he was especially concerned with healing the physical and spiritual scars of war.

To me Nhat Hahn is a superb example of a person who recognizes the essential connection between spiritual wholeness and effective political action. About him, James Forest, a Fellowship of Reconciliation member who traveled with Nhat Hanh, says, "What American peace activists might learn from their Vietnamese counterparts is that, until there is a more meditative dimension in the peace movement, our perceptions of reality (and thus our ability to help occasion understanding and transformation) will be terribly crippled."

At the end of one of his chapters, Nhat Hanh concludes with a very important observation about the need to balance spirit and action.

> I thought about conference rooms where people argue and debate, where angry and reproachful words are hurled back and forth. If one placed flowers and plants in such rooms, chances are they would cease to grow.

> I thought about the garden tended by a monk living in mindfulness. His flowers are always fresh and green, nourished by the peace and joy which flow from his mindfulness. One of the ancients said, "When a great Master is born, the water in the rivers turns clearer and the plants grow greener."

> We ought to listen to music or sit and practice breathing at the beginning of every meeting or discussion.

Free-Floating Activism

One of the more disabling spiritual errors is attachment to results.

A friend and I were talking one morning over breakfast about peace. The Reagan administration had just announced its latest plans for sending millions of dollars in "humanitarian aid" to the Contra terrorists killing women and children in Nicaragua. And we were both confounded that this could happen in the face of polls showing that 60 percent of the American people opposed U.S. intervention in that Central American country.

"Is there any hope at all?" he asked. And then, as he put his head between his hands, came the key question: "I don't see the point of going off to another demonstration at the federal courthouse! What good will it do?"

This man was a long-time friend. We had had many conversations over such spiritual essentials as living in the present but without attachment. He knew as well as I did the importance of living mindfully, of responding to what is before one now. And, despite its special ambiguity for us possession-obsessed Westerners, he appreciated the importance of being devoted to what is socially and spiritually worthwhile without getting attached to it.

But we had never talked about the hazards of making our responses to moral challenges conditional upon whether those responses will succeed.

And so, we talked. Finally, I said to him, "What about nuclear war? You and I agree that nuclear war is a real possibility. Yet you're an active members of PSR (Physicians for Social Responsibility), and we both support several nuclear concern groups. Why do we do that?"

After a moment's thought, he replied, "Well, you can't just stand around and wait for the world to blow up—even if you think it might. It matters too much. You do what seems right, at least for your own sake."

He was correct, of course. I recalled novelist Bernard Malamud's advice in *The Fixer* where he has his nearly defeated and totally dejected character say, "I live as an optimist because I find I cannot live at all as a pessimist."

Carefully, I explained to my comrade my conviction that, just as love and attention can transform our social change activities, so can practicing nonattachment. What nonattachment means in such a context is not getting hung up on specific results. Attachment to a particular outcome can befuddle our thinking, distort our actions, and even immobilize us. Yes, we should pay attention to injustice or whatever, and we should respond to it appropriately, even passionately. But we should beware of insisting that the outcome conform to the details of our own expectations. Nonattachment says, "Do the best you can, and let the result take care of itself." And really! When you think about it, what choice do we have?

The late afternoon sun was bathing the side of the federal courthouse in an orange glow as we met, grinned, and gave each other a hearty hug.

7

Suffering and Pitfalls

No pain, no gain. No shortcuts either!

One of my favorite descriptions of the proper function of a religious institution is that it should "comfort the afflicted and afflict the comfortable." One of the reasons so many churches are not effective in helping their people grow spiritually is that they do not appreciate or implement this advice. Far too many churches merely comfort the comfortable, and a distressing number of others afflict the afflicted.

Spiritual growth is not easy. Every established mystical tradition says this. Along with the ecstasy or joy that comes with enlightenment, or salvation, or satori, or realization, comes the suffering that any creative activity requires. There are also numerous dead ends, pitfalls, and false paths to be avoided. All of these need looking at.

Let's begin with the suffering of growth. The impulse toward spiritual growth begins rather modestly; after all, in the early years we're involved in egotistical concerns of the "identity search" and that sort of thing. Early on, there are significant shifts in what we now call faith development, but the real urge toward self-discovery in the spiritual sense doesn't usually commence until middle age.

Often it is said that the purpose of spiritual growth is loss of the ego. That's a menacing statement for people who think that the isolated ego is their sole identity. But the purpose of spiritual growth is not really loss of the ego but recognition that the ego is not the ultimate Self—the Atman which is identical with Brahman. And once that recognition begins, the ego's dominance is surrendered willingly and even joyfully.

But until then, most of us get thoroughly identified, tightly attached, to the ego. Thinking it is us, we are deathly afraid of losing it. So we hang on for dear life, suffering all the fears and anxieties that accompany the letting go of life's material and temporal attachments. During this phase, death, of course, represents the ultimate loss.

As we grow older, the urge toward spiritual growth begins to intensify. Even then, the first intimations are more nearly nudges or vague discontents than they are soul-wrenching upheavals. And there are many false starts.

Over the years, I have been approached by several men with requests that I serve as their spiritual guide. Aside from doubts as to whether I am competent to undertake such a responsibility, I also hesitate under strong impressions that my petitioners are not ready. I am all too personally aware of Thomas Merton's conclusion: "The spiritual life is something that people worry about when they are so busy with something else they think they ought to be spiritual."

There is one man, a psychologist in his mid forties, whom I can count on to show up whenever his love life is troubled or becalmed. But his interest in spiritual literature and disciplines lasts only until a new woman comes into his life.

Not that I think there is any necessary conflict between spiritual growth and an active erotic interest. But, for this man, it appears that his spiritual proclivities are somewhat analogous to the conventional religious impulses of soldiers under fire in foxholes. As soon as the crisis is past, they forget all about "higher" things.

In his book *Journey of Awakening* Ram Dass (who was born as Richard Alpert) has some cogent and humorous descriptions of the emotional and spiritual seesaw of growth during the middle years. "You start cleaning up your life when you feel that you can't go on until you do. Cleaning up your life means extricating yourself from those things which are obstacles to your liberation."

But the path is seldom smooth or continuous. Most pilgrims move at a rather erratic pace. They oscillate between spells of fairly strict spiritual practices and longer periods of willful backsliding. They are often much more preoccupied with outer appearances than they are with inner progress. And, for sure, they aren't yet interested in loosening any of the attachments by which the ego assures itself of its preeminence.

As one alternately follows and neglects one's discipline, however, a kind of spiritual yearning develops. At first it is not discernible, except as a feeling of relief when, after a layoff, one resumes one's meditation. Then a soft but deeply felt sense of "coming home" flows over one. And the quiet question asks itself: "Why haven't I been doing this all along?"

Many people, of course, shield themselves from all authentic spiritual yearnings by compulsive stimulation-seeking or by affiliating with some authoritarian system that saves them the sacrifice and struggle of true growth. Others flirt with the possibility of growth until they can no longer stand themselves the way they are. At that point, their discomfort may turn into real suffering. There may even be times of deep despair or disorientation when all hope seems lost. The Christian mystics call this desperate condition a "dark night of the soul."

The classical spiritual literature contains many vivid accounts of struggle, doubt, and anguish that may go with spiritual growth, especially where the pilgrim tries to resist the change. One of the most graphic modern descriptions is Francis Thompson's haunting poem, "The Hound of Heaven." In fact, the poem is so close to the core of the matter that most of those who have not experienced some of the pain of real growth do not understand it.

Thompson's imagery is generally Christian, but the imaginative non-Christian can readily translate its language. The "Hound of Heaven," in Thompson's epic poem, is the irresistible transformation of self represented in realization of the Self. Consider these opening lines:

> I fled Him, down the nights and down the days;
> I fled Him, down the arches of the years;
> I fled Him, down the labyrinthine ways
>   Of my own mind; and in the mist of tears
> I hid from Him, and under running laughter.
>   Up vistaed hopes I sped;
>   and shot, precipitated,
> Adown Titanic glooms of chasmed fears,
> From those strong Feet that followed, followed after.
>   But with unhurrying chase,
>   And unperturbéd pace,
> Deliberate speed, majestic instancy,
>   They beat—and a Voice beat
>   More instant than the Feet—
> "All things betray thee, who betrayest Me."

That is but the mere beginning of this nearly overwhelming poem. And in the whole of Francis Thompson's shattering utterance, there is no hint of the dilettantism which seems to characterize much of the contemporary activity that masquerades as spiritual growth. Oh, yes—we do hear the call to become who we really are, but we resist! Psychiatrist M. Scott Peck, in his work *The Road Less Traveled,* asserts that laziness is the most common cause of evil, or separation from wholeness.

Christmas Humphreys is adamant on the cause of most spiritual suffering: "The number is legion of those who wander from meeting to meeting searching for someone to do all the work for them." He also says: "We are all members of the Escaping Club. In one way or another we are all trying to escape from the very thing we say we are trying to find. Some of us know we are trying to escape. Others don't."

Humphreys concludes with this warning, "Stagnation and death is the future of all that vegetates without change. And how can there be change for the better without proportionate suffering during the preceding change? Suffering is, in brief, a friend, and to admit it, suffer it and use it is neither pessimism nor being dreary; it is common sense."

In *The Road Less Traveled,* M. Scott Peck says we have no creative alternative to growth. The failure to choose growth is the "primary basis of all human mental illness." I agree. More and more, I recognize that the personal and relational problems most of us experience are really spiritual problems. Carl Jung was correct in saying, "Neurosis is a substitute for legitimate suffering."

Now let's look at the suffering of growth in more positive terms. The spiritual literature is filled with lyrical accounts of the successful pilgrim's journey. None is more fascinating or instructive than that of Bernadette Roberts, a former Catholic nun, who sets forth her own spiritual odyssey in a recent book, *The Experience of No-Self.* In it she tells the story of her twenty-year "journey beyond union, beyond self and God, a journey into the silent and still regions of the Unknown," a pilgrimage in which she gains a new and powerful understanding of Jesus's words: "He who brings himself to naught for me discovers who he is."

What we learn from Bernadette Roberts's account (and that of every other articulate mystic, from Saint John of the Cross to Saint Therese of Lisieux) is that coming to spiritual maturity is the epitome of the creative process. Every creative act involves preparation, struggle, doubt, and suffering. Then, when least expected, the breakthrough comes, *if* we stay with the process, and if we have the good sense to back off occasionally, unfocus our attention, and let the good news come in its own time. Brother David Steindl-Rast puts it beautifully: "When I drop the question, the answer is there." Says Thomas Merton: "We have what we seek. It is there all the time; if we give it time it will make itself known to us."

It is then that the pain and effort pay off. The insight, the burst of illumination, comes in a rush. Where it comes from is anybody's guess—the unconscious, the intuition, the Cosmic Consciousness, the universal holographic knowing, God itself. Who knows?

But there is no mistaking its arrival. There is a rush of energy and excitement, of joy—the joy of release and knowing. This creative flash,
whether it concerns secular or sacred matters, is a peak experience. It is
awe-inspiring and humbling. It is transforming and unifying. It erases the
boundaries between self and the rest of creation and, for an eternal instant,
one stands in harmony with the All.

The moment is savored, and the work of consolidation and elaboration
is done. But the moment passes, and is gone, although surely not forgotten.

Then comes the inevitable next step. The path leads on. "The path
has many steps and the next is always the hardest we shall ever know,"
writes Christmas Humphreys.

What we need is the imagination and courage contained in Claire
Morris's *Edges:* "When we walk to the edge of all the light we have and
take the step into the darkness of the unknown, we must believe one of two
things will happen—there will be something solid for us to stand on, or we
will be taught to fly."

Pitfalls!

What about pitfalls?

First, let me repeat a thought that I've offered before. Anything having
creative power is also associated with the possibility of destructive power.
Some spiritual practices are risky. Kundalini, for example, one of the most
powerful of the yogas, can be a perilous undertaking for the untutored. And
some meditative techniques can result in dynamics which encourage not
unity with the Divine Ground but an intensified attachment and egoism.

Drugs

You don't hear much about it now, but in the heyday of LSD, many
people thought of such chemicals as shortcuts to spiritual growth. Harvard
professors Richard Alpert and Timothy Leary were among the more
notorious proponents of this practice. Alpert went to India, took up meditation, gave up drugs, and became Ram Dass. Leary, with his "Turn on, tune
in, and drop out" slogan, went to jail.

Ironically, psychedelic drugs may be useful adjuncts to mystical experience. But in the hands of the uninitiated and unguided, the drug experience may overload the novice's circuits, leaving him or her traumatized
or worse. The more common result of drug-induced mysticism is that
spiritual novices may mistake it for the real thing, which it isn't.

It is now clear that LSD and similar drugs can provide a glimpse of
what's possible in authentic mystical experience, but that is all. Via the in-
gestion of a chemical, one can climb a promontory from which previously
unseen mystical wonders may be seen, but one cannot go into the territory

itself. Repeated trips may, in fact, cause the user to confuse the view with the real thing—to become a spiritual voyeur, neglecting or not recognizing the possibilities that go with true growth. It is well-known that drug users who become serious meditators almost invariably give up the drugs.

Meditational Cul-de-Sacs

In my description of meditation, I noted that novices sometimes have paranormal experiences. And I warned that these should be treated like any other white bear (distraction) and gently waved off. The rationale for this is not trivial.

Whether through meditation or in other ways, novices occasionally discover that they have psychic abilities, including extrasensory perception, psychokinetic powers, and the ability to heal and work miracles. This realization can be heady, enormously seductive to the ego, and may cause the seeker to stop his or her serious spiritual work and become a psychic, a healer, a wonder-worker, or a dabbler in the occult arts. The Hindus call such powers *siddhis* and have about the same regard for them as Christians do for sorcery.

It is not that such powers and practices are intrinsically evil or even harmful but that they are distracting, and for those who misinterpret or misuse them, they may lead to power trips or attachments prohibiting further growth. The Sufis regard miracles and such as "veils" intervening between the soul and God. Meher Baba called them card tricks. And the Buddha is reported to have reacted to a feat of levitation by reminding one of his disciples: "This will not conduce to the conversion of the unconverted, nor to the advantage of the converted."

These are chastening judgments to one who has walked on fire and who works regularly with psychic healing. I regard them soberly. I am wary of the possibility that such feats may gain an exaggerated and corrupting influence in my life. I know they are not a signal of spiritual progress or maturity, nor are they adequate substitutes for spiritual practices. On the other hand, like all finite skills, psychic skills may serve as instructive experiences and tools in the living of everyday life. I have no doubt, for example, that authentic psychic readers have access to information—even spiritually useful information—that other people do not generally have. And at least some of this information can raise questions and suggest possibilities for growth that might otherwise be missed.

In my opinion, psychic readings should be treated in much the same way as devotional literature or myths. Being often metaphorical or mythic, they may point to a truth without being literally true themselves. And persons reacting to such information should ask themselves the questions: "What does this say to me? How should it affect my approach to life?" At the same time, any powerful event the psychics experience can be either creative or destructive. I have witnessed situations, for example, where persons appeared to be receiving messages that were demonic, and they were unable to cope with them. Some of these episodes were similar to what, once upon a time, would have been called "possession."

As with the more powerful spiritual disciplines, psychic experiences and powers, as well as what is sometimes called miracle working, need to be treated cautiously. The guidance of a teacher or spiritual counselor may be indicated, at least to facilitate understanding and avoid power trips.

Mysticism Versus Magic

In her classic work *Mysticism*, Evelyn Underhill makes a useful distinction between mysticism and magic. Mysticism she defines as the attempt to come into oneness with the cosmic power. Magic, on the other hand, is the attempt to harness and exploit cosmic power for one's own purposes. Thus, mysticism is harmonizing; magic is manipulative. One is humble; the other is arrogant.

Underhill wrote her book in 1924, well before the current interest in spirituality and the occult had mushroomed. But she recognized the possibility that the two would get confused. "In every period of true mystical activity we find an outbreak of occultism, illuminism, or other perverted spirituality and—even more dangerous and confusing for the student—a borderline region where the mystical and the psychical overlap."

She also recognized that some overlap is inevitable and that religious institutions even welcome certain kinds of magic. "Religion can never entirely divorce itself from magic," she wrote, "for her rituals and sacraments must have, if they are to be successful in their appeal to the mind, a certain magical character." Thus, magic is not to be avoided at all costs, but it must be clearly distinguished from mysticism, else the unwary pilgrim will end up becalmed in some occult backwater or swept through the rapids of an egotistical power trip.

The Stink of Zen

This graphic term includes a whole family of pitfalls. It refers, first of all, to the all-too-common temptation to see one's spiritual experiences as badges of accomplishment. A few years ago I heard a lecturer describe in great detail all of the spiritual disciplines he had mastered and all the peak experiences he had had. It was a pathetic performance. The speaker might as well have been showing us his military medals or collection of sports cars. And his audience literally writhed in discomfort as this man's overly active ego trampled his barely viable spiritual yearnings. He was, most of us realized, a desperately lonely man.

Related to the "Stink of Zen" is "guru chasing." Some novices go through teachers in much the same way that a tourist might go through seven European countries in nine days. Again, the ego is in charge, and the spirit gets left behind. Where a teacher seems necessary, finding the right teacher is important. But finding the perfect teacher, or the most famous teacher, or following a succession of teachers, does not add to our spiritual status or understanding. And where we habitually make these errors, chances are high that spiritual growth for us is one more stimulation, just another consumer experience. By the same token, any teacher who, like the speaker above, is eager to impress the student with his or her elevated position or special powers should be scrupulously avoided.

Then there is the "pilgrim-in-a-hurry." In keeping with their approaches to secular life, many novices believe that the harder they push themselves, the more rapidly they will progress. More likely the reverse will result. Achieving enlightenment is like letting silty water clear; it happens in its own time, and attempts to rush it do not accelerate the process.

Akin to the drug user is the "bliss ninnie." This vivid term, which originated with Jean Houston, refers to people addicted to peak experience. Forcing such an experience is a little like faking a sneeze. It is obvious to the bystander and of scant satisfaction to the actor. To be sure, authentic peak experiences are important signposts on the spiritual journey, but they are not the purpose of spiritual searching. They tell us of our progress, they leave us shaken and transformed, but then they pass, and it becomes our duty to return to ordinary reality, pay attention, and take the next step on the path.

Finally, there is "spiritual materialism." This is perhaps the most subtle pitfall of all. Spiritual materialism is simply a special form of attachment. In Buddhism, it is said that the final attachment that must be surrendered is the attachment to enlightenment itself. Remember the rule that we are already enlightened, we just don't know it. In order to achieve that realization, we must let go of it—sort of an ultimate koan.

I-Found-It Mania

This pitfall is so obvious that it may not need mentioning, but let us note Krishnamurti's comment about truth being a pathless land. While there are obviously better paths and worse paths, no one path can claim to be the best. Beyond its crippling effects on the individual pilgrim, I-found-it mania may be the deadliest of spiritual epidemics. As Aldous Huxley points out again and again, creedalism, literalism, and fanaticism are signs that a spiritual tradition has become temporal and materialistic, fixed in time and space. Corrupted and fragmenting religions invariably foment wars, persecutions, and heresy trials. They have lost their sacred aspect and become demonic. As examples of the abuse of power, they are categorically evil. Because they separate people from their higher selves (God), they epitomize sin. Sadly, there is no lack of examples of I-Found-It mania in the modern world.

No Big Thing

Many of the mistakes of spiritual practice come about because of attachment to sensation and the failure to appreciate the very ordinariness of most spiritual growth. The popular misconception is that seriously and successfully following a path involves exotic disciplines, renowned and mysterious gurus, spectacular experiences, and even desperate and prolonged suffering. As a well-known Zen story tells us, quite the reverse is closer to the truth.

A particularly eager spiritual novice went to the master of a monastery and said, "I am ready for every sacrifice; please teach me the way."

"Have you eaten your rice porridge?" asked the master.

"Yes," replied the student, "I have eaten."

"Then you had better wash your bowl," said the master.

Summer of the Calves

It is widely known that the Chinese name their years after common animals. I'm thinking of doing the same with my summers.

Thus, this might be called the summer of the bovine. A few weeks ago, I might have chosen the bluebirds which abound around the farm. But now the cattle have it. Hands down.

Among the cattle on our pasture are a half dozen calves four to eight weeks old. Calves, especially in groups, lead idyllic lives—drinking fresh milk, gamboling about like puppies, seeking adventure. The immediate area about our house in the woods is fenced with nasty, four-point barbed wire on three sides, and prettier, rustic wooden rails in front. The nimble calves sometimes crouch low enough to slip under the rails. But not often, partly because my roaring emergence from the house discourages them. Or so I'd thought.

A couple of weeks ago, the concrete truck came with four and a half cubic yards for the garage floor. Rob, my son, and I carefully worked it up—screeding, floating, and troweling—all the correct things. In the evening Rob went back to Spokane, I off to visit the neighbors. The calves crossed my mind as I left, but the gate bars were firmly in place, and besides, the calves had shown no interest in intruding into the yard for well over a week.

Two hours later at dusk when I returned, the calves were hanging around near the gate, outside where they were supposed to be, looking innocent and wide-eyed. I let myself in, replaced the bars and, just before going inside for a relaxed evening, went to the garage to admire the handiwork.

Egad! The once-smooth floor looked as though Pan and all his kinfolk had held a bacchanalia in the place! Hundreds of hoof-prints an eighth- to a quarter-inch deep covered the new floor. I looked at the scene dismayed. The calves, meanwhile, stood in a row just beyond the gate watching. For an instant I pondered the contents of their consciousness.

Two hours later, by dint of hard labor, I had retroweled the embossed concrete. But the cloven-hoof impressions will still last as long as the floor does.

Later, I recalled an anecdote about a Zen-like housewife whose freshly laundered clothing stretched on the grass had been muddied by a tribe of passing dogs. "Land sakes," exclaimed the incredibly good-natured woman as she surveyed the damage, "they didn't miss a one!"

8

Sex and Spirit

When the carnal and the sacred come together

A recurring theme in ancient mythologies is that male and female were originally one being, complete and unified. Then, for some transgression against the divine powers, that being was sundered into two sexual poles, each incomplete in itself and destined thereafter to yearn for wholeness by uniting with the opposite pole.

It's a fetching notion, one that conforms rather closely to the behaviors of the sexes. It also has a spiritual relevance, referring, as it does, to the striving toward wholeness which is a core feature of all the great religious traditions.

Furthermore, the similarities between sexual orgasm and peak experience have been similarly noted. Both experiences, at their best, are marked by an at least momentary loss of the sense of oneself as an isolated individual. The word "ectasy" is often used to describe either happening.

Then, too, the fact that the natural result of heterosexual union is the appearance of a new being—another manifestation of life—also evokes religious associations.

Because of all of these, it is inevitable that religious traditions and religious institutions would take sex seriously. At a very practical level, sex is simply too powerful a human dynamic to escape the notice of religion. It is a simple and harshly pragmatic fact that whoever controls a person's sexual expression probably controls the person as well. Authoritarian institutions, both political and religious, have long recognized this connection, and have usually rushed to exploit it.

In the Western world, it is impossible to resist the conclusion that our current repressiveness toward women and exploitation of sexuality are a direct result of our predominating theologies. The evidence is painfully clear from Jewish and Christian scriptures where women are regularly accorded a second-class status and usually treated as chattel. Curiously, while the Koran as written is somewhat less severe than the Old and New Testaments, the predominating attitudes toward women and sexual expression in Islamic cultures seem even more hopelessly benighted.

Among the ancient Greeks, Plato had some thoroughly thought-provoking notions about sex and spirit. For most of us the mention of the philosopher's name probably brings up the term "platonic relationship." The popular connotation of that term is non-sexual or ascetic. But that is both a misunderstanding and a gross simplification of Plato's thought on the matter.

To the philosopher love was a cosmic principle having a hierarchical structure. He fully expected and approved of liaisons in which two people, physically attracted, would fall in love with each other. And he called this "a madness which is a divine gift and a source of the chiefest blessings granted to man."

Plato did not expect this madness to last, however. Noting that, to people in love, the universe seems concentrated in the other person, Plato suggested that this passion should lead inevitably into a cosmic kind of love—to what we, today, might call mystical oneness. Thus, sexual involvement with another person should lead both partners toward personal or spiritual growth.

When Plato talked about the madness of love, he meant more than sexual expression. To him genuine passion meant selfless unconditional love. And it was this selfless, unconditional love which began in the appreciation of a beautiful physical form and led, via the love of all Beauty, including Wisdom, to the infinite Source of All Being. It was to this latter love—the love of the infinite Source of All Being—that the term "platonic love" originally referred.

The same idea pops up among contemporary philosophers. Father Bede Griffiths, a Benedictine monk living in an Indian ashram, takes a rather Catholic view of the subject, saying sex is holy and, when it is expressed properly, makes the partners one with God.

When we move to the Eastern cultures, we again encounter religious practices, such as the Hindu suttee, which are repugnant to us. And the lot of women in such cultures is little, if any, better than it is in the West. Curiously, however, these injustices seem to be less founded in myth and theology than they are in other cultural dynamics.

A central teaching in the Eastern spiritual traditions is that each human being is a manifestation of the divine principle, but that this knowledge gets obscured by the egotistical concerns of everyday life. Typical of this thought is Hinduism, where wholeness or enlightenment comes as we recognize Atman (the essence of Brahman) in ourselves, or as we realize that the self is actually the Self. Holding this essential principle in mind, we can then appreciate the Hindu principle that all authentic love is founded in the yearning of the self for the Self.

The love being thought of here is not limited to erotic love. It includes the love of the craftsman for his work, the love of the mother for her child, the love of friends for each other, the love of the artist for beauty, the love of the scholar for wisdom, the love of the mystic for transcendent oneness or wholeness. Thus, however little sexual lovers may be conscious of it, the basis of their desire for one another is really the spiritual hunger that urges us all toward the divine beings that we are.

This idea recurs in the sacred books of the East, and even in their erotic literature: "Therefore if you like, Lady, I will explain it to thee, and mark well what I say: Verily a husband is not dear that you may love a husband, but that you may love the Self, therefore a husband is dear."

Such a statement seems vague and even a little childish to Western ears, so accustomed are we to believing that the formation of a committed relationship is an ultimate end in itself. And it is nearly repugnant to those who focus exclusively or very largely upon the sexual component of a relationship. Thus, Western society's obsession with sex is revealed as an exceedingly immature stance from a spiritual perspective. It is rather like an adult who has never grown past his or her love for childish pastimes and pursuits.

Jiddu Krishnamurti, who seldom commented on sexual activity except when asked, was rather impatient with the popular contemporary focus upon sex. "Why have you made sex a problem?" he demanded. "Really it doesn't matter at all [to your spiritual growth] whether you go to bed with someone or whether you don't. Get on with it or drop it, but don't make a problem of it. The problem comes from this constant preoccupation."

Mind you, I make no claim that youthful (or even aged) passions and practices are somehow evil, but that the persons who know only these are in an arrested state of development and will regard spiritual enticements in very much the same way a child would. More than likely, as the years pass, various physical, emotional, and spiritual deficiencies will weigh ever more heavily upon them, including upon their sexuality.

As we have often observed in others, and probably upon occasion in ourselves, the sexual contact based on selfishness is seldom satisfying and inevitably adds to the alienation and loneliness that sexually self-centered persons live with. One test for a wholesome sexual relationship and, indeed, for any relationship, is to ask the question, "Upon whom is my attention fixed? Myself or the other person?" A wish to exploit or control the other person is entirely egotistical. And the result will never be elevating, to either person.

Ananda Coomaraswamy, a Hindu scholar, describes an attitude between lovers in which the aim is spiritual freedom (which is the precise opposite of what most people mean by sexual freedom). Such a love, says Coomaraswamy, "has nothing to do with the cult of pleasure. It is the doctrine of the Tao, the path of non-pursuit. All that is best for us comes of itself into our hands—but if we strive to overtake it, it perpetually eludes us." So much then for the sexual sweepstakes that seem to preoccupy the majority of Western men and women!

In case Plato's model of love seems too ancient and the Hindu model too esoteric, let me offer a thoroughly mundane possibility which exhibits the same principles.

From my own experiences and observations, it seems rather clear that two potential lovers approaching each other are rather like mirrors facing. At some level—most commonly, unconscious—each person is seeking self-knowledge: the kind of divine identity which is the ultimate task of all humans to search out. But in the ignorance or innocence of egotism, the person does not want to take the risks or undertake the discipline that goes with such a discovery.

Nonetheless, the yearning is there. In the mirror of the other person we hope to gather some self-affirmation—to glimpse the shape of our own identity. Lovers inevitably tell each other that they want the truth, but they quake even as they say so. What they really want is admiration, signals of being okay. And where such signals are not forthcoming, the relationship is almost surely doomed to a short duration.

So it happens that, when we approach another person, we peer into the mirror, expecting, hoping, even maneuvering for a favorable reflection. This is the courting dance which includes all the erotic games people play with each other. Not only do we trust a comely mirror more than we do an uncomely one, but we want it to emphasize our attractive features and ignore our less attractive ones. We want it to show us how clever, intelligent, compelling, and irresistible we are. And we know that the same signal is expected from us. So we distort our mirrors, at least until we get whatever it is we want.

All this assumes that we start off with a reasonably trustworthy mirror at the beginning, which most of us don't. Lacking self-knowledge, we are in a very poor position to help others toward self-knowledge. Still, the dance of the mirrors goes on until one or both mirror-holders become dissatisfied with the images they perceive. Then they drift away in search of other mirrors that send reflections which are more novel and (at least momentarily) more stimulating. Little or no growth or self-discovery occurs, gradually the ultimate goal of life gets forgotten altogether, and existence becomes a lonely searching. Small wonder that our popular literature is filled with articles analyzing our sexual habits and offering prescriptions and nostrums for trying harder at what hasn't been working to begin with.

About this, Clara Codd, a British feminist, has written: "The worldwide prevalence of sex problems comes from the exaggeration of one factor in it, physical gratification." And then she goes on to note that where two people open themselves to honest discovery and disclosure, a "mystical experience" results which passes "ever more deeply into an interior consciousness, so the lovers become to each other as a door to God."

In using the term "door to God," Codd is not talking about some sort of Victorian self-surrender. She is talking about discovering the secret purpose of life—growth toward an awareness of one's own higher Self.

Clara Codd concludes with the admonition, "Love must sanctify sex." Again her language sounds a little quaint and stodgy. But the intent is practical rather than pious. Love means respect, tolerance, responsibility, honesty, and a genuine concern for mutual growth. Where these are lacking, love is lacking too. And as for sexual difficulties, she agrees with Carl Jung and Krishnamurti, both of whom advised that the only certain cure for sexual problems is love.

The sad truth, however, is that, as the word "sex" has been corrupted, so has the word "love." Whether sex is viewed positively or negatively, there is precious little authentic loving in either viewpoint. The most fervently righteous members of our society have long regarded sex as sinful, in the sense of moral unfitness. And that is a designation as socially useless as it is inaccurate. About all the pairing of sex and sin achieves is to cause guilt and deceit, further inhibiting responsible decision-making. The contemporary association of sex and sin is ironic in that the word "sin" originally referred to separation. If we still thought of sin as separation, rather than as moral unfitness, then it would be highly appropriate and instructive to discuss sex and sin.

The plain everyday truth is that sex is simply one of the most powerful of human drives and experiences. And, like all powerful dynamics, it can be equally creative or destructive. To my way of thinking, where two persons mutually employ sexual expression as a joyful or even playful way of celebrating the human condition, there is no fault. But where a person becomes obsessive about sex, there is not one jot of joy in it, only desperation. And where others are being exploited, that, indeed, is morally wrong.

In either case, a spiritual tragedy has taken place in that no growth whatever occurs.

I don't think I have ever seen the essence of this tragedy more graphically portrayed than in the film "Carnal Knowledge." The hero, a now-aging Lothario, finally resorts to purchased sexual stimulation in order to assure himself that he is still a worthwhile and potent human being. The loneliness and desperation in this scene, which is where the film ends, transform whatever contempt one may have had for the hero's earlier exploits into a profound sorrow.

Again and again I sense that one of the most painfully puzzling aspects of contemporary human experience is why sex, which is touted at a public level as easily available and wonderful, should be so often frustrating at a personal level. Part of this, I'm sure, is that modern sexual experience is heavily laden with all sorts of Catch-22s, starting with the fact that we try to make it into an ultimate experience when it isn't. However wonderful it may be momentarily, sex is preliminary in the scheme of things, just as other finite activities (eating, walking, talking, working) are. It's only a part of the human growth process leading toward ultimacy. Theologian Paul Tillich has pointed out that we create a demonic situation anytime we take something which is not ultimate and try to install it as ultimate in the center of our lives. This, says Tillich, is idolatry. And millions of Americans make sex into an idol while their spiritual selves languish.

One of the more lucid commentators on sex and spirit is Elizabeth Haich, a yoga teacher who lives in Switzerland. She calls the sexual act "an exalted fulfillment of the desire for oneness, for love, as a life-giving act of imitation of God, affording real contentment and happiness." Like some of the other authorities I have cited, Haich invites us to "look upon sexual energy as the key which opens the door for us between the spirit and the world of matter, from the higher to the lower but also from the lower to the higher. Let us regard it then as the divine impetus which enables us to create further generations, to propagate life from above downwards in the body but also to transform man upwards out of his ferity into a spiritual man and to help conquer death. We must be grateful that sexual energy, used properly, gives us so much happiness on both paths. On the downward path it is brief and transient, on the upward path it is eternal happiness.

"Let us use its fire," Elizabeth Haich concludes, "to make our race of life flourish and blossom."

Ultimately, when all the philosophical speculations are said and done, the average person is still left with the very personal questions of judging his or her own life experience. The most immediate index of a creative sexual relationship is, I believe, contained in a single question: "Do I feel more whole, more connected to the cosmos, as a result of this relationship?"

If the answer is yes, one may rejoice modestly in having grown. If the answer is no, one may still rejoice modestly, providing the experience is recognized as an opportunity for change, for growth.

It's that simple, and that challenging.

Bluebirds and Honeybees

For me, the surest sign of spring is a flicker of blue against a blue sky.

The bluebirds are back at the farm! Every time they return, I have the same reaction I used to have over autumn foliage in New England. How can anything be so beautiful? How come I'm so amazed all over again?

Bluebirds are such understatements in contrast. Against the noise of their color is the quiet of their call and movement. The loudest sound bluebirds make is a soft coo. And their goings and comings, compared to the dartings of the ever-present swallows, are almost unnoticeable.

Whereas the swallows relentlessly pursue their prey, the bluebirds sit motionlessly on a fence or the barn roof, alert to the barest movement in pasture or garden. Almost casually they flit over to the disturbance, gather up a bug, and return to their perch to wait for more. Baby bluebirds must be insatiable.

* * *

I took a day and went to the farm last week to check out the honeybees. And while I spotted and enjoyed the bluebirds first, I gave most of my attention to the bees.

In beekeeper's terms, my bees did just fine last winter. Therein lies another generally unknown astonishment. I used to think that honeybees hibernated during the coldest weather. They don't. Instead, they form a great living ball in the center of the hive, feeding on honey and generating eighty-degree temperatures. Except on unseasonably warm days, they don't come out. At least, most don't. Those that do fly a short distance, losing heat and altitude and spotting the snow with their corpses.

Inside the hive, all is not safe. By spring the bottoms of the hives are an inch deep in bodies. Wintertime for a bee colony is a neck-and-neck race between the food supply, the death rate, and the return of spring.

Last Wednesday, however, the sun shone brightly upon the hives. And already the workers were setting forth and returning, their hind legs heavy with yellow pollen. Now begins another race—actually two races—one to build up the colony population sufficiently to outlast another winter, the second race to store enough nectar and pollen so that a minority can survive the ordeal.

Life! What a wonderful, terrible mystery!

9

Faith Stages and Oxherding

Searching for the ox while riding its back!

One of the deadlier perils in spiritual growth is the all-too-human tendency to look down one's nose at those who are less elevated than oneself. A Sufi tale about Moses and a humble shepherd teaches this lesson very clearly.

Moses is out walking one day when he chances upon a shepherd kneeling in prayer. Thinking that it would be interesting to hear how the shepherd addresses the Lord of the Universe, he stops and listens. This is what he hears: "Oh, Thou Almighty who has bestowed many blessings upon me, it is my sweetest pleasure to serve Thee. If thou wouldst permit me, I would comb Thy hair, and wash Thy robe, and kiss Thy hand. . . ."

Moses is both startled and dismayed by the shepherd's prayer. He is offended by the shepherd's chummy familiarity with the Almighty, and he is especially upset that the man knows no better than to regard God in primitive, anthropomorphic terms. Immediately he rushes up to the shepherd shouting, "Stop! Stop, you fool, you blasphemer! Have you no better sense than to address the Lord as a mere human being with hair and hands and clothes? Have you no shame, offering to do good deeds for that which is all-powerful and all-present and needs nothing from you, save your obedience?"

The shepherd is, of course, astonished, and deathly afraid. But before he can reply to Moses's fierce admonition, God himself speaks up, "Wait, Moses, 'tis thee who is ignorant and guilty of an arrogant presumption. Wouldst thou drive this sincere shepherd away from me when, in his heart and mind, he is offering me the very best that he has? Take heed, Moses!

There is a gradation of understanding in all persons. Each perceives according to his understanding, and worships as he perceives. Verily, I say unto you, Moses, before the Lord of Hosts the shepherd's humble offering is as sweet to my nostrils as thine own."

As this tale teaches, concern about who is higher and who is lower on the ladder of spirituality is hazardous in the extreme. For those on a lower rung of the ladder, such comparisons may be demoralizing, yielding resentment. For those on a higher rung, such comparisons may generate pride, the most enslaving of attachments.

And yet if we are to grow in any respect, we do need some indications as to the direction in which maturity lies. If we are to avoid the problem just mentioned, then we must use such knowledge not to measure our fellows but to assess our own progress.

The ancient Chinese recognized that there are levels or stages of spiritual development in human life. They postulated four such stages—student, wage earner, householder, and spiritual mendicant.

Today names like Erickson, Piaget, Kohlberg, Smith, and Fowler remind us in religion of what every mother knows about her children. We grow in discernible stages. An awareness of these stages helps us make sense of life. Thus, a mother with a two-year-old hellion is comforted upon hearing about the "terrible twos," and an intimate watching a forty-year-old man do something wildly uncharacteristic is at least moderately mollified by the term "midlife crisis." Millions of people have used Gail Sheehy's *Passages* both to understand the lives of others and to see some order in their own lives.

In religious circles, James Fowler's stages of faith have become practically a shorthand or code for talking about spiritual growth. Fowler, a specialist in the psychology of religion, studied at Harvard and a few years ago moved to Emory University, where he is director of the Center for Faith Development. He has written several books, including one key to our subject: *Stages of Faith—The Psychology of Human Development and The Quest for Meaning.*

Like most academic systems, stage theory can be as heavy as it is useful. Fowler's work is no exception, but it is of compelling relevance to almost anyone interested in how human beings grow spiritually.

Fowler defines six stages of religious development which, at least in the early years of life, are generally related to a person's age.

Pre-Stage (Undifferentiated)

Infants, of course, do not appear to have a discernible faith. But the time from infancy up to about two years of age is a critical period, during which trust, autonomy, courage, and capacity for self-esteem are shaped.

For his or her psychological health, the child needs to progress satisfactorily toward fulfilling these basic needs. Obviously, these qualities are also at the very center of one's religious outlook. It is clear that we are especially dependent upon our parents for shaping the person we will later become and for the kind of meaning we find in life.

I. Intuitive-Projective

As the child begins acquiring language and cognitive skills, he or she begins assembling a world view. The years roughly between three and seven are marked by rapid change. Both fantasy and imagination are very important, and the youngster is most aware of his or her own helplessness with respect to the rest of the world. Fears of abandonment are easily triggered. So are fears of not measuring up. In terms of faith development, this is stage one; Fowler gives it the name "Intuitive-Projective."

My wife, Patty, tells a charming story illustrating both the fantasy and ritualistic aspects of stage one. Her six-year-old daughter, Kaky, had a parakeet named Spike. Spike was prone to biting the hand that fed him. One day Spike surprised Kaky with an especially vigorous nip. Kaky's response was a loud, shrill, "Spike!" The bird promptly keeled over, dead. Later on, Patty was intrigued to hear Kaky and several of her small friends singing "God Bless America" on the back deck. Looking out an upstairs window, she saw the youngsters gathered around Spike's corpse, all laid out on crumpled Kleenex in a kitchen matchbox. Stage one children may not be theologically advanced, but they do have a keen sense of ceremony.

II. Mythic-Literal

Stage two ordinarily lasts until about puberty. By this time the child is hard at work sorting out what is real from what is not real. The urgency of the task tends to make the youngster into a literalist. Symbols are one-dimensional, and mythic material is either true or false—no in-between subtleties! God is definitely anthropomorphic, and there is a strong sense of justice and fairness. Trust is heavily dependent upon how closely things hew to the either/or distinctions characteristic of this age. Although the onset of puberty usually signals the transition to stage three, some people never move much beyond stage two and, for the rest of their lives, continue to be narrow, rigid, literalistic, and moralistic in their theology and ethics.

III. Synthetic-Conventional

Stage three brings a softening to one's religious attitudes and an increased ability to handle abstract ideas. Symbols and myths, as a special sort of language for referring to abstractions, become useful. During stage three, which Fowler calls "Synthetic-Conventional," the developing person's world expands rapidly beyond the family, and the rebellion of adolescents against parental authority is entirely normal. Beliefs and values continue to be deeply felt, but they are held more tentatively. Authority is sought but may be rejected vehemently if it does not measure up to the young person's ideals, or if a more persuasive authority comes into view. Differences in beliefs and values tend to be personalized. In other words, a person who does not agree with one's own beliefs and values is apt to be rejected as unworthy or even dangerous. Stage three is probably normative for the majority of adults. They know what they believe, and that's that! They also have strong opinions as to what other people should believe. A common type of statement by stage three people is, "I don't believe you can think that and call yourself a Christian!"

IV. Individual-Reflective

Movement into stage four is much more deliberate and cognitive than the earlier transitions. Entry into stage four often occurs as the result of a "crisis of faith" ("My religion didn't stand by me when my mother died") or by a rational process ("Too much of what my church taught simply didn't make sense anymore"). Fowler calls this stage "Individual-Reflective," and it is characterized by a willingness to take responsibility for one's own commitments, lifestyle, beliefs, and attitudes. There is an acceptance of ambiguity, of the unavoidable tensions between individualism and community, subjectivity and objectivity, absolutism and relativism. Since stage four is often a reactive phase, one during which a person is reacting negatively against where he or she was as a stage three person, religious attitudes may be marked by excessive skepticism or too much trust in logic, with a corresponding suspicion of what might be called the poetry and art of religion.

Most persons coming into the Unitarian Universalist Church as adults are early stage four. They have often experienced a crisis of faith. And they are usually counterdependent—they know what they don't believe, but may have trouble saying what they do believe. Unfortunately, many early stage four people never get beyond their counterdependency, and hence their religious perspective lacks affirmation.

V. Conjunctive Faith

As a person becomes less emphatic about what has been rejected during stage four, he or she begins moving into stage five. Stage five which, if it is achieved at all, usually is not reached before midlife, is called "Conjunctive." One doesn't reject the strong rationalistic emphasis of stage four, but one recognizes there is more—rationality doesn't include all that is important to being a complete human being. There is acceptance of the nonrational which resides in mystery and paradox and is more intuitive than cognitive.

Often the stage five person recognizes deep meanings in stage three concepts which were rejected upon passage into four. One reinterprets the myths, rituals, and symbols that one has discarded and discovers a higher meaning within them, a meaning that would have been regarded as heresy if it had been suggested years earlier. Inevitably, the stage five person becomes something of a mystic, one who accepts and appreciates that ultimate truth is unknowable and can be approached more readily through intuition, metaphor and symbol. The stage five individual apprehends the interconnectedness—the unity—of all things, yet manifests an active concern that the everyday world is untransformed and menaced by its fragmentation and suspicion.

VI. Universalizing Faith

Few persons arrive at what Fowler describes as the sixth and final stage. The ones who do are often recognized as prophets or saints but may well end up suffering a savage rejection. As modern examples, Fowler cites such enlightened individuals as Gandhi, Mother Teresa, Martin Luther King, Jr., Thomas Merton, Dag Hammarskjöld and Dietrich Bonhoeffer. I would hasten to add Albert Schweitzer and Martin Buber to this list. I also imagine that there is a sizable body of others who, even though they attract little or no public attention, still qualify in the quality of their being. The stage six individual is not perfect but is highly centered and self-actualized. He or she has, in some sense, hooked into the power of the cosmos and, in turn, unself-consciously brings that power to bear creatively on human lives. In Buddhism, such a person would be called a Bodhisattva. One who qualifies for nirvana, a Bodhisattva delays accepting it in order to return to the human scene and promote the growth of others.

While James Fowler's studies of faith development provide us with a precise and rather clinical way of understanding the stages of religious growth, there are other systems, far older, that are also useful and more poetic. The most famous of these are the so-called oxherding pictures.

Dating back more than a thousand years to the period when Chinese Buddhism and Taoism were combining into Zen, these drawings make use of the taming of a wayward ox or bull as a metaphor for a person's spiritual journey. Appropriately, the same idea crops up in the literature of the time. Thus, Pao-chih, a Chinese poet from the sixth century, wrote:

. . . how you labor in vain!
if you don't understand
that the mind is Buddha!
That is truly like riding an ox
looking for one.

In other words, those who are ignorant of the in-dwelling Buddha (en-lightened state) and persist in looking outside of themselves for enlighten-ment are like a person searching for a lost ox without recognizing that he or she is already mounted on its back!

In typical Taoist humor, there is the ninth century anecdote told by Ch'ang-ch'ing Ta-an about his master Isan's ox:

I lived with Isan more than thirty years. I ate Isan's food, I excreted Isan's excrement, but I did not study Isan's Zen. All I did was look after an ox. If he got off the road, I dragged him back; if he trampled the flowering grain in others' fields, I trained him by flogging him with a whip. For a long time how pitiful he was, at the mercy of men's words! Now he has changed into the white ox on the bare ground, and always stays in front of my face. All day long he clearly reveals himself. Even though I chase him, he doesn't go away.

This tale is the epitome of a Zen art. In the course of diligently caring for a undisciplined ox, Ta-an achieves enlightenment. (There's no hint of what Isan achieved.)

The oxherding pictures are found in numerous artistic styles, and the set may contain six or eight pictures, but more often there are ten. They were, and continue to be, popular among Oriental students of spiritual growth for much the same purpose as Fowler's faith stages: they allow the pilgrim both to assess and be encouraged in the progress toward Whole-ness.

The oxherding pictures shown here are whimsical, cartoon-like ver-sions of the original illustrations. They are the creations of Tomikichiro Tokuriki, a Kyoto woodblock artist who worked in the early part of this century.

Traditionally, the oxherding pictures are each accompanied by a poem which describes (somewhat enigmatically) what is going on. Instead of using the poems, I add my own commentary.

1. The Search for the Ox

What the pilgrim is searching for is not really lost. It's inside him waiting to be discovered. At this point the novice has only the vaguest impression of what he's looking for. But he is growing dissatisfied with his life. He is subject to attachments that don't really satisfy, but he is fearful of losing his egotistical identity. He is in a growing predicament.

2. Discovering the Footprints

Having perused a teaching or two and undertaken a discipline, the pilgrim sees the footprints of the ox (which is a metaphor for her unrealized Self). She suspects the ox is there, but she doesn't know where or even what the beast looks like. But she now has some incentive to keep looking.

3. Glimpsing the Ox

Now the novice has actually glimpsed the ox, albeit the hind end. Could this be the first payoff for the novice's having taken up meditation? Here the metaphor falters a bit, because even though the novice sees the ox "out there," still the teaching says that the novice is already realizing that the bull is not separate from himself. D. T. Suzuki, a renowned Zen master, says that the ox is perceived in the same way as salt in the ocean, as a part of one, not as a separate entity.

4. Catching the Ox

Encouraged by her glimpse, the novice intensifies her practice and actually lassoes the ox. Now the action begins! In laying hands on the ox, the pilgrim realizes that she has hooked into something with a great deal of power—much of it not under her control. In a sense, the struggle of the ox to escape represents the struggle of the pilgrim's own ego to stay in control.

5. Taming the Ox

The novice's efforts are paying off as he more and more is able to practice his meditation and other disciplines with some consistency. But he
must not relax or let his attention wander. The novice and the ox are not
yet one in the novice's own knowing, and unless he keeps a firm hand on
the tether, loss of control will result. But he is catching on!

6. Riding the Ox Home

The ox is now pacified and obedient. The pilgrim's concentration is no longer held or lured by attachment. Her mind cannot be deceived, nor may she be led astray. As one text says, "I sing the song of the village woodsman, and play the tunes of the children. Astride the ox, I observe the clouds above. Onward I go, no matter who may wish to call me back."

7. The Ox Transcended

Now that the ox is tamed, it is perceived as one with the pilgrim and, hence, is no longer needed. The ego, too, is transcended. And the pilgrim sits quietly before his hut having even given up his attachment to the struggle. Thus, he has conquered the last attachment, attachment to enlightenment itself. He is home again!

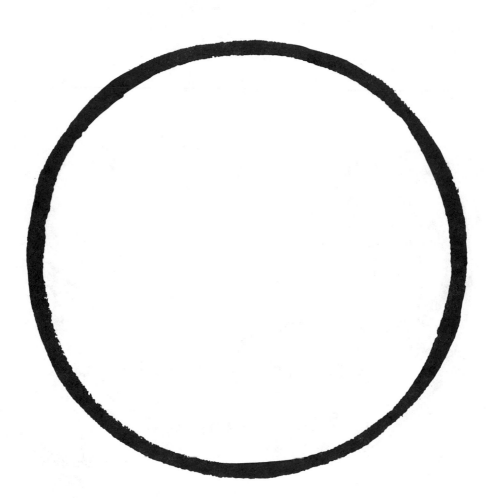

8. Both Ox and Self Transcended

All dualism has ceased. The ancient prescription, "Not two. . . . Not two!" prevails. The pilgrim no longer follows a path but lives a truth. And the ecstasy experienced is sublime beyond words. As one text says, "Mediocrity is gone. Mind is clear of limitation. I seek no state of enlightenment. Neither do I remain where no enlightenment exists. Since I linger in neither condition, eyes cannot see me. If hundreds of birds strew my path with flowers, such praise would be meaningless."

9. Return to the Source

Here the pilgrim realizes his identity with the Supreme Reality. This is the goal of all mystical questing. He has realized his Buddha nature and enjoys the bliss of that knowing. Now he may elect nirvana or return to the world as a Bodhissatva.

10. Back in the World

It may come as a surprise that there is anything beyond what is represented in the ninth picture. Here we see the result of the pilgrim eligible for Buddhahood (nirvana) who has elected instead to return to the world and help all other souls toward enlightenment. This is what it is to be a Bodhissatva. But no one knows of her elevated spiritual station because her life is so simple. She is not recognized as a sage—"The beauty of her garden is invisible." In the marketplace and wineshop, she goes quietly about her business.

Because Bodhissatvas, practicing no attachments, do lead such simple lives, it is next to impossible to know who they are. But spanning from times ancient to times modern, we might name two: Socrates and Mother Teresa of Calcutta.

Socrates said that his task was as a midwife, helping others to give birth to themselves. Because he had already cured himself of attachment, he could be present to others without fearing for his own safety.

Similarly, Mother Teresa leads the most humble life in the poorest large city on earth. Many mistake her example as some sort of deliberate self-denial. But that assessment misses the mark. She lives humbly because she already has all that she needs.

The Fence and the Shoulder Pains

"You can take the boy out of the country, but you can't take the country out of the boy."

This old saying may account for the fact that I've had a yearning most of my adult life to lead a simpler existence. Usually on a farm. Half a dozen years ago, I partially realized this dream when Patty and I went into partnership with a pair of friends and bought an eighty-acre farm in Pend Oreille County, Washington.

Almost immediately I went to work in the summers building the house and other buildings that were to become a very special place for me. But the partnership did not last. Our friends decided they wanted to live in a different part of the country. And the care of the farm with its two and a half miles of barbed wire fence fell largely to me.

The fence, especially, became a burden. Every spring more than a hundred rotted-off fence posts had to be replaced by hand. This past spring I was at work on this relentless task.

It was a lovely day. The sunshine warmed the air, the meadows were lush and green, the swallows soared and swooped, and the mountains stretching off to the north fairly sparkled. It was a sublime sight.

But I was not happy about doing such a laborious task by myself. In fact, it would be fair to say that the spot which had so recently been a joy for me was suddenly the scene of deep disappointment and resentment. And stretching across my shoulders, there was a telltale pain which informed me in no uncertain terms that I was stressed. I could not figure out what to do. And it would be accurate to say that I felt trapped by that which I had formerly loved.

As the sun sank lower into the west, I labored on. Then suddenly it hit me: the cause of my misery was my own refusal to let go. In an instant, I decided: we would sell the farm!

Tossing the tools into the wheelbarrow, I returned to the house, loaded up the pickup, locked the house, and, with scarcely a look backward, headed for town. The gate down by the county road was barely closed before I realized that the shoulder pains were gone. And I was free!

We later decided to sell just the lower half of the farm and retain the part that included our buildings. Since then I have continued to enjoy the place. But with attachment no longer contaminating my devotion, I don't have to fear giving it up.

10

Taoism, the Natural Spirituality

Or, the joy of dragging one's tail in the mud

Let's consider Taoism, a spiritual tradition which stands in rather sharp contrast with the others. In recent years there has been a flood of books with the word "Tao" in their titles. By and large, they've been significant books, but not because they taught about Taoism.

Except for Zen, which arose out of it, Taoism is more enigmatic, more contemplative, more naturalistic, and less creedal, intellectual, and meddlesome than all the other religions. Although my own way of life and thinking comes nowhere close to being Taoist, still my spiritual impulse esteems Taoism above all others, and hungers for it.

One of the best ways to describe Taoism's approach to the living of life and to spiritual growth is by citing the example of water. Water is soft and yielding. It conforms to the shape of every vessel. It settles into tranquility even after the most violent agitation. It seeks its own level by flowing along the most natural path. And yet, as Taoist writings are fond of pointing out, water is not weak. Over time it changes the appearances of all things, wearing away the hardest rock and moving mountains. Water, moreover, does not become attached to any place, accepting change and moving on when the time comes. Taoism thus emphasizes the idea of adaptability, acceptance, harmony, and tranquility. Because of the water metaphor, Taoism is sometimes called the Watercourse Way.

In China several centuries before Christ, a series of teachings was brought together by unknown persons. Lao-Tzu (which literally means "old philosopher") is said to be the author of these teachings, but he is, no doubt, a legendary figure. The compiled teachings were called the Tao-Te-Ching, and their wisdom is both mythic and mystical.

To understand the nature of Taoism, it helps to understand the historical times during which the Tao-Te-Ching took shape. The fourth and third centuries B.C. in China were the period of the Warring States. It was a time of intellectual ferment and social and political unrest. China was divided into a number of principalities, and many of the rulers sought a philosophy which would assure prosperity for the people and political stability for the leaders. Learned persons were summoned—Confucians, Mohists, Legalists, Sophists, Logicians. In return for their counsel, they were offered powerful and prestigious positions. The Taoists refused all such blandishments.

Hence, there is a popular story told about Chuang-Tzu, the best-known historically authentic Taoist sage. Chuang-Tzu was sitting and fishing in the river P'u when two messengers of the king appeared and asked him to become a high official in the royal court. Chuang-Tzu heard their offer and, without looking their way, replied, "I have heard that the king possesses a sacred tortoise which has been dead for three thousand years. The king, I am told, has it wrapped in exquisite silk and keeps it in an ornately carved box where it is stored in an especially holy part of the ancestral temple. Tell me—would the tortoise rather be dead with its bones preserved and honored, or would it rather be alive with its tail dragging in the mud?" The two messengers agreed that it would rather be alive with its tail dragging in the mud. "Be off with you then," said Chuang-Tzu, "I prefer to drag my tail in the mud."

This story is highly illustrative of the Taoist perspective. Taoists preferred simplicity and nature. They were individualists and they honored a mystical philosophy which taught that things were best when left alone. Within the Taoist tradition, there are tales of sages who could perform miracles, live entirely on air and dew, roam at will through the universe, and by doing absolutely nothing could heal, avert calamity, and bring prosperity. The learned Taoists, no doubt, took such tales allegorically, but the simple folk regarded them literally. The latter believed in "immortals" who had attained everlasting life via the practice of yoga, hygiene, and alchemy.

The early Taoists were horrified by the political corruptions and barbarism of their day. But they regarded such excesses as being the result of too much interference in the natural order. They believed that organized attempts toward reform would lead to other problems as bad or worse. Hence, they advised retreat into the country where one could conform more readily to the natural and spontaneous rhythms of birth, growth, death, and decay.

Freedom, peace, and happiness, they taught, could be achieved only by recognition and conformity to natural and not human laws. Withdrawing into the countryside, living frugally with few desires, they spent their days contemplating the works of nature. Doing so, they hoped to discern—though not comprehend—the working of the ultimate force which they called Tao.

Although the word simply means "way," some Western scholars have translated Tao as "God." This is an error. While many Taoists believed that the whole cosmos was populated by spirits, and that there was a profound spiritual dimension to human beings, almost none saw any reason to believe in a sensate, purposeful god. Tao was simply there, eternally. The aim of religious life and contemplation was to seek and find Tao, that mysterious principle which resides within one's inmost being and works throughout the entire universe. To become utterly engulfed in the quietude and serenity of Tao became the supreme goal of the Taoist mystic.

The sages did not expect to understand Tao. In fact, their writings appear almost designed to frustrate cognitive grasping. Consider this passage from the Tao-Te-Ching:

Before Heaven and Earth came forth there was something form-less yet complete. How silent! How still! Standing alone and un-changing, all-pervasive and unwearying, it may be regarded as the mother of all things. I do not know its name but, if forced to give it a name, I would call it 'Tao.' Forced to designate it, I would call it 'great.' So great is it that it may be said to go on and on, so far that it turns back on itself.

Tao is the origin of all things. It is that by which all things come to their completion. By it all things exist.

Tao is that which fills all forms, yet man is not able to hold it secure. It departs but does not return. It arrives but does not abide. Desire it and you do not so much as hear a sound of it. Yet suddenly it is found within the mind. So obscure is it that its form cannot be seen. So pervasive is it that it is within all our being. One cannot see its action nor hear its sound, and yet it brings to perfection whatever it seeks to accomplish. Such we call Tao.

As an example of devotional literature, this passage is superb. Its mean-ing cannot be extracted but must be received. Cognitively regarded and grasped, it is almost nonsensical; dwelt with and lingered over, it conveys a profound impression that takes shape over time. The student's patience with Taoist texts grows into a *knowing* which is as much visceral as it is mental. One of the closest parallels in Western theological writings is Martin Buber's *I And Thou*. It, too, takes many readings and much reflection before its essence begins to be grasped.

Of course, not all Taoist scriptures are this esoteric. The literature also contains numerous polemics and tales. The tales, especially, are instructive, for they contain a subtle humor and often resort to wild exaggerations in the name of making a point. For this reason, the overly linear student of Taoism is apt to get into all sorts of trouble. Consider, for example, the upshot of taking the advice of this story too literally:

> A drunken man who falls out of a cart, though he may suffer, does not die. His bones are the same as other people's, but he meets the accident in a different way. His spirit is in a condition of security. He is not conscious of riding in the cart; neither is he conscious of falling out of it. Ideas of life, death, and fear cannot penetrate his mind; and so he does not suffer from contact with objective existence. And if such security is to be gotten from wine, how much more is to be gotten from spontaneity.

Now the literalist reading this might conclude that the best route to spiritual wholeness is via drunkenness, or discipline in falling out of carts, or even in having no concern for ordinary hazards. But the story is a lesson

in nonattachment. Don't be attached to anything, even your own life and limb. Be there, pay attention, but don't get enmeshed in fears or dark imaginings.

Most people associate the yin/yang symbol with Taoism. A few think it the symbol of the Northern Pacific Railway, and a few others think it was invented by a defunct organization called Technocracy. I often wear the symbol as a pendant around my neck. A while back, a clerk in a store spotted it and wondered if I worked for Safeway.

The concept of yin and yang is crucial to Taoism. It represents the perpetual interconnectedness, harmony, and transformation of everything. Within a single unity, it depicts two equal and opposite forces, one quiescent, the other active, but each essential to the whole. Light and dark, summer and winter, heat and cold, male and female, good and evil—all is described in terms of polarities. Yet neither is ever absolute—within yin there is yang, within yang there is yin. That's what the two smaller dots within the major fields represent. And they remind us that Tao redresses all extremes, inevitably, and sometimes furiously. We should be both warned and comforted by this awareness. For example, in the Tao-Te-Ching there is a passage which anticipates by almost twenty-five centuries a very contemporary notion.

> Knowing the male but keeping the female, one becomes a universal stream. [Knowing the female but keeping the male, one becomes a universal stream.] Becoming a universal stream, one is not separated from eternal virtue.

Taoism is basically the art of doing what comes naturally. It might seem, therefore, to be the easiest form of spirituality, but that conclusion would be a snare and a delusion.

For if we are to live naturally, we must know what is natural. That means we must pay attention, pay attention while interfering as little as possible. How many of us are willing or able to do that? When we stay in touch with "the all," that (which is us, too) will tell us what we need to do in order to be whole. Thus, we are presented with some rather puzzling and paradoxical advice: in order to be whole, be whole! What this means is to be totally present. Be here now. Let the cosmos (which is you, too) tell you what to do.

There is a story of Ch'ing, the chief carpenter, who was making a music stand. When the work was finished, it was of such fantastic beauty as to seem supernaturally inspired and wrought. The Prince of Lu asked Ch'ing, "What mystery is there in your art?"

"No mystery, Your Highness," replied Ch'ing, "And yet there is something. When I am about to make such a stand, I guard against any diminution of my vital power. I first reduce my mind to absolute quiescence. Three days in this condition, and I become oblivious of any reward to be gained. Five days, and I become oblivious of any fame to be acquired. Seven days, and I become unconscious of my four limbs and my physical frame. Then, with no thought of the Court present in my mind, my skill becomes concentrated, and all remaining elements from without are gone. I enter some mountain forest. I search for a suitable tree. It contains the form required, which is afterwards elaborated. I see the stand in my mind's eye, and then set to work. Otherwise, there is nothing. I bring my own natural capacity into relation with that of the wood. What was suspected to be of supernatural execution in my work was due solely to this."

Actually, this attitude is not so foreign to the other spiritual traditions as we might think if we read only their popularized writings. Alan Watts was thoroughly eclectic in his religious tastes, but Watts was as close to being a Taoist as he was to being anything. In his last book, *Tao: The Watercourse Way*, he addressed the Taoist perspective on ambition, striving and planning ahead:

> The Contemplative Taoists, while rejecting the quest for immortality, were certainly concerned with "living out one's natural term of life. . . ." But they are also saying that the chances of survival are best when there is no anxiety to survive, and that the greatest power is available to those who do not seek power and who do not use force. To be anxious to survive is to wear oneself out, and to seek power and to use force is to overstrain one's system. One is best preserved by floating along without stress, all of which is the same as Jesus' doctrine of not being anxious for the morrow, and the Bhagavad-Gita's principle of action without concern for results. This theme runs throughout the spiritual literature of the world: that you will get if you do not want [i.e. lack] it, and that to him that hath shall be given.

Testifying to Watts's point about the chances of survival being best where there is no anxiety to survive is the story of a sage who was walking along a rushing, boiling river one day when he looked up ahead and saw an old man suddenly leap into the cascades. Expecting never to see him alive again, the sage stood, at first horrified, and then transfixed, as the aged one popped to the surface of the raging water and then glided along on the crests and troughs of the waves, flowing easily around all the jagged rocks of the riverbed. Finally, the floater, his arms folded serenely across his chest, was swept into calm waters where he worked his way to the riverbank and climbed out. Breathless with astonishment, the sage rushed over to him and asked what he was doing, and how he managed to survive such an experience. And the old man replied that he did it often. Then, in answer to the second question, he said, "I become as one with the water, and, as you can see, the water suffers no harm. So why should I?"

Allowing for the occasional exaggeration of such tales, one can appreciate the Taoist principles of "letting be," of accepting and trusting, of "being there," and of "going with the flow." No exceptions! Listen to Chuang-Tzu's description of Lao-Tzu's death:

> The Master came because it was time. He left because he followed the natural flow. Be content with the moment, and be willing to

follow the flow. Then there will be no room for grief or joy. In the old days this was called freedom from bondage. The wood is consumed but the fire burns on, and we do not know when it will come to an end.

Paradoxically, Taoism is a success-oriented spirituality. Its secret of success is in paying attention, not striving prematurely or excessively, but in going with the flow and accepting what happens. Such people succeed—not just periodically—but in their entire lives. As Alan Watts says: "The real and astonishing calm of people like Lao Tzu comes from the fact that they are ready and willing, without shame, to do whatever comes naturally in all circumstances. The unbelievable result is that they are more sociable and civilized than those who try to live rigorously by laws and watchwords."

It is a recipe as readily applied to political life as to personal life. About government, Lao-Tzu is supposed to have taught:

The more restrictions and avoidances are in the empire,
the poorer become the people.
The more sharp implements the people keep,
the more confusions are in the country.
The more arts and crafts men have,
the more are frivolous things produced.
The more laws and regulations are given,
the more robbers and thieves there are.

And the way Chuang-Tzu summarized Lao-Tzu's advice was this: "One successfully governs a large kingdom the same way one cooks a small fish—lightly."

Flying Fish

The course of our lives from birth to death is somewhat analogous to the arching flight through the air of a flying fish. The fish's natural habitat is the ocean. It is, in fact, part and parcel of the ocean. But for some reason, it elects to leave its natural element and take flight through the atmosphere. Then it plunges back into the water.

So, too, we humans (and all other creatures as well) come out of the Infinite. For some unclear reason we leave the boundless deep and are propelled into the finite realm. Breaking the surface, we take flight.

We are born. What a different environment we enter! As we pass into the air (world), we lose all sense of who we are, where we came from, or the purpose of our passage. So the ascending arc of our flight is spent in reorienting ourselves, in gaining a sense of identity.

Significantly, as all of this takes place, we increasingly forget our source, the Infinite ocean. We become convinced that this world is "it." Awed by its size and power, we struggle to establish enough control over the world that we can feel as though we belong here. Of course, it is a forlorn struggle. However successful we may be in our attempt to have power over the world, still we are minuscule when our finite significance is measured against the totality of existence.

Somewhere around the midpoint of our life flight, we may begin to have intimations that there is more—intuitions about the ocean and our unlimited connection to it. Perhaps these intimations come in the form of transcendental experiences during which the veil of forgetfulness is momentarily parted and we glimpse the Infinite in all of its grandeur and simplicity. Perhaps they come more ordinarily as the result of silence or contemplation or the teachings of another who has had such a transcendental experience. We may not know it, but every authentic relationship with our fellows and every occasion when we come into harmony with the rhythms of the cosmos are transcendental experiences.

In any event, if we are attentive and diligent, our awareness grows. And, as that happens, we become both more loving (i.e., more conscious of the oneness of everything) and, paradoxically, less attached to the transient items by which we would control the world and feel significant as separated beings. It is as though, by being able to let go of the fragments of our finitude, we begin to regain our sense of "having it all," since, as part and parcel of the Infinite, we *are* It All.

Some few of us actually "awaken" to our true identity as denizens of the deep. More of us, however, simply become more accepting of the transient nature of our flight, of our approaching "end," of our inevitable re-entry into the ocean. And, with our splashdown back into Infinity we rejoin that nourishing mystery in which we have, throughout our journey, lived and moved and had our being. Like all true homecomings, how could this one possibly be other than okay?

11

Self-Discovery

Reluctant penguins and the "five delusory Ps"

At the same time I've been telling you how important spiritual growth is, I keep saying it is not easy. The obstruction lies not so much in the difficulty of growth itself as in our own timid perceptions. We are reluctant to give up our present, familiar state and accept a better but unfamiliar one. Part of the problem is that we do not recognize a better way of being until it has been shown to us many times. And the other part is that, even after we recognize the better way, we delay following it.

This whole point is made in a charming anecdote told by Eknath Easwaran in his book, *The Supreme Ambition: Life's Goal and How to Reach It:*

> A few years ago I saw a documentary about penguins, which depicted the lives of these droll creatures almost from the first moment. They looked so human that I found it easy to identify with them as they grew into adults, impeccably attired in evening coats and tails, and set about learning to live in the world around them.
>
> To me it seemed a most inhospitable environment. Penguins hatch in craggy Antarctic rookeries high above frigid waters, which are probably covered with ice for half the year. But the little ones evidently felt quite cozy in those precarious nests. For some time, while they are protected by their parents, they eat, sleep, and do precious little else.
>
> But once the young birds begin to molt, their parents make a drastic move. Up to this time they have been loyal and attentive, in-

spiring examples for the rest of the avian world. But when it comes time for the children to grow up, the parents simply walk out. There is a great parade of them away from the rookery, and the scene they leave behind is sorrowful indeed. The fledglings I saw looked so dazed that I had to keep reminding myself it was all part of a larger picture. Unless the parents leave them, the children will sit in the nest and never grow up, having their five meals a day, quarreling over who gets what, and never learning to fend for themselves.

With their parents gone, the children naturally began to feel hungry. One day passed; they suppressed their hunger. Two days passed, and their stomachs grew insistent. Finally, after three days or so, they could stand it no longer. Some of them ventured out of their nests.

Penguins are inquisitive by nature, and one of the fledglings in this film was more inquisitive and daring than any of the others. I called him Peter, and he really captured my imagination. I could almost see what was going on behind those curious, beady eyes as he waddled to the edge of the cliff and peered down at the cold, gray waves crashing against the rocks below. Instinctively he must have known that the sea meant fulfillment. If he could only get into the water, he would not die on the rocks but live as a penguin should. But his senses were telling him just the opposite. He hurried back and told the others, "This is death! Better to stay here and go hungry than to face such a terrible fate."

The rest of the rookery were all too willing to agree. "This may not be much of a life," their faces said, "but it's better than violent death. Who knows? Mom and pop may still come back."

But mom and pop did not come back, and finally the hunger grew so fierce that they could not live with it any longer. One morning Peter made his way slowly back to the edge of the cliff. He was still afraid, but anything must have seemed better to him than starvation. He closed his eyes and repeated his mantra. Then with one brave leap, he hurled himself out into the air. The expression on his face said clearly, "My number is up!" We heard a great splash; I could almost feel the shock of the icy waters. Peter disappeared beneath the waves.

There was an agonizing pause. Then, to my great relief, up bobbed a bright-eyed, slightly sheepish little face. Peter churned with his wings and waggled his tail vigorously. Within minutes he was swimming gracefully through the waves, at home at last. "Hey," he squawked up to his friends. "Come on down! This is what we were born for."

Some of the other penguins waddled to the ledge and poked their heads over to see. But even after seeing Peter's exuberance, only two or three were willing to take the plunge. Most of them decided to approach their destiny by stages—that is, they hunted for ledges by which they could walk down. They took a lot of time about it too, looking for just the right ledge and then descending with excruciating care. Only after they were perched about six feet above the water would they cautiously fall in. But once they were in, they too began to crow. "Hey, Pete, wait up! You were right; this is really living."

Still some were not prepared to take this last little six-foot plunge. They just sat there on the lowest ledge, and no amount of frolicking on the part of their friends could induce them to dive in. But even for them, all was not lost. Gradually the tide rose, and one by one the waves washed every penguin into the sea.

I found this a very heartening ending. The whole of life, the mystics of all religions tell us, is moving inexorably toward the sea of joy and fulfillment that we call God. Some—great saints like Teresa of Avila or Mahatma Gandhi—plunge into this sea boldly. Many of the rest of us, busy with other pursuits, wait for the tide to rise. But none of us is lost. Life has a goal, and in the Hindu and Buddhist perspective, even if it takes hundreds of lifetimes, evolution itself will carry us to the fulfillment of life's purpose, which is Self-realization.

There is a story told of Arthur Schopenauer. The German philosopher was wandering aimlessly through a city park at night when he was spotted by a policeman. "Who are you?" demanded the policeman. Schopenauer answered, "I wish I knew!"

Not long ago I was speaking with a young man who had come to me to discuss his difficulty in finding his niche in life. He had graduated with honors from a good university. He had spent almost a year wandering through Europe. He had attended countless workshops and seminars at places as far-flung as Bar Harbor, Maine, and the Esalen Institute in California's Big Sur. He had sat at the feet of several gurus and psychics. He had experimented with four psychedelic drugs. He had tried Kundalini yoga, past life therapy, est, and a dozen hours in a sensory deprivation tank.

About all he had to show for his efforts was a whole assortment of esoteric memories, none of which seemed to be a source of joy, and two quite frustrated parents who had "bailed him out for the last time." He had come to me, he said, "for help." I asked him what he meant by that, and he replied, "I'm trying to find the key to my life. And every time I get close, something goes wrong."

As I listened to this young man's quite desperate but thoroughly undisciplined search for himself, I was reminded of a Sufi tale about Nasrudin. Nasrudin had lost the key to his house while going home one night. He was down on all fours by the streetlight looking for it. Presently, a stranger came by and asked Nasrudin what he was looking for. Nasrudin replied, "My house key." So the stranger, being a helpful sort, got down onto the pavement, too, and began looking, but without success. Finally, in some frustration the stranger asked, "Are you sure you dropped the key here?" "Oh, no!" replied Nasrudin, "I dropped it over there in the alley." "Then, why are you looking for it here?" exploded the stranger. "Because the light's better here," answered Nasrudin.

So it is for most of us when we ask that crucial question, "Who am I?" For one reason or another, we look in the wrong place. And yet, self-discovery is the ultimate spiritual task. The fundamental question of life is, what is the true self?

Is it this image I see when I look into my mirror? A fellow bearded, bald, ten pounds too heavy, just past sixty—is that who I am?

Is it the description I read when I pull out the file folder labeled "resume"?—Bill Houff—born on a farm in the Shenandoah Valley of Virginia, three college degrees in chemistry and one in theology, ten years' work in chemical research, twenty-four years in the ministry? Is that who I am?

Is it this man whom two grown men call Dad and a woman named Patty calls spouse? A person who enjoys being a minister but occasionally wishes he were a farmer or the caretaker of a spiritual retreat—is that who I am?

Once I was certain that the true self was something I would become. I was busy "making something of myself." I studied hard in school; I labored to push back a scientific frontier or two; I enjoyed seeing my name in chemical journals and the *Patent Gazette*; I traveled hither and yon, camera in hand, collecting memories; I imagined myself the senior minister in one of the so-called cathedral churches of our denomination.

And there have been times when I fantasized of establishing my true identity by what I owned—a distinguished library on many subjects, a spectacular color slide collection, sound recordings of all the significant classical works, a vegetable patch that *Organic Gardening* magazine might someday feature, a house built with my own hands—in short, an assortment of interests and talents establishing my standing as a true Renaissance Man.

Even as these "marks of self" periodically compelled my attention, I dreamt of another direction. I would find myself by intensive self-searching—by "peeling the onion." Layer by layer, I would strip away the successive façades until I came at last to my one true self—a precious and essential being, the only one of its kind. Unique and irreplaceable, at last would be revealed an individual who had never lived before and would never live again.

What a bewildering array of possibilities for establishing who I am! And all of them rather like Nasrudin searching under the street light for the key he dropped in the alley.

The problem with all such modes of self-discovery is that they reveal nothing that endures. And when looked at closely, it must be obvious that what we are searching for is something not limited by space and time. So arises the rather juvenile hope for some sort of physical immortality that is found in many religious systems.

It is curious, however, how often the very people who reject fanciful theologies that still depend upon time and space turn right around and come up with other notions similarly limited. Thus, we may have the concept of ourselves as a part of a dynamic continuum—a droplet in the everflowing stream of life. A good many others of us anticipate some level of immortality through our deeds and descendants. And a few, being existentialists, simply see our current being as a kind of evolutionary accident or cosmic joke—"absurd," as John Paul Sartre put it. Finally, there are those who, seeing only the temporary nature of all material things, decide to make an ultimate of the process; they worship progress. Our own culture has done that. So, too, upon occasion, has my own religious movement.

There was a time when I included myself among the existentialists, and among the followers of "progress." Essentially, I took the sensory metaphors of existence and tried to make them literal. As a scientist—one trained to apply all the tools of observation and logic to the problems of existence—I could find no other thing "out there" to fasten upon, so I focused upon matter and its events as the real stuff. Still, there was the "real life" fact: time changes and ultimately destroys all things. No accomplishment, no possession, no attachment can halt the work of time. As Omar Khayyam says hauntingly:

> The bird of time has but a little way to go
> And lo, the Bird is already on the wing.

How the Hindus gained such an insight so long ago, we may only guess, but we are indebted to them for the idea that the so-called "real world" is only an illusion. This is why, they say, that whenever we try to find certainty or security in the things that change, we simply end up making ourselves less sure, and less secure.

It is an idea that makes its appearance in all of the great religious traditions. As the founders and mystics of those traditions all tend to advise us, we should not identify with our bodies, or our possessions, or our accomplishments.

Look upon your body, they tell us, as your house, as the vehicle you travel in, as the coat that keeps you warm and dry—even as the temple of your soul. Take proper care of it as you would of anything else useful to you; but don't confuse it with who you really are.

The same goes for your possessions. They are not yours, even though you use them as signs of your self-worth. The self they point to is the illusory self—the self that thinks it is the body, the self caught in time and space.

As for your accomplishments, they too are "out there"—signals of your impact in time and space. But do not expect them to last. That is why ordinary happiness never lasts. Such happiness is founded upon the fulfillment of desires that, once accomplished, fade away into the past. It is the nature of the mind to desire, and the nature of desire to pass.

Possessions, power, prestige, profit, and pleasure—the five delusory Ps, I call them—all of these must be questioned as ultimate goals of being. None last; none satisfy for long. All must be jealously guarded and constantly reinforced. All are traps. No matter how hard you try, you can never accumulate enough of the five delusory Ps to assure you once and for all that you are somebody. The prophet Jesus was talking about the five delusory Ps when he warned us, "Lay not up for yourselves treasures upon earth, where moth and rust doth corrupt, and where thieves break through and steal."

Now, please hear me carefully—I am not calling the five delusory Ps utterly evil. Possessions, power, prestige, profit, and pleasure are all okay when achieved in moderation and when not elevated to a position of high priority, and most especially, when not allowed to distract us from the real goal of life, Self-discovery.

Many centuries ago, Chuang-Tzu stated the essence of the balance required when he said, "When one tries to expand his power over objects, those objects gain power over him." Thus the five delusory Ps are rather like electricity, which can light a house or burn it down, keep the tenant warm or cause swift electrocution.

Another of the great gifts of Hindu thought is that the individual self—the I—is not to be confused with the sensory world, not with its possessions, or experiences, or the physical body. It is not even to be confused with its thoughts. The essential I is far greater than these. It is integral to the fundamental principle of all existence which both stands behind and encompasses what we ordinarily take to be real. The Hindus have a word for this fundamental principle. They call it Brahman—a word roughly equivalent to God or Tao. They also have a word for the essential I; they call it Atman. And the Atman is the true Self, with a capital "S" to distinguish it from the bundle of individual characteristics, the small "s" self, which is dominated by the five delusory Ps.

Thus, we are not who we think we are. When we are successful in the journey of Self-discovery, we realize we are Atman. And then we know that Atman and Brahman are of the same essence.

Ideas and theories such as these can be most helpful in getting us past our usual limiting theologies; they can also introduce us to entirely new conceptions. But there comes the time when neither religious nor scientific speculation can take us as far as we need to go. Rationality "works" in the material world. Only mystical insight finally "works" in the spiritual realm.

Trying to discover your real Self—the Atman that is Brahman—via linear analysis is like using a light to discover its own source. When you turn on a flashlight, you can discover everything else within sight but the flashlight itself! By the light all else can be seen. But the source of the light can only be inferred, recognized intuitively. Using a slightly different analogy, the color red is not a thing in itself, but it can be used to draw, to "show" things.

Thus, on our spiritual quest we need more than anything else to be gentle and patient. There is a Zen-like aspect to spiritual growth. We mustn't push too hard! Alan Watts puts it this way: "The more you look through the drawers, under the bed and bureau, in the closet and on the bathroom floor for the spectacles you are already wearing (on your nose), the further you will be from finding them."

Even with gentleness, patience and perseverance, Self-discovery is no easy task. The ego, the illusory world, these are distracting. The flash and noise of everyday life tends to blind and deafen us to an awareness that we are far more than we ordinarily know. Not only is the world of appearances—the illusory world—extremely seductive, but the mind itself constantly chatters away with all the data and feelings that go to make up our myriad thoughts and sensations.

Just as we have to limit the power of the five delusory Ps, so we must somehow gain control of all of this mental chatter. We think that we control it, but only an enlightened few really do so. Even Plato compared the human mind to a ship in which the crew has mutinied and locked the captain below deck.

Quieting the chatter is essential to Self-discovery, to finding that we are Atman, to hearing what has sometimes been called "the quiet still voice within." This is why meditation and the other spiritual disciplines are integral to every one of the mystical traditions. Meditation and its allied practices are simply ways of quieting the chatter—of tying up the cognitive mind—so that the "good news that flows out of silence" can be picked up and recognized. It is not that we hear something outside ourselves, but that we hear and recognize something that has been inside all the time. It is then that we find out who we really are. We find the Self.

This is satori in the Hindu tradition. It is the approach to enlightenment in Buddhism, and to "no mind" in Zen. And yes, despite all the popular and sentimental mumbo-jumbo that has co-opted the word, it is salvation in Christianity.

Please note, none of this is easy. Spiritual growth—Self-discovery—takes discipline and dedication. It also takes something else: letting go and waiting. The timing of the final step is not ours to determine.

However, as in all creative endeavors, we must do our preparation well and then we can but allow the muse to strike. All of the study, all of the meditating, all of the selfless service is but preparation. The Hindu Upanishad puts it this way: "That Self cannot be [finally] attained by the study of the scriptures, nor by the intellect, nor by much learning. He whom the Self chooses, by him the Self can be attained."

In other words, the insight that we are Atman comes to us like a thief in the night—unexpectedly. Indeed, the biographies of spiritual persons are filled with accounts of enlightenment coming when least expected, at the sound of a temple bell, or the sight of a hawk against the sky, or a word or glance from an enlightened person, or a sudden realization amidst a moment of suffering or selfless service. This is what C. S. Lewis meant by his phrase, "surprised by joy." The surprise is one of recognizing who we really are, and it is a joyful recognition! It is the delight of coming home after a long absence and seeing with new eyes what has been there all along.

Just as it is impossible to know one's real Self (the Atman) by purely cognitive means, so it is equally impossible to talk about that knowing in linear language. Yet we must communicate. And, when we do so, the "state of unitary awareness" inevitably gets misunderstood, misinterpreted, abused, corrupted, and exploited.

It is because of the limitations of language that some religions simply discourage discussion of ultimate truths. This taboo is behind the ancient Jewish prohibition against the utterance of the name Yahweh. And it is the basis for the Taoist declaration: "Those who know do not speak; those who speak do not know."

While language and cognitive knowledge are limited, they are, of course, useful. They are critically important to the choices we must make concerning spiritual paths and the practice of selfless service. Words and logic are essential to classifying experience, and in discerning and turning away from error.

Thus, although spiritual activity must finally be silent, still there are times when words are helpful. Even Taoists talk. We tell stories, relate myths, crack jokes, use metaphors, chant, sing, and write poems.

Some poets are masters in conveying a sense of the mystical. T. S. Eliot is one of the best. His book *Four Quartets* is filled with gems of sublime insight. In the poem "Burnt Norton" there is a fragment that touches the essence of that Self which is the usually unrecognized center of each of us. Eliot calls it "the still point":

> At the still point of the turning world. Neither flesh nor
>   fleshless;
> Neither from nor towards; At the still point, there the dance is,
> But neither arrest or movement. And do not call it fixity,
> Where past and future are gathered. Neither movement from
>   nor towards,
> Neither ascent nor decline. Except for the point, the still point,
> There would be no dance, and there is only the dance.

And then there is William Blake, perhaps the best-known of our mystical poets. It was Blake who penned a brief and pointed verse alluding to what it is like at that primal instant when one becomes aware of one's true Self:

> To see a world in a grain of sand
> And a Heaven in a wild flower,
> Hold Infinity in the palm of your hand
> And Eternity in an hour.

As we are able to discover our own true Self, we become more able to recognize the true Self in others. This realization first occurred to me upon one of my many rereadings of *I and Thou*, Martin Buber's marvelous little classic which sets forth his basic thesis, "All real living is meeting."

The great Hebrew theologian's fundamental insight was that humans have two quite different ways of meeting the universe. They can do so objectively, by holding themselves apart from whatever they are meeting. Or they can do it subjectively, by seeing themselves as part of whatever they are meeting. The first relationship Buber called "I-It," the second "I-Thou."

In an I-It relationship, the I is interested in the other only from the standpoint of reaction or exploitation. This is what we're doing when we consider a tree as lumber or firewood, or a cow as meat or a source of milk, or a human being as an employee, a student, or a sex object.

In an I-Thou relationship, the I is intimately interdependent with the other. This is what is going on when we get swept up with a sunset as a religious experience, or feel a deep kinship with an animal, or love another human being unconditionally.

Buber was not so naive as to think that it is possible to live constantly in terms of the I-Thou. He knew that the conditions of finite existence require us to regard the rest of the world, including other people, objectively. But he was utterly certain that those who never get past the I-It orientation are spiritually malfunctional. While I-It describes our everyday mode of doing business, I-Thou describes a spiritual encounter.

Buber tells of an I-Thou encounter with a fellow creature:

He was stroking the head of a dapple gray horse. As he did so he experienced a strong feeling of kinship with the animal. Buber sensed that the horse shared the feeling as well. For a timeless moment man and horse were one.

Then, abruptly, Buber became aware of his hand upon the horse's head. He sensed the special connection and, in his mind's eye, stepped back to observe it. At that instant the spell was broken. I-Thou shifted back to I-It. The horse, too, recognized the shift as it lifted its head away from Buber's hand.

What I conceive to be going on in an I-Thou encounter is that the Divine essence within both beings meets and greets itself. Two manifestations of Thou (God, Brahman, Cosmic Consciousness) come together. In the much more common I-It, however, the presence of the Divine is unrecognized and ignored. A meeting of "its" has occurred.

We have all had that special kind of "knowing" that comes quite unbidden upon those rare occasions when our eyes happen to simply meet the eyes of another person. This happens only, I'm sure, when there is no agenda, beyond the acceptance and acknowledgment of the other.

As Martin Buber writes, it can happen with animals. Or even a pine tree (Buber's example)! In a haunting poem titled "Two Look At Two," Robert Frost describes a pair of human beings meeting a pair of deer while walking in the woods. The two sets of beings pause, transfixed in some creaturely identification. Frost concludes the scene:

Two had seen two, whichever side you spoke from.
"This must be all." It was all. Still they stood,
A great wave from it going over them,
As if the earth in one unlooked-for favor
Had made them certain earth returned their love.

I have had similar encounters with my mongrel collie dog when, per-chance, our eyes meet and linger, and, simultaneously, he wags his tail and I smile. Yes, I believe that wherever the spirit of life abides, the Divine is present and yearning to meet itself.

Only more recently, however, have I concluded that the I-Thou mutuality represented in the meeting of two pairs of eyes can be consciously willed. Ideally it requires the consent or cooperation of the other person. I have experienced such "created" encounters in spirituality workshops, where the setting is "safe" and permissive. Often, near the end of a workshop, I will suggest to the participants that behind the eyes of another person, a manifestation of "God within that person" is looking out, seek-ing recognition—even when that person may not know it. And I've found again and again that people, when reminded of such a possibility (and ac-cepting of it), are able to see one another in a new and thoroughly open and non-threatening way. I'm convinced that there is a shift in the nature of relating, in which there is a perceptible lessening of the awkwardness that exists where eyes meet one another with unclear purposes.

Sometimes in public places such as airline terminals, where people are waiting for time to pass, I have tried this technique of seeing God in the eyes of a stranger. No, I don't stare! Rather, I look softly, with an inner awareness that acknowledges who they really are.

The reactions (if any) are varied, of course. But I have never sensed wariness or hostility. Most importantly, within me there grows an under-standing for which the word "love" seems appropriate. It is, I'm sure, a spiritual technique that more of us could creatively practice—perhaps even with profound social consequences.

Three "Practical Rules"

It was during the coffee hour after the eleven o'clock service that an occasional visitor to the church approached me saying, "Bill, this is the second
time I've heard you talk about mysticism and spiritual growth. And I must
admit that it's not the sort of thing I've done much thinking about. Usually when I hear terms like Tao and 'no mind' and Cosmic Consciousness
and nirvana, I just tune out. But while I don't want anything to do with ordinary church beliefs, I do think there's more to existence than earning a
living. What I want to know is, if you were going to boil spiritual concern
down to a few practical rules, what would you say?"

"Whew!" I replied. "I need some time to think about that." About then
someone joined us, and I was mercifully spared having to give an immediate
answer. But the visitor had asked a legitimate question.

After some reflection, I'm suggesting three "practical rules" for the
authentic spiritual life. Let's call them attention, love, and nonattachment.

Attention can be summed up in a two-word command: "Pay attention!" It asks us to live mindfully. Even Emerson talked about this spiritual
rule when he wrote,

> These roses under my window make no reference to former roses
> or better ones; they are for what they are. . . . There is no time for
> them. There is simply the rose; it is perfect in every moment of its
> existence. . . . But man postpones or remembers; he does not live
> in the present, but with reverted eye laments the past, or heedless
> of the riches that surround him, stands on tiptoe to foresee the fu-
> ture. He cannot be happy and strong until he too lives with nature
> in the present.

Love has little or nothing to do with mere liking. That's why the com-
mandment "Love your enemy" makes so little ordinary sense to us. Love
refers to the fact that we are interconnected—part of a larger whole. When
we are told to love, what we are being asked to do is to recognize our kinship to another—identify with another—walk in his or her shoes for a mile.
The reason we should love our enemy is that we need to recognize that that
person, even if we despise what he or she has done, is really an extension
of ourselves. "There but for the grace of God go I!"

Love and nonattachment seem diametrically opposed. After all, we
should be attached to whatever we love; that's what the movies, storybooks,

and our own hearts tell us. The trouble with "attached" love is that it is controlling and possessive, jealous and stifling. That's why it so easily turns into hatred. Nonattachment does not preclude devotion; on the contrary, it promotes it. But it shows its devotion by encouraging growth and by being able to let go when the time comes.

So, the three essentials of authentic spiritual life are:

Attention to what is before us at this moment in time,
A sense of inclusiveness (love) that rises above all separation,
And a life of devotion unhampered by attachment.

Attention, love, nonattachment—may these three ever guide us.

12

Better Living through Mysticism

After letting go of the banana

I cannot say whether it is a cultural accident or an aspect of the resistance most people have to Self-discovery, that is, to spiritual growth, but it is unfortunately true that in Western society we have a grossly distorted view of what it means to be a mystic, of what it means to be a person actively pursuing Self-discovery.

To most of us a mystic is an aging, antisocial recluse. The word "mystic" is often confused with the words "magic" and "occult." In the common vernacular a mystic is a person who shuns the major spiritual traditions and goes off in pursuit of esoteric perspectives which are both secret and a little bit crazy. I have heard liberal ministers suggest that mysticism has no place in a rational person's religion.

Well, I am here to testify that true mystics are at the same time the most hardheaded of thinkers and socially concerned people, and yet open to the most intuitive and creative of insights. Alan Watts put it well when he said, "The most spiritual people are the most human people. They are natural and easy in manner; they give themselves no airs; they interest themselves in ordinary everyday matters, and are not forever talking and thinking about religion. For them there is no difference between spirituality and usual life, and to their awakened insight the lives of the most humdrum and earth-bound people are as much in harmony with the infinite as their own."

Evelyn Underhill, who in 1924 wrote the authoritative book on the subject, defines mysticism as "a highly specialized form of that search for reality, for heightened and completed life, which we [find] to be a constant characteristic of human consciousness." She warns,

> Mysticism . . . is not an opinion: it is not a philosophy. It has nothing in common with the pursuit of occult knowledge. On the one hand, it is not merely the power of contemplating Eternity: on the other, it is not to be identified with any kind of religious queerness. It is the name of that organic process which involves the perfect consummation of the Love of God. . . . Or, if you like it better— for this means exactly the same thing—it is the art of establishing [a] conscious relation with the Absolute. . . . It is . . . an ordered movement towards ever higher levels of reality, ever closer identification with the Infinite.

As for the misconception that real mystics are softheaded and fuzzy minded, I counter that spiritual seekers are enormously attentive to life and open to its possibilities, as well as being dauntless skeptics.

They have to be. Among the teachings of the great spiritual traditions is the one that we should not trust the sensory world, nor become entangled in its attachments. There is the Hindu concept that the things which seem most real are *maya*—illusory. Moreover, while in everyday life material objects seem quite separate from one another, religion at its core is concerned with the interconnected wholeness of things. It is not even safe to insist upon one's own individuality. The Buddha warns that the cause of all suffering is in our insistence in holding ourselves apart from the whole, while becoming attached to fragments of the whole.

Thus, even though they are the popular goals of modern life, the five delusory Ps—possessions, power, prestige, profit, and pleasure—are actually traps.

How alien this sort of thinking is to most Westerners! We have become habituated to the belief that matter and its permutations are the fundamental stuff; so how can they be *maya*, illusory?

Does this mean that we should dismiss the material world, the universe of time and space, and henceforth ignore it? No, it does not. For we humans are momentarily stationed in such an existence, much as we have all, upon occasion, felt stuck in a dream. Only when we awaken do we recognize the dream as an alternative state of being, different from the waking state.

What we need to appreciate is that this illusory world does have its own reality and its own rules. The person who ignores a speeding truck or who denies the law of gravity is apt to be in trouble.

Some few highly enlightened persons may be able to ignore or even defy the rules of ordinary life—to perform miracles, for example. But most of us are not so learned or elevated. And getting involved in such escapades is not only hazardous to life, limb, and sanity, but can also become a spiritual cul-de-sac which limits further growth. This is why most of the spiritual traditions warn against sorcery. It is not that sorcery (magic) is impossible, but that it tends to become a personal power trip which can set the uninitiated apart from the whole rather than connect him or her to it.

These essential points made all too briefly, let me now turn to my primary concern: the practical consequences of spiritual growth, or of being a mystic.

I define a mystic as a person who is serious about coming into harmony with the cosmic whole. Such a person is alive in every conceivable respect. He or she is self-actualizing in the sense that Abraham Maslow used that term. He or she lives mindfully day to day, in the here and now, but also sees through the veil of the everyday to the infinite and the eternal. To use a Biblical phrase, such persons live "in the world" but are not "of the world." They have had some significant personal experiences which assure them that they are far more than the possessions, the physical self, and even the thoughts that are such an integral part of everyday life.

This is not to say that mystics are perfect. As a matter of fact, to the degree a person is preoccupied with being perfect, he or she is not a mystic. Mystics are morally and spiritually fallible. The following Zen story makes this point precisely.

Seeking to promote his spiritual growth, a novice went off to a remote monastery where he practiced *zazen* many hours every day and led a very simple and humble existence the rest of the time. For twenty years the regimen continued. At last, convinced that he had freed himself of all attachments and was now at the very threshold of enlightenment (if not in fact past it), he returned to the village whence he had come.

Immediately he went to the marketplace which was crowded with many people going noisily about their worldly business. Serene in his spiritually elevated condition, he plunged directly into the crowd. He had no more than gotten into the milling throng when someone, intent on some single-minded pursuit, jostled him so hard as to nearly knock him off his feet. At once his serenity vanished and a flash of anger surged through him. In that instant he knew that his enlightenment was far from imminent, and he returned to the monastery for another twenty years.

Obviously there is an element of presumption and chance in declaring who is a mystic and who is not. And yet, in the name of making explicit what it means to progress on the mystical paths, let me suggest the names of some well-known persons who were probably well along.

I think of Thomas Merton, the Cistercian monk who wrote so many books on spiritual living. I think of Jiddu Krishnamurti, the East Indian who, into his eighties, attracted large crowds to his lectures. I think of Dag Hammarskjold, Swedish Secretary General of the United Nations, and of U Thant, his successor. Certainly, Martin Luther King, Jr., and Albert Schweitzer, Mahatma Gandhi, and Mother Teresa of Calcutta come to mind. So do Mary Baker Eddy, the founder of Christian Science, Evelyn Underhill, who wrote what is still the fundamental book on mysticism, and Saint Therese of Lisieux, a French nun at the turn of the century who led such an exemplary life of service that she was elevated to sainthood shortly after her death. I also have a growing conviction that all truly creative people are mystics. As examples I offer the authentic pioneers of modern physics: Albert Einstein, Niels Bohr, Werner Heisenberg, and Wolfgang Pauli. In other fields there are Carl Jung, T.S. Eliot, Simone Weill, and Doris Lessing.

For every mystic who has somehow captured the world's attention, there is a multitude of unknown persons who, through the practice of spiritual disciplines and the living of lives useful to others, are also authentic mystics.

A few years ago, E.I. Du Pont de Nemours, the giant chemical corporation, advertised widely its slogan, "Better living through chemistry." I'm suggesting another slogan, "Better living through mysticism."

Let's consider some of the practical benefits of being a mystic, beginning at the personal level. One of the first things discernible in a person who seriously undertakes meditation and other spiritual disciplines is a lessening of stress and an improvement in health. This effect is sufficiently well-documented to be called established.

There is no mystery here. Stress and poor health, I believe, represent disharmonies: disharmonies within oneself and between oneself and the world out there. Meditation is automatically harmonizing. It brings us into tune, so to speak. Meditation is a spiritual modulator. By slowing down and diminishing both the noise of the world and the chatter of the cognitive mind, one allows the powerful and healing rhythms of the cosmos to come into play within one's own life. Meditation releases the creative power that is there all the time, but which so often gets squelched by the attachments, fears, and illusions of everyday life.

I am sure that emotional problems are as amenable to mystical remedies as are physical ones. More and more, I recognize that relational and personal problems are, in the last analysis, spiritual problems. The Buddha's pioneering discovery at the moment of enlightenment was that all suffering is caused by desire—attachment. Time and again I realize, as I am listening to someone describe serious emotional difficulty, that he or she is trapped by something that, for one reason or another, is clung to.

In India there is a time-honored method of catching monkeys which involves putting a banana or some other piece of fruit into a jug with a suitably sized neck. The jug is then tied to a tree or stake with a stout cord. Soon a monkey comes along and, being inquisitive, peers into the container. Immediately seeing the tidbit and wanting it, the monkey reaches in and grabs it. But the neck of the vessel is too small for the animal to withdraw its hand while wrapped around the fruit. At that point, the person who has set the trap comes out of hiding. And as often as not the monkey is so attached to its desire for the fruit that it allows itself to be captured rather than let go. It's amazing how often something similar seems to be going on when we persons are suffering emotionally!

One of the most common and painful emotional afflictions arises through our attachment to unmet expectations. How often I sit in my study and listen to people mourn the disappointments, unkept promises, and betrayals of life! Again and again I am chagrined as I recognize that they are caught in a recurring cycle of archaic dreams. "My mother never loved me as much as she did my brother!" "My father doesn't accept me for who I am!" "My spouse had a love affair!" "My friends take more than they give!" "My children don't appreciate all I did for them!" "My boss told me I'd be a department head at the end of two years!" "My ex-husband never paid attention to our children!"

Inevitably, as such sorrows are poured forth, blame and indignation mount until the burden is nearly unbearable. "He made me angry." "She made me guilty." "They left me with poor self-esteem." So goes the litany of complaints and recriminations—all relics, all irretrievable. Yet they dominate and distort the only time we have: now! So it is that we squander the present. So it is that we fashion our own prisons. How seldom we pause in our pain to recognize that our present feelings are our own, and we can do something about them.

Nobody "makes" us feel anything. This truism, which made its popular appearance during the heyday of the human potential movement (and which can be misused to justify insensitivity or irresponsible behavior), is actually a cardinal principle in Zen Buddhism.

In Zen cause and effect are not seen as separate; they are part of a single process in which all parties are active participants. Yet how obstinate we are in trying to relieve the stresses of life by struggling with the effect while putting the cause "out there." It never works. Zen teacher John Daido Loori is correct: "When we can acknowledge that we create our own stress and begin to look at how we create it, then we can begin to do something about it."

That's an exceedingly risky statement in these times. "Blaming the victim," it's called. But blame is the very thing it does not do. Empowerment is its purpose. It invites us to address our own suffering by asking us to see how we contribute to it and what we might do to relieve it. It meets the same challenge that Victor Frankl met when he was confined in the Nazi death camp, a place of enormous suffering and deprivation. Determined not to be a victim, Frankl decided that, while he could do almost nothing to change or resist his oppressors, he could elect how he would relate to his own suffering. The result was that he not only survived but did so with such courage and dignity that his example still serves as an inspiration to others.

Declining to be trapped and hurt by our unmet expectations in no sense excuses those who mistreat or neglect others. But neither does it waste time trying to change others to be as we would like them. Rather it asks us to determine what the present moment requires and to respond to that need (something that is within our power). The first requirement is that we must own our disappointment and suffering. The second is that we must recognize our participation in that which hurts us. And the third is that we must let go of the attachment represented in our unmet expectations and bad feelings. We can, in other words, heal ourselves by changing the way we think.

How much better our lives go when we are able to appreciate the wisdom set forth in *The Faith Mind Sutra*, which was written by Master Sozan, the third Zen Patriarch:

The Great Way is not difficult;
It only avoids picking and choosing.
When love and hate are both absent,
Everything becomes clear and undisguised.
Make the slightest distinction, however,
And heaven and earth are set infinitely apart.
If you wish to see the truth,
Then hold no opinions for or against anything.
To set up what you like against what you dislike
Is a disease of the mind. . . .

How alien, how bizarre such a teaching may sound! In the Western world where ambition, judgment, and rising expectations are honored virtues, such a passage may only serve as evidence that the Oriental mind is passive or inscrutable.

But wait! Like all great teachings, *The Faith Mind Sutra* is a mind-blower to the uninitiated. Grasping its essence takes living with patience and practice. The literalist and absolutist won't get it. But for those accustomed to living in the questions of life (Rilke's immortal phrase), something remarkable happens. Gradually, nearly unnoticed at first, a sense of freedom and peace of mind will come in while attachment and suffering diminish.

Because of such teachings some people imagine that Zen Buddhists somehow eschew all choice making and do no planning. But that is a misperception. Instead, by living within the wholeness of things and with full attention to the here and now (letting go of attachment to future results), each step becomes clear and appropriate. It is almost as though the choices make themselves, although not without prior discipline and effort. As anyone who has closely observed a Zen artist knows, there is much careful preparation. And when the right moment to begin arrives, the ongoing process essentially "uses" the artist to fulfill its proper goal. As with all true creativity, the result appears unbidden.

It shouldn't surprise us, then, that mystics are also creative. The spiritual search itself is a perfect model of the creative process. Spiritual growth requires discipline and patience; so does any other creative endeavor. Spiritual growth requires an open attentiveness; so does any other creative endeavor. Spiritual growth requires an ability to relax toward one's primary goal and to trust that the answer will come at the proper time. Again, every other creative endeavor requires an ability to back off and wait.

In his research on peak experience and his study of self-actualized persons, Abraham Maslow observed that peakers and self-actualizers are composed, stable, and creative members of society. Such persons, in Maslow's assessment, have a sense of purpose and worth and are part of "an unceasing trend toward unity, integration, or synergy." They spend little or no time in ego maintenance, and they have a strong sense of identity with humanity as a whole as well as a sense of oneness with the cosmos.

While all growth is at times painful (and spiritual growth is no exception), it is clear that, when one is faithful to one's spiritual process, life proceeds more harmoniously. It is also clear that, when the suffering of change or growth is accepted, its intensity diminishes and even is transformed.

Once a person becomes regular in his or her spiritual discipline, choices open up and possibilities appear. Boredom disappears. One does not worry about what the day will bring. Difficulties are expected, yet the capacity to overcome them is also anticipated.

One of the most surprising and welcome results of seeking the true self is that life's anxieties are diminished. Gradually, often without knowing it, one becomes less attached and, therefore, less controlled by the five delusory Ps. I do not mean that one becomes careless and slovenly about one's welfare. I mean that one puts all of this into a different perspective, so that instead of being obsessed or possessed by this want or that, one is able to let go and be free.

There is a story told of Saint Ignatius of Loyola, the founder of the Jesuit Order. Saint Ignatius was asked what his feelings would be if he were ordered to disband the work of his whole adult life. "A quarter of an hour of prayer," he answered, "and then I should think no more about it." That's detachment!

Many persons, hearing such stories, protest vigorously. What about commitment? What about loyalty? What about righteous indignation and patriotism? What about passion, joie de vivre, and sweet nostalgia? What about all of the wonderful bursts of emotion to which we assign nobility and beauty?

Think about these for a moment. Are they not all thinly disguised expressions of attachment? Are they not directly connected to wistful desires, fears of loss, and impulses toward self-importance? One need not be in an emotional fervor to be constant in one's worthwhile purposes. It is so easy to confuse sentimentality and spirituality!

But then is there no joy, no laughter, in the life of a serious seeker? Oh yes, indeed, there is! The bliss of spiritual growth and enlightenment is not a mere figure of speech. The laughing Bodhisattva is firmly established in the Buddhist tradition. But the bliss is the joy of discovery. And the laughter is the good humor of acceptance. In both cases it is an "aha!" expressed in the full exuberance of knowing and feeling wholeness. Indeed, humor has a very prominent place in the spiritual traditions.

Stories are favored teaching devices in every spiritual tradition. The Taoists are especially adroit at putting the rules for spiritually sound living into clever little verses. Wishing to comment on the importance of not rushing off in a panic to accomplish something, Po Chu I said:

Better by day to sit like a sack in your chair;
Better by night to lie [like] a stone in your bed
When food comes, then open your mouth;
When sleep comes, then close your eyes.

And, in the Tao-Te-Ching, we find this stark plea for nonviolence:

To delight in victory
Is to delight in slaughter.
Let a victory be celebrated
With the funeral rite.

And also from the Tao-Te-Ching there is this prescription for effective living:

I have three treasures:
The first is love;
The second is never too much;
The third is never try to be first in the world.
Through love one has courage;
In moderation one has strength;
In never trying to be first
One gives one's talents time to mature.

Something that bothers many people looking at spiritual growth is the perennial directive that one must let go of the egotistical self in order to tap into the power of the cosmic Self. To the uninitiated this feels like the loss of everything unique and worthwhile, as though such a process exhaustively pursued yields both nothingness and powerlessness.

Father Bede Griffiths, an unusual Roman Catholic priest living in India who has incorporated Hindu wisdom into his writings, comments on this.

It must not be thought that when reason surrenders to the [Cosmic] Self it loses any of its powers. On the contrary, it is only then that it rises to the height of its power. The mind of a Sankara [Hindu mystic] or an Aquinas is equal to that of any modern scientist or philosopher, but it draws on sources of wisdom which raise it to a higher power and carry it beyond their reach. Bertrand Russell was a baby compared with Sankara or Aquinas. His mind, in spite of its excellence, could never get beyond the world of senses.

As have many other spiritual writers, Father Griffiths suggests a hierarchy of knowing. He says,

Science is the lowest form of human knowledge—the knowledge of the material world through discursive reason. Philosophy is above science, because it goes beyond the material world and explores the world of thought, but is still confined to discursive reason. Theology is above philosophy because it is open to the world of transcendent reality, but its methods are still those of science and philosophy. It is only wisdom which can transcend reason and know the Truth not discursively but intuitively.

Father Griffiths is not advising that we discard scientific knowledge, philosophy, and theology. He is saying these are not enough. He is saying that where we immerse ourselves only in these and do not seek the kind of knowing which comes through spiritual practices, we will live only partially. And such partial living not only cuts us off from the kind of richness I've been talking about, but also opens us up to all the personal and social problems of modern alienated existence. I believe one of the reasons our popular social reform programs often are so hampered is because many of those involved have not paid sufficient attention to their own spiritual growth. (See chapter fifteen.)

Coincidentally, as spiritual maturity is essential to the evolution of a creative society, so selfless service is an essential part of spiritual growth. Every religious tradition reminds us to practice charity, justice, and peace in our dealings with others. "Right action" is one of the tenets of the Buddhist Eight-fold Path. Mahatma Gandhi once said that it is not possible to be completely happy unless everyone in the world is happy. Premier Nehru of India used to say of Gandhi that though his "eyes were often full of laughter . . . yet there were pools of infinite sadness." Thus the true mystic, in his or her sense of oneness, cannot help being aware of suffering and wishing to do something to relieve it.

And yet we must remember that working for the welfare of others is not a grim life of drudgery. The Bhagavad-Gita, a Hindu scripture which offers spiritual choices rather than commandments, says: "Here are two ways of living. If you live for your own pleasure and profit, that very way of life will eventually make you lonely, bitter and unfilled. If you forget yourself in living for the happiness of others, you will be secure, happy, loving and loved."

Similar sayings are found in every major spiritual tradition. Still we hesitate. Here in America we live under the guiding light of the free enterprise doctrine. What that doctrine advises us is that, if everybody serves his own economic interests, the interests of others will also be served. It is a clever and seductive piece of propaganda. It legitimizes selfishness, as we can tell by comparing the lifestyles of the rich and the poor.

Curiously and tragically most of us believe that if we do not worry a lot about our own economic well-being, swift disaster will befall us. And yet again the Bhagavad-Gita advises, "Empty yourself of all self-will, throw yourself into my work without asking about money or recognition or success, and I will not only take care of your spiritual needs, I'll underwrite all your material needs as well."

Jesus said very much the same in his Sermon on the Mount. Curiously enough, so did R. Buckminster Fuller, the tireless inventor. "Bucky" Fuller was a man of enormous energy. It might seem that he was continually "pushing the river." And yet, in his final essay, Fuller made a statement which was a sort of technological rewording of one of Jesus's utterances in the Sermon on the Mount. Remember the advice to consider the birds of the air and the lilies of the field, which neither sow nor reap, nor toil nor spin, and yet seem to do rather well? The way the great inventor put it was, "I see the hydrogen atom doesn't have to earn a living before behaving like a hydrogen atom."

And then Bucky went on to express the philosophy that he had followed most of his life—a philosophy that, while it uses traditional language, really says on a cosmic scale what I've been trying to say here. "So we—my wife and family—have for fifty-six years realized a series of miracles that occur just when I need something, but not until the absolutely last second. If what I think I need does not become available I realize that my objective may be invalid or that I am steering a wrong course. . . . I simply have to have faith and just when I need the right-something for the right-reasoning, there it is—or there they are—the workshops, helping hands, materials, ideas, money, tools."

What all of this says is that if we as whole persons respond to what is truly before us at the moment, accepting what is and moving on from there, going with the flow and letting it work on our own behalf, we'll probably get to where we need to be. And it will be good.

We are One!
Let us live in terms of this principle
And the rest of life will take care of itself.

I have a growing conviction that as more and more people grow in authentically spiritual ways, the whole world will become a more harmonious place. Both theologians and psychologists have long told us that as people live separated—alienated—from each other, they fear and even practice violence upon one another.

How ironic it is that the nations of the world still believe that they can assure their own security by stimulating suspicion and fear of their neighbors! Progress away from this erroneous notion is painfully slow, but I believe it is happening. More and more, private citizens are applying the principles of networking and ecological interconnectedness to conflict resolution at both a local and global level.

This is even happening with respect to the practice of spiritual disciplines. Several years ago the organization that promotes Transcendental Meditation announced that it was going to test the pacifying effects of having a large number of people meditate simultaneously in neighborhoods with high crime rates. They chose several different times and several areas in the city of Atlanta. Sure enough, when the violent crime statistics were later published, it was found that there had been a modest but significant decrease.

This is consistent with the theory that health—wholeness—can be encouraged through the meditative intervention of another person. Thomas Merton believed that the prayerful contemplations of the brothers in his monastery at Gethsemane were instrumental in preventing nuclear war in the 1950s.

Such a notion is supported by the novel theories of Rupert Sheldrake, a British scientist, who offers fascinating evidence that, once an idea is embraced by enough people, it acquires a greatly enhanced persuasive power and tends to become widely accepted.

Earlier I shared Eknath Easwaran's charming anecdote about penguins and the courage to take the plunge into the spiritual life. Near the end of the same book, Easwaran offers a single sentence which summarizes the practical advantages of Self-discovery. Meditation and the allied spiritual disciplines, he says, develop something precious: "The capacity to turn anger into compassion, fear into fearlessness, and hatred into love."

The Whitewater Mystic

So what's the difference between the way a mystic looks and lives and how ordinary unenlightened folks look and live?

Well, first off there may be no visible difference at all. Most mystics don't live in mountaintop caves, and they don't wear yellow robes, and they don't chant "Om" half of every day, and they don't look spiritual (whatever that is), and they don't levitate or radiate a lavender glow at the drop of a hat. In fact, as far as outward signs are concerned, the only possible way that you could tell a genuine mystic from an ordinary person is that the mystic might look more ordinary.

The main distinction, other than metaphysical perspective, between a mystic and others is in the *approach* to life. It's rather like the difference between jet boating and whitewater rafting.

Most of us are jet boaters. For us power and speed are what life is all about. We love the roar of the motor and the smell of the exhaust. The river seems to be an enemy ever ready to consume us. How invigorating to meet it, defy it, and subdue it! No matter how swift the current or how high the cataracts, we need pay little heed because our power is greater. True, the jet boater does roar through life, seldom touching the nature of things. But with enough speed it doesn't matter. As long as the motor keeps turning out those rpms and the tank stays full, the jet boater can run circles around those who travel at a more pedestrian pace. Of course there's nothing so helpless or ludicrous as a jet boater with a dead motor. And sometimes the jet boater does get to wondering who's really in charge of life.

The whitewater rafter, by contrast, doesn't cover a lot of distance. By necessity, the whitewater rafter must go with the flow of the current. There's no way those big yellow inflated rubber doughnuts are going to go against the flow. But they do get very good gas mileage. Despite first appearances the whitewater rafter isn't powerless. He or she observes the current, studies the rapids, calculates the force of the water as it goes around obstacles, and then decides how to use the power of the river to go in a natural direction. It's an ecologically sound and satisfying way to travel. More gets seen, nature seems closer, and the adventure is leisurely enough to enjoy. Something else: the whitewater rafter seldom worries about equipment failure and never wonders who's in charge of the trip.

A funny thing: many of us extol the lifestyle of the mystic. We say we'd like to live that way ourselves. But there isn't time. . . .

13

The Right Rite

Avoiding *wuzi-wuzi*

The Mbuti of Africa believe that every person is surrounded by a sphere, an invisible bubble, which is all one's own. Move too fast and your bubble can be outdistanced. An impostor can take your place. Those going too fast for their bubble are in a state of *wuzi-wuzi*. Without the slowing, the attention to our personal speed, the fulfillment of our need for ritual, we operate in a state of *wuzi-wuzi*. So writes Colin Turnbull in *The Human Cycle*.

The conscious renewal of ritual and celebration is a way to return to the sacred from the clamor of the world. Ritual and celebration give us the revelation that the spiritual is part of life. We are religious beings. If we make a conscious choice away from religious ritual, we will fill the vacuum with other unconscious rituals, such as habits, neuroses, and symptoms.

Like a bowl catching rainwater, ritual is the form we put forth to catch the spiritual. We must leave some part of our lives "out of control" so the unexpected can happen. We must leave a hole in space and time. Sometimes it's scary to decide how much to structure and how much to leave out of control. The hole in time is the sabbath, the holiday, the feast, the celebration. It is the time we take to play with the gods, the Great Spirit interacting with our own, in order to be fully human.

The most important ceremonies of the human cycle have to do with transitions, when we are vulnerable. These are likened to the long process of a reptile shedding its skin. Once accomplished, the new, vulnerable skin is exposed and the animal is exhausted. The animal cannot fit the old skin any longer. Likewise, it seems just when we fit best we must change.

—Connie Blair, Montessori teacher

Except for the most superficial examples such as table manners, driving a car, tying one's shoes, and the routine followed upon rising in the morning, rituals have profound secular and sacred dimensions. Involving both the finite and the Infinite, most rites, sacraments, liturgies, ceremonies, and celebrations are essentially spiritual.

Today there is a new and burgeoning awareness of the importance of ritual. Not only is ritual essential to the successful negotiation of life passages, crises, and holy days, it also facilitates our connections to one another, affirms operant cultural and spiritual values, and evokes a sense of wonder and gratitude about life and the cosmos. In sum, ritual is a crucial feature of the path of devotion.

Our growing awareness of ritual is in contrast to the situation only two decades ago when the counterculture was challenging and rejecting both secular and sacred ritual as irrelevant or worse. Curiously, in our innate insistence upon rituals, at the same time this breakdown was taking place many of us were turning to the Eastern religions, native American traditions, and paganism and witchcraft. Without realizing it, millions of Americans were also turning sports and entertainment into ceremonial occasions.

How quickly fads and trends shift! Suddenly we are consciously returning to ritual—in some cases resurrecting and adapting old forms, in others trying to originate new ones. This search is highly spiritual in its implications. It responds to the eternal questions: "What do we believe in? How can we find meaning in our lives? How do we create structure and order? How shall we get to where we are going?"

The quest, however desperate and poignant, is not an easy one. Meaningful rituals, like compelling symbols, are not readily contrived. They come from a place deeper than whim or rationality. Poet Gary Snyder is correct: "They must come from dreams and visions, and from the particular place where you live." And historian Morris Berman says, "You know what you need to do, dammit; just listen."

The current discussions about ritual are not new. Writing in 1945, religious philosopher Aldous Huxley saw very clearly the development of our modern ambivalence toward ritual. That ambivalence is not limited to our own times. Indeed the great religious prophets, in their advanced stages of spiritual development *and* customary hostility to alien faiths, regularly took a dim view of religious rituals; they recognized how readily such observances lose their symbolic meaning and become idolatrous and turn into magic-making.

Yet in their reservations about ritual, sages and saints no doubt expected too much of those who were inspired by them. As history shows most abundantly, both the vested stewards of religious institutions and their adherents habitually refuse to follow such lofty paths. They insist upon more sentimentality, pageantry, and mystery.

Thus in *The Perennial Philosophy* Huxley wrote:

> That very large numbers of men and women have an ineradicable desire for rites and ceremonies is clearly demonstrated by the history of religion. Almost all the Hebrew prophets were opposed to ritualism. [Thus in the Old Testament we read:] "Rend your hearts and not your garments." "I desire mercy and not sacrifice." "I hate, I despise your feasts; I take no delight in your solemn assemblies." And yet, in spite of the fact that what the prophets wrote was regarded as divinely inspired, the Temple at Jerusalem continued to be, for hundreds of years after their time, the center of a religion of rites, ceremonials, and blood sacrifice.

> What the Jews did in spite of their prophets, Christians have done in spite of Christ. The Christ of the Gospels is a preacher and not a dispenser of sacraments or performer of rites; he speaks against vain repetitions; he insists on the supreme importance of private worship; he has no use for sacrifices and not much use for the Temple. But this did not prevent historic Christianity from going its own all-too-human way. A precisely similar development took place in Buddhism. For the Buddha of the Pali scriptures, ritual was one of the fetters holding back the soul from enlightenment and liberation. Nevertheless, the religion he founded has made full use of ceremonies, vain repetitions, and sacramental rites.

No doubt Aldous Huxley shared the prophets' reservations about ritual, but he also understood something that we religious liberals in our caution about rites need to appreciate too:

> First, most people do not want spirituality or deliverance, but rather a religion that gives them emotional satisfaction, answers to prayer, supernormal powers, and partial salvation in some sort of posthumous heaven. Second, some of those few who do desire spirituality and deliverance find that, for them, the most effective

means to those ends are ceremonies, "vain repetitions," and sacramental rites. It is by participating in these acts and uttering these formulas that they are most powerfully reminded of the eternal Ground of all being; it is by immersing themselves in the symbols that they can most easily come through to that which is symbolized. . . .

And so until the majority of humanity has achieved nirvana and can live in the rarified atmosphere of unadorned spirituality, we must expect that all of the ceremonial trappings of religious searching and practice will remain precious. Similarly, the so-called rites of passage will be necessary to our sense of identity and place in the world.

In our current rediscovery of ritual, we are starting to recognize the essential role of certain mainly secular rituals in the harmonious functioning of all contemporary cultures. Where these ceremonies are lacking, we must expect more or less continual trouble in the moderation of ambiguous behavior and in the maturation of the young.

The current concern about drug abuse is illustrative. Human cultures, even the most primitive, have had to contend with the availability of mind-altering and sensation-intensifying natural substances. Modern Western civilization, which obsessively pursues stimulation for its own sake and routinely overmedicates itself, is particularly beset by an epidemic of illegal drug use. And we are well-advised to be alarmed.

By contrast various native American people knew about and used peyote, cannabis, datura, psilocybin mushrooms, and other psychoactive materials to produce ecstatic states of consciousness which they generally interpreted as the ingested gods or spirits working from within. Yet, except for periods of high cultural stress or breakdown, misuse of these powerful and readily available substances did not occur. Their use was permitted within a ritualistic framework that made abuse essentially unthinkable.

We moderns lack the mass discipline of such rituals. In our inability to handle drugs, we are in a predicament similar to that of the native American people when alcoholic drinks became available to them. Lacking both rituals and experience in using such beverages, the Indians became addicted in droves. We non-Indians have not done much better. Our youth, being just as rite-deficient as their elders in the use of alcohol and other drugs, are following suit.

Beyond the drug problem, our lack of harmonizing rituals and moderating ceremonies is manifested in the difficulties that our young have in growing up and in dealing with such potentially destructive activities as sexual expression and the operation of motor vehicles. The same lack can be observed in the difficulties adults have in negotiating marital disruptions, job losses and retirement.

Of course, more than the absence or inadequacy of operant rituals is involved. Along with a paucity of rites, there is a corresponding lack of compelling creative values and myths. The understanding that these deficiencies are closely and critically related and even mutually reinforcing should not be neglected by us. Until cultural rituals, myths, and values are brought into concert, our contemporary social discords will continue and perhaps even worsen. We need all of these to tell us who we are and how we should behave.

One of the more insightful recent articles on the essential role of ritual was written by Francine du Plessix Gray and appeared in the September 1980 issue of *Vogue*. After ruefully recalling her college girl refusal to participate in a 1949 Maypole dance, Gray continued:

> Since then it has become painfully clear to me that we've been secularized and deritualized beyond forbearance; that the Enlightenment's promise of salvation through technology has radically failed; that in the great debate between Freud and Jung concerning the role of religious ritual, Jung's view has been the prophetic one: Our expressions of joy, sorrow, hope, and particularly our need to honor some form of transcendence will always seek ritual channels if our psychic balance is to survive.

A feminist, Gray nonetheless regrets what she regards as the loss of women's historic role as guardians of essential cultural rituals. In the "women's work" of the past—the quilting bees, sewing circles, reading circles, and church fairs—she sees creative and sustaining motifs that modern civilization is the worse without. She bemoans "the dehumanizing efficiency of science [that] makes it increasingly hard for [women] to experience the intimacy of childbirth, to preserve our ancient roles as comforters of the ill and the aged. Our isolation deepens with the decades in this immense continent; we're increasingly separated from kinsmen, siblings, parents. The rituals of the extended family are growing most infrequent."

Unlike some feminist theorists, Gray does not believe that the future of ritual lies in the past. She recalls the mass fascination of the late sixties and seventies, during which millions claimed an allegiance to Oriental and occult liturgical expressions. Gray interpreted this as a nostalgia for some golden era during which our lives were securely structured by powers or wisdom greater than those of our own time. And she also warned—quite correctly, I think—against the kinds of corruptions and excesses this can lead to. The craving for authoritarian motifs and exotic figures has resulted in the exploitation of millions as well as in the disillusionment and cynicism prompted by the meteoric rise and tawdry fall of such televangelists as Jimmy Swaggart and the Bakkers. And then there are those occasional tragedies, an extreme example of which occurred at Jonestown, Guyana.

The evidence mounts up that we cannot long abide our current ritually ambiguous condition. In the absence of meaningful rituals, we are apt to adopt those that are trivial, silly, or even hurtful. I have seen more than one too-true-to-be-very-funny parody of football (which I admittedly enjoy upon occasion) as a replacement for ancient pagan rites. Especially among the young, the frenzied worship of weirdly costumed and bizarre acting musical groups testifies to the hunger for both ritual and heroes. The epitome of the urge toward ritualistic participation is perhaps represented in the long-term popularity of "The Rocky Horror Picture Show"—where the devotees show up time after time in spectacular garb and, with lit candles and other ceremonial objects in hand, engage in stylized dialogue with the actors on the screen. Finally it should not be lost upon us that our presidential campaigns and elections have become a nationwide ritual in which the playing of the winner/loser game increasingly appears to be more important than the real issues, values, and responsibilities at stake.

As rituals are essential to the identity and well-being of most individuals, so they are equally necessary to the formation and functioning of coherent communities. Again feminist writers are taking a leading role in the discussion.

Starhawk, author of *Dreaming The Dark* and *The Spiral Dance*, writes in her newest book, *Truth or Dare*,

> Ritual affirms the common patterns, the values, the shared joys, risks, sorrows, and changes that bind a community together. Ritual links together our ancestors and descendants, those who went before with those who will come after us. It helps us face together those things that are too painful to face alone. . . . A truly life-affirming culture would be filled with ritual: personal rituals, birthday parties, family and household celebrations, neighborhood rituals, street fairs, promenades, processions, fiestas, vigils, carnivals.

A special form of community ritual is represented in the term "red-letter days"—holiday rituals. And not just Christmas, Easter, and Thanksgiving, although these are indeed signal events with enormous power to bring people together around common experiences and values. One also thinks of Valentine's Day, May Day, Halloween, Mardi Gras, and New Year's with its bittersweet singing of "Auld Lang Syne," which is Scottish for "old long since" or, roughly, the good old days.

Churches, as special communities, have their red-letter days and other rituals which foster group coherence. Besides the so-called religious holidays or high holy days, there are more regular observances such as communion and of course the predictable Mass or liturgy. Among religious liberals rituals are viewed with a more skeptical eye.

In the Unitarian Universalist congregation that I served for fifteen years in Spokane, we were in the habit of holding hands and singing "Shalom Havayreem" as a benediction to our regular worship services. Thinking that the people would enjoy variety, I suggested that we add a Fivefold Amen to our repertoire. The first reaction was immediate and strong; "Leave our religious customs alone!" was the majority message. Even at Thanksgiving, when we had a highly liturgical Abraxan service, the absence of "Shalom" at the ending was noted wistfully by several persons.

Of course religious ritual is all too often used to affirm and reinforce theological concepts that will not stand up to vigorous rational analysis. This is what Aldous Huxley was talking about in the quotation cited above. So there is ambiguity in church liturgy. Like art and poetry, it serves as an aesthetically pleasing shorthand for both teaching and celebrating. But it can also be used to resist change and compel conformity.

As far as I am concerned there is no avoiding this problem, except via an intellectual awareness that causes us to pause and ask ourselves: "Does this make sense to me? Is it congruent with where I am now?" Free and mature religions have nothing to fear from such inquiries; the others do what they can to discourage all questions except those that lead to approved answers.

One query that comes up regularly concerning religious rituals is whether a person can find credible meaning in practices from religious traditions other than his or her own. I believe that one can. It can be tricky, and one must be careful not to bring in specious understandings; but, as Huxley pointed out so persuasively in *The Perennial Philosophy*, behind the myths, forms, and rituals of all the major faiths are common truths. These common truths may be hard to ferret out of the popular expressions of the various religions, but by returning to the fundamentals the diligent student will find them.

Of the Eastern religions, the one to which I resonate the most is Taoism. But that is a theological attunement, not a liturgical one. For a number of years I have had both at home and at the farm a Buddhist altar, complete with icon, candle, incense, and flowers. Sometimes days will pass without my paying much attention to it. But it is there, I know it's there, and upon occasion, I will place myself on my meditation bench before the altar and go inward for twenty minutes or so. At the end of that period I rise and go about my daily pursuits more centered, refreshed, and at peace with myself.

I have found that, as a result of my involvement with the Eastern religions and the discovery of the common elements between these and the best of the Judeo-Christian heritage, I have been gradually able to reexamine that heritage, and I find much to affirm that I had not even noticed before. For example, once the complex altar of a Roman Catholic church was not only enigmatic but disturbing to me. Not anymore. I don't buy the popular theology represented, but I do understand and appreciate the aesthetic and symbolic aspects of the altar. And I find an empty or nearly empty Catholic sanctuary to be a most comforting place.

During the past decade or so many community and religious rituals have been drawn or adapted from ancient pagan traditions, even including witchcraft. Partly through prejudice and partly through skepticism about historical credibility, many people are disturbed by this borrowing and revisionism. Yet what the doubters may not recognize is the degree to which all ritual is drawn from the past. Almost every aspect of Christian liturgy, for example, was borrowed from the Egyptians and the Greek mystery religions. Besides, much of the purpose of ritual has not changed in several millennia. That being the case, some of the old tried and tested forms at least deserve an examination.

In her book *Drawing Down the Moon*, Margot Adler defends the use of pagan rituals. "From my own experiences of neo-Pagan rituals," she says, "I have come to feel that they have another purpose—to end, for a time, our sense of human alienation from nature and from each other. Although we know that on some level we are always connected, our most common experience is one of estrangement. . . . Rituals have the power to reset the terms of our universe until we find ourselves suddenly and truly at home."

Such sentiments should not, however, serve to reinforce the already prevalent notion that community rituals are concerned only with honoring and preserving the past. Not so, says Starhawk: "Any ritual is an opportunity for transformation. To do ritual, you must be willing to be transformed in some way. That inner willingness is what makes the ritual come alive and have power. If you aren't willing to be changed by the ritual, don't do it."

And so we return to those rituals that are almost indispensable to those points in life where our own development or accident throws us into strange and troubling emotional territory. Even today we have many rites by which we celebrate life's normal passages: christenings, graduations, weddings, birthdays, anniversaries, retirement parties, and funerals. But these all go with clearly discernible transitions. On the other hand, we have almost nothing to designate coming-of-age or to facilitate that amorphous but terribly real event called a midlife crisis.

What we need to appreciate about such rituals is that they are not merely reactive; they are also proactive. A rite of passage does not simply acknowledge a particular change; it also encourages and validates that change. Starhawk says, "Ritual affirms the value of any transition. When we celebrate life changes together, we create strong bonds of intimacy and trust that can generate a new culture. [But] when we undergo a change uncelebrated and unmarked, that transition is devalued and rendered invisible."

Not ordinarily recognized is the dual function, both mystical and magical, of many religious rituals. While such observances serve the mystical purpose of bringing the participants into harmony with the rhythms of the cosmos, they also have a magical function in that, when done properly, the ritual causes the cosmos to keep certain implied bargains with human beings. Old Testament scholars have long pointed out that, while the mercurial Yahweh was strict in his ritualistic expectations of the Children of Israel, there was an equally strong expectation on the part of the people that if the ritual were performed correctly, the intended effect was assured. There was, in other words, a two-way bargain between the finite and the Infinite.

Although it is seldom explicit, this dual function is found in most modern religious rituals, including those of mainline churches and in such neopagan celebrations as witchcraft. In making petitionary prayers, most people imagine that they are making a humble request to the divine; but the very fact that such a request seems necessary with an all-knowing deity indicates the petitioner's modest expectation that, by asking, extra force is added to the appeal. Similarly a study of the rituals developed by Starhawk and others will reveal a more direct expectation on the part of the members of covens.

All told, while a greater sophistication may be involved, most religious rituals are entered into with a frame of mind on the part of the celebrants which is not remarkably different from that of the small child who puts a baby tooth under his or her pillow anticipating that by morning it will have been replaced by a coin from the tooth fairy.

I emphasize all of this not for any derogatory purpose, but because I think it important for us to appreciate the significance of our ritualistic practices. I would not wish to press the matter too far, but I do find credible evidence that magical acts, for whatever purpose, are occasionally effective. It behooves us, then, to be sure we're going to want what we are asking for! (The spiritually active reader's attention is directed to the discussion on pitfalls and magic in chapter seven.)

The rigor and power as well as the beauty of rites of passage become quite clear in narrations such as Anne Cameron's *Daughters of Copper Woman*, where the traditional customs of the native people of Vancouver Island are graphically set forth.

Among the Nootka people, for example, at the time of puberty there was a very specific procedure whereby a young woman was admitted into the privileges and responsibilities of adulthood. Already she had gone through a training period at the hands of the older women. Then, with her first menses and a sojourn in the waiting house, a large celebration involving all the people and including relatives from afar was planned.

The climax of this celebration came when the initiate was garbed in a fine robe made of exotic feathers and taken in a special dugout canoe out onto the coastal waters. There, following a sacred chant and a prayer by a wise old woman, she was stripped of her robe and caused to dive naked into the frigid waters.

It was a long, lonely, chilly swim back to the village—an ordeal both physical and psychological. But as she neared her destination, she'd see many bonfires blazing on the beach and all of the people waiting to greet her with a victory song telling of the girl who had gone forth and the woman who had returned. As she staggered onto the beach exhausted and cold, she was met by the wise old woman who would drape her cape over her and welcome her home. Only with the completion of this memorable rite of passage was she considered ready to marry and bear children as she wished.

Among certain tribes of American Indians, similar ordeals into the wilderness, called vision quests, were common for young males. Curiously, the vision quest has nearly disappeared from contemporary Indian rituals, but during the past decade it has been revived by Caucasians in search of personal transformation.

Now adapted to spiritual pilgrims of all ages, the vision quest is really a journey into the unknown. More than anything else it is a sneaky way of getting people to confront the things they would prefer to avoid. Since the exercise calls upon the individual to risk physical and psychic safety by going out alone and without food or shelter into the wilderness for three days, the main inner challenges confronted are fear, loneliness, and boredom—conditions that, in contemporary society, we go to extravagant lengths to avoid.

Individual vision quest experiences vary widely—hallucinations, nearly mystical encounters with animals, intense dreams, and perhaps most of all a recognition of the harmony and symmetry of all existence. The net result? Change! After three days and nights alone, almost everyone becomes different. And a major feature of that difference is a lasting ability to see day-to-day life in a new and more holistic way. Finally, there comes a quiet confidence that says, "If I did that, I can do anything."

Besides the rites of passage, there is another ritual that I'd like to recommend to the harried. You won't read much about this one in the literature on ritual. But I'm going to call it "the ritual of making your everyday life a meditation." That's the way Saint Teresa of Avila wanted her life to be lived: as a meditation.

Fundamentally meditation is a special way of focusing attention, seeing what is really before us and being there with it. The best instruction on the meditative approach to living—and that's what it is, an approach to living—is found in the slim volume *The Miracle of Mindfulness*, written by the wise and gentle Vietnamese Zen Buddhist monk, Thich Nhat Hanh.

Near the beginning of the book is the sentence, "Mindfulness is the miracle by which we master and restore ourselves."

And how does it work?

In the morning, after you have cleaned and straightened up your house, and in the afternoon, after you have worked in the garden or watched clouds or gathered flowers, prepare a pot of tea to sit and drink in mindfulness. Allow yourself a good length of time to do this. Don't drink your tea like someone who gulps down a cup of coffee during a workbreak. Drink your tea slowly and reverently, as if it is the axis on which the whole earth revolves—slowly, evenly, without rushing toward the future. Live the actual moment. Only this actual moment is life. Don't be attached to the future. Don't worry about things you have to do. Don't think about getting up or taking off to do anything. Don't think about "departing."

Be a bud sitting quietly in the hedge
Be a smile, one part of wondrous existence
Stand here. There is no need to depart.
This homeland is as beautiful as the homeland of our childhood
Do not harm it, please, and continue to sing.

There is more to the ritual of making your everyday life a meditation, and Thich Nhat Hanh talks about it in this book. There are even some simple exercises described. If you would like to live life more smoothly, I recommend this book, even if you can only practice the exercises between three o'clock and four o'clock on alternate Thursdays.

For those who take life too seriously to live like "a bud sitting quietly in the hedge," let me offer one final quotation. This one comes from a very famous Zen master named D. T. Suzuki: "You have to be present to win."

You have to be present to win!

Traditional "Charge of the Star Goddess"

I who am the beauty of the green earth and the white moon
    among the stars and the mysteries of the waters.
I call upon your soul to arise and come unto me.
For I am the soul of nature that gives life to the universe.
From Me all things proceed and unto Me they must return.
Let My worship be in the heart that rejoices, for behold—all
    acts of love and pleasure are My rituals.
Let there be beauty and strength, power and compassion, honor
    and humility, mirth and reverence within you.
And you who seek to know Me, know that your seeking and
    yearning will avail you not, unless you know the mystery:
    for if that which you seek, you find not within yourself, you
    will never find it without.
For behold, I have been with you from the beginning, and I am
    that which is attained at the end of desire.

—Poem version by Starhawk

14

Evil and Misfortune

When the cosmic whole is broken

Where is the Life we have lost in living?
Where is the wisdom we have lost in knowledge?
Where is the knowledge we have lost in information?
. . . .
The world turns and the world changes,
But one thing does not change.
In all my years, one thing does not change.
However you disguise it, this thing does not change:
The perpetual struggle of Good and Evil.

—T. S. Eliot

In these stunning lines from "The Rock," Thomas Stearns Eliot leaves little question that the "perpetual struggle of Good and Evil" is as inescapable as death itself. In the introduction written for Baudelaire's *Intimate Journal*, he tells us, "So far as we are human, what we do must be either evil or good; so far as we do evil or good, we are human. . . ."

Few would deny that in these two statements, T. S. Eliot has grasped one of the essentials of the human condition. Evil is pervasive. Evil is an integral part of being human.

Evil, however, fractures our sentimental and finite notions of a cosmic wholeness. When in the midst of great suffering or injustice, we often cry out, "How can a just and loving God permit evil? How can a nourishing universe that gave us life suddenly yank that life away, or demean it with suffering and betrayal?"

If we are "part and parcel of God," why are we less than perfect in body, mind and deed? Why are some of us born congenitally deformed, as thalidomide babies, or with Down's syndrome, or with childhood leukemia already coursing through our veins? Why do some come into the world with the genes to be fleet of foot, quick of hand, and strong of back, while others are quite the opposite? Why are some of us destined to become Mozarts, Shakespeares, and Madame Curies, while others are shallow-minded and creatively dull?

Even more confounding, if we are all finite fragments of the Infinite, how is it possible for any of us to be evil? Why are we not all Buddhas, Christs, Mother Teresas and Mahatma Gandhis? Whence comes the shadow self that tempts even the saintly? Why are there Hitlers, Mansons, and Borgias?

Such questions as these are as unanswerable as they are unavoidably perennial. But I am inclined to agree with Anatole France's contention: "Nature, in her indifference, makes no distinction between good and evil." And I suspect that, whereas animals and even plants may display aversion toward life-threatening actions and conditions, we humans are the only creatures to make moral judgments about them. On the level of nature, as in the cosmic realm, good and evil are simply part of what is. In other words, the Infinite includes everything (good as well as evil), and only in the finite sphere do the differentiations and preferences arise.

When philosophers and metaphysicians hear statements along the line of, "I am God (or whatever)," they are put off by what they call monism. Monism is the view that reality is one unitary organic whole with no independent parts. Although the language used in this book may sometimes sound monistic, that is not my intention at all. The distinction is best made by comparing the monistic "I am God" with Emerson's "I am part and parcel of God." The key feature is interconnectedness rather than identity.

Those for whom the Brahman/Atman model is useful can avoid the monist trap by remembering that by definition the Infinite includes the finite but the finite does not include the Infinite.

Therefore, while we are part and parcel of God, we are not the whole of God. We are partial (finite or limited) manifestations of the Divine. The Supreme Reality, to which we belong, comes through us incompletely and imperfectly. And that is the source of our individual uniqueness. We vary from one another; and we vary, over time, within ourselves. Because of our differing talents and situations, we take only partial advantage of our opportunities for growth. Hence we fail to be the best we can. We progress erratically (sometimes we regress) in discovering our innate enlightenment.

The upshot is that we fall short of grasping the creative spiritual power that is already available within us. And in our egotistical yearning or existential despair, we abuse the finite power that is all around us. Power, like all creative qualities, is ambiguous; it easily turns destructive or evil.

I define evil as an abuse of power growing out of a sense of powerlessness (separation or brokenness or sin). Let's look at what this definition might mean in everyday life.

M. Scott Peck, who wrote the best-selling book *The Road Less Traveled*, which has inspired thousands, later wrote another book which shocked and repelled many of his admirers. The second book is on evil and is titled *People of the Lie*. Whereas the first book is tough but hopeful, this one is, as Peck admitted, "not a nice book. It is about our dark side, and in large part about the very darkest members of our human community—those I frankly judge to be evil."

With such an introduction, the reader of *People of the Lie* prepares to meet such characters as Adolf Hitler and Charles Manson. But these are not the examples Peck cites. Instead he describes people like the traveling salesman who becomes obsessed with premonitions of an early death and makes a nonverbal deal with the devil as a way of escaping his obsession; the parents of a son dead by his own hand who then gift their second son with the suicide gun; a lonely middle-aged female patient who spends most of her therapy sessions attempting to seduce or otherwise manipulate the psychiatrist.

Only in the chilling case of the parents of the boy who committed suicide does the word evil at first seem appropriate. Like Erich Fromm, M. Scott Peck defines evil as that which is life-denying. Then he goes on to distinguish between occasional misdeeds and authentic evil by saying that authentic evil is characterized by its consistency and by the entrenched self-deception that evil people practice. Hence the term "people of the lie."

Evil persons are not only persistent in their wrongdoing, they also refuse to recognize the harm that they do. Thus they are psychopathic, or people who refuse to accept responsibility for their acts and who treat the problems arising from hurtful actions as though the acts were disconnected from themselves. The key figures in all of Peck's case histories feigned innocence when confronted.

Peck writes:

A predominant characteristic . . . of those I call evil is scapegoating. Because in their hearts they consider themselves above reproach, they must lash out at anyone who does reproach them.

They sacrifice others to preserve their self-image of perfection. Take a simple example of a six-year-old boy who asks his father, "Daddy, why did you call Grandmother a bitch?" "I told you to stop bothering me," the father roars. "Now you're going to get it. I'm going to teach you not to use such filthy language. I'm going to wash your mouth out with soap. Maybe that will teach you to clean up what you say and keep your mouth shut when you're told." Dragging the boy upstairs to the soap dish, the father inflicts this punishment on him. In the name of "proper discipline" evil has been committed.

In Peck's first book, *The Road Less Traveled*, evil is defined as "the exercise of political power—that is, the imposition of one's will upon others by overt or covert coercion—in order to avoid . . . spiritual growth."

This is perhaps a curious but useful definition. What is meant is that evil persons attack others rather than acknowledge their own failures and imperfections. Were they to make such an acknowledgment they would stand to grow spiritually—to become more whole, loving persons. But they cannot bear the thought that they are imperfect or guilty of mistakes, so they attack the real or imagined imperfections of others, just as did the father who washed out his son's mouth with soap.

Perhaps now we can see how some of the most evil deeds occur in a religious context. Inquisitions, witch trials, and holy wars are all examples.

Martin Buber, the Jewish theologian, talks about this in his book *Good and Evil*. Appreciating that evil persons are most of all eager to avoid evidence of their own imperfections, Buber suggests that religious institutions and roles serve to conceal the evil act while providing a maximum opportunity to scapegoat others. "Evil people," writes Buber, "tend to gravitate toward piety for the disguise and concealment it can offer them." And indeed, how often it happens that the demonic dresses itself in the robes of the holy!

From Peck's definition of evil as the exercise of political power in order to avoid spiritual growth, we can go on to recognize evil as a misuse or distortion of power, arising from a sense of powerlessness.

This description, I believe, has a universal validity—that evil arises from a sense of powerlessness, which then gets translated into an abuse of power. We see it in a multitude of ordinary life situations. I think, for example, of the impulse to lie. There is one kind of lying represented in telling tall tales. Here it is the self-esteem of the teller that is weak—a form of powerlessness. There is also the kind of lying represented in cover-ups of myriad sorts. Here the liar is trying to avoid the embarrassment and penalty that go with discovered wrongdoing. Again, powerlessness is the motivation. There is the kind of lying necessary to avoid some injury, as when one bluffs an attacker by pretending to have a weapon. It may be that, within the context of the situation, the lie is necessary to avoid a greater evil; nevertheless the definition holds. Sadly, children have very little power to begin with and can often be put into a position where they tell lies, or worse. Sometimes it takes years for the abuse of power to show up.

One of the best-known and most chilling examples of childhood powerlessness leading to adulthood abuse of power is the case of Charles Manson. As a child Manson was badly mistreated, and he grew up with a consuming hatred of authority and privilege. Having learned early in life that he could not exercise power creatively, he lived in a delusory world filled with destructive fantasies. He imagined himself leading a gang of murderous cutthroats on a fleet of machine-gun-equipped dune buggies and causing enough havoc to destroy civilization.

The fleet of dune buggies was out of Manson's reach, but he was sufficiently charismatic to attract a modest following of other spiritually broken people who were burdened by feelings of worthlessness and powerlessness. Rather than engaging society in open battle, the Manson tribe silently invaded wealthy homes in the middle of the night and eventually went on the bloody rampage that killed actress Sharon Tate and several others.

The same abuse of power by the powerless can be seen in other terrorist acts, as well as in vandalism, industrial sabotage, and even white-collar crime. One matter that concerns me gravely is what will result from the feelings of helplessness that the prospect of nuclear war generates in the world's people, especially in its children. Another is the powerlessness that racial minorities and women and the impoverished experience when confronted by the abuse of power represented in our unjust and oppressive cultures.

Tragically, people often feel so powerless that the only evil they can do is to themselves. The fear of success which gets translated into apathy or chronic failure is one example. Another is hypochondria and somatically caused illness. Cancer often appears in people who have received repeated "drop dead" messages as children. Many suicides are the product of rage born of past or present feelings of helplessness. The aggressive component of suicide is also well-known. Finally, many lifestyles are characterized by extravagant risk which is life-threatening. The line that separates thrill seeking and self-destruction is indeed a narrow and fuzzy one!

Now it may seem that the evil perpetrated on the very weak by the very powerful does not fit my definition of evil as arising out of a sense of powerlessness which then gets translated into an abuse of power. What about the evil represented in the possibility of nuclear war? Does the United States have a sense of powerlessness? Does the Soviet Union? The answer obviously is yes. It has in fact become common to talk about the powerful nations being rendered powerless by their very ability to destroy. Our weapons are too awful to contemplate using, we sometimes say. There is an illusory comfort in that. Except, except: we must remember that feelings of powerlessness always exact a toll!

"Power tends to corrupt." What happens to powerful nations and their leaders when they possess the firepower to destroy the whole earth, yet are not able to intimidate revolutionaries, terrorists, and two-bit dictators?

We know what happens. Monstrous evils get committed. We saw proof in Vietnam. We are seeing more proof every day in Central America, and in Afghanistan, and to a lesser degree in half a dozen other locations around the world. Moreover, if we examine the high-flown rhetoric that gets used, we will realize that tragic appropriateness of M. Scott Peck's term, "people of the lie." In this connection I cannot help remembering President Ronald Reagan's persistent use of the term "freedom fighter" when referring to our client terrorists, the Contras of Nicaragua, nor his regrettable reference to the Soviet Union as "an evil empire"—an illustration, if I ever heard one, of the pot calling the kettle black. What we have on today's international scene is reciprocal scapegoating. Until it ceases I have little expectation for an improvement in the relations between nations.

If evil is peculiar to humans, does the causing of evil require conscious intention? That's a tough question, arguable in either direction. While I believe that intention at some level is usually involved, I'm also inclined to say that we can unintentionally cause evil. It is possible, for example, for evil to be done through ignorance, neglect, or even greed (egoism or self-centeredness).

One may say that the effects of ignorance, neglect, and greed are all predictable or at least knowable. And on that I would agree. But the basic cause of those unintentional evils arising from ignorance, neglect, or greed is inattention. In *A Sense of the Cosmos*, Jacob Needleman writes that "lack of attention may be the original sin." Needleman was thinking of the spiritual cost of not paying attention, but the ethical cost is there, too. Spiritual growth and ethical concern must, after all, come together! It is no mere happenstance that several of the great religious traditions strongly recommend "being here now."

This counsel is mainly peculiar to the Eastern religions, but we need to remember that even Jesus was fond of saying, "He that hath ears to hear, let him hear, and eyes to see, let him see." Another way of saying, "Pay attention!"

Curiously, one of the more common defenses used by those who blunder or accidentally hurt others is "I didn't do it on purpose." And this, of course, is important. But it does not mitigate the lack of attention.

As we've already noted, there are real life situations where there does not appear to be a way to avoid evil completely. I mentioned the example of the person who uses a ruse, a lie, to ward off an attacker. Here we would say that the lie, including the evil it represents, is justified. Surprising? It shouldn't be! Life is shot through with such situations. And we can learn something significant about moral decision making from them.

One of the best contemporary examples is abortion. There are those who assert stoutly that all abortion is nothing less than murder. And there are those who assert just as emphatically that bringing an unwanted child into an overpopulated world is wrong. Who's correct? And who's wrong? My response is that both are correct, and both are wrong! They are each guilty of oversimplification. The fact is there is no way to come out clean, to avoid the existential ambiguity present in an unwanted pregnancy. Those who try are rebuffing the fact that we are finite and fallible beings living in an imperfect world.

Let's look at it this way. By the time the unwanted pregnancy is discovered, a serious mistake or accident has occurred. The situation is already muddled, and a moral quandary is present. And while there are usually better resolutions and worse resolutions, there is no way one comes out of a moral quandary innocent and unscarred.

Abortion, to be sure, is not what even the most ardent pro-choice advocate would want, if complete choice were an option. And abused children or a violated mother or an overpopulated world is not what a wise and compassionate pro-lifer would advocate. The problem is that too many people on either extreme of the abortion question try to settle the matter by resorting to absolute rules of one sort or another. This means they do not want to wrestle with the ambiguities inherent in all true moral dilemmas. In reality, rather than tolerate the relative powerlessness that goes with such situations, they, in their rhetoric at least, abuse power. And that's evil!

Coming back to Jacob Needleman's suggestion that lack of attention is the original sin, I believe we can bring some understanding into moral quandaries. The invocation of an absolute rule is a failure of attention. It is a form of uninvolvement, a shortcut. Rather than deal with the individual situation, sorting through all the considerations and options as carefully as possible (including time-tested principles), the dogmatist stays fundamentally uninvolved. This is seen in the fact that many pro-life people are opposed to welfare for needy families, including those where children are suffering. While they claim a fervent interest in the unborn child, they are really serving their dogma and standing back from the total human situation.

In order to go on with our discussion of good and evil, we need to return now and pick up some of the theory that I deferred discussing in the beginning. I will add that theories are useful rather than true. Theories must, of course, be congruent with human experience, but they are not literally factual. Rather they are models—ways of making sense of our experience and communicating about it. And as our understanding evolves, so inevitably must our theories.

Because we human beings are able to distinguish between good and evil, we are tempted to ascribe a similar power to the cosmos. "Why does God allow Evil?" we sometimes cry. Our first mistake here is theological— it makes the Supreme Reality into a person, a thing, an object among other objects. And it separates that which is infinite from creation, automatically making Supreme Reality *not* infinite, a logical contradiction. Second, it ascribes intention, similar to human intention, to Supreme Reality—a conclusion not justified by the evidence available to us.

It's an old and perennial problem. Even Albert Einstein wrestled with it. Like any true scientist Einstein was devoted to the idea that the universe is orderly and predictable. Thus when quantum theory came along, the father of relativity theory was very disturbed. Quantum theory pictures the fundamental workings of the universe as random—unpredictable except in statistical terms. This suggestion—which was founded on hard experimental evidence—upset Einstein so badly that he often insisted, "God does not play dice with the universe."

A random universe, to Einstein's way of thinking, was not only unpredictable, it was uncaring. And Albert Einstein very much wanted a universe that "cared." A question he asked about the universe was, "Is it friendly?"

And so when we wonder why God permits evil, or however we might phrase our questions, we are really asking Einstein's question about the universe: "Is it friendly?"

For certain, I do not know the purpose of creation. I do discern a direction to it—a movement toward higher and higher levels of consciousness. But since the highest consciousness must be what I have called the Cosmic Consciousness, and we are already manifestations of that Cosmic Consciousness, the exact purpose of the process eludes me. Like T. S. Eliot, I admit the inevitability of the search, and I sense that it will eventually take us back to our point of origin.

But why? I cannot finally say. And neither can any other mortal person. The best we can do is to speculate, as the Hindus do, that the created cosmos is simply a dream Brahman is having for its own edification. Or, as the Buddhists claim, that we are searching to become what we already are, enlightened. Or as the Jews, Christians, and Moslems assert (somewhat chauvinistically), that we are God's Chosen People, and, depending upon our level of obedience and love, He will bless us in various ways. Among the major religions, only the classical Taoists avoid such speculations and content themselves with trying to discover and conform to the practical realities of creation.

On evil, I do not discern that the cosmos intends evil any more than it intends good. The cosmos, like the Tao, just is. It is we humans who seek purpose and discern meaning. This does not mean that I think the universe indifferent or even hostile. To the degree that we are integral to the universe, we must participate in its power and process. And that I would call "friendly" in the same sense that I find meaning in the phrase: "that nourishing mystery in which we live and move and have our being."

About the cause of evil, both Alan Watts and Ernest Becker—two quite different religious thinkers—say the same thing. Both attribute evil to the human failure to accept its own finitude. By this they mean that we do not admit that we are partial creatures, imperfect in our understanding, imperfect in our choice making, imperfect in our sense of connectedness, and blessed with a nearly unlimited capacity for getting attached to all sorts of finite concerns. It is within this imperfection and attachment that we fall short, sense ourselves to be powerless, and thus resort to the abuse of power which I have called evil.

On a cosmic scale neither evil nor good has validity. The fall of an animal to a predator is no more understandable in terms of good and evil than is the movement of the tectonic plates of the continents, or the Big Bang itself. These are just events—changes of greater or lesser magnitude, depending upon who's looking.

So am I saying that we should have no concern for good and evil? Absolutely not! While we must not become attached to the finite world, we, being finite and part of it, must respond to it. Pay attention! Not to do that is what Becker and Watts were talking about when they referred to evil as being the human failure to accept its own finitude.

Let's move now from theory to practice. Theoretical discussions are edifying and stimulating. They are central to the understanding of spiritual growth. But except to discern our responsibility in the causes of evil, there is minimum practical benefit in asking why evil occurs.

Rabbi Kushman, the author of the best-selling and excellent book *When Bad Things Happen To Good People*, advises that instead of asking, "Why did this happen to me? What did I do to deserve this?" we would be ahead to ask, "Now that this has happened to me, what am I going to do about it?"

Naturally, as with all significant loss, it will take us some time to process and come to terms with what has happened to us. This work is called grieving. We need to recognize our agonized questions—such as "why me?"—as part of that grief work.

Dorothy Soelle, a German theologian who researched the Holocaust extensively, notes that even in the presence of the most outrageous evil, there finally comes a time to move on. At this point "the most important question we can ask about suffering is whom it serves. Does our suffering serve God or the devil, the cause of being alive or being morally paralyzed?"

What Soelle refers to is a phenomenon: that some people, when they are victims of evil, refuse to continue as victims but rather resolve to learn what there is to be learned and to continue with their lives wiser for the experience. Others, however, get stuck as victims; they become attached to their hardship. Disbelief, anger, and despair become a way of life, and the tragedy becomes chronic.

The bitter irony in the latter event is that stricken persons turn from being victims of evil to victimizing themselves. Consider Erich Fromm's words: "Good is all that serves life, evil is all that serves death. Good is reverence for life . . . and all that enhances life. Evil is all that stifles life, narrows it down, cuts it to pieces." It seems an intuitive truth to me that it is our first moral duty to enhance life, including our own, and avoid evil.

This is an attitude that can serve us well, not just when we are the victims of evil, but in limiting the future impact of evil upon us. Because I accept the randomness of the universe, I don't want to push this point too far. But it does seem clear to me that life-affirming people not only do less evil and recover faster from the misfortune that befalls them, but they also, in some ineffable way, are a little less likely to be the victims of evil.

The Rabbi's Gift

Once long ago there was a monastery verging on collapse. The buildings were falling down, the gardens had grown up in weeds, the animals had died or wandered away, and there were only a few monks left in the place.

This was all very sad because at one time this monastery had been alive and vigorous with many monks who did lots of good deeds. The monastery was especially important to the people of the area because of the hope it gave them. No matter how hard times got for the people, the monks would cheer them up by promising that sooner or later a Messiah—a great spiritual leader—would come and help straighten things out.

But the Messiah did not come. As a matter of fact, instead of getting better, things got worse. The ruler of the land was cruel, food became scarce, and the people were very discouraged. Matters were as difficult in the monastery as they were among the people in general. Finally there were only five monks left, including the abbot.

In the woods near the monastery there was a little hut that the rabbi in the village occasionally used as a retreat. The monks had gotten so that they could sense when the rabbi was in the hut. They would go about saying: "I think the rabbi is in the woods. . . . Yes, I'm sure the rabbi is in the woods."

One day as the monks were talking about the hard times that had come to their monastery and wondering what to do, it occurred to the abbot that perhaps the rabbi might have some helpful advice. So the next time there was the feeling that the rabbi was in the woods, the abbot took up his walking staff and went to the hut.

Sure enough, the rabbi was there. And he welcomed the abbot warmly. But when the abbot told him the sad story of how bad things had gotten at the monastery, the rabbi could only nod in agreement. "Yes, I know," said the rabbi. "The times are bad everywhere, and the people are desperate. Everyone seems hopeless. Even the synagogue is nearly empty on the sabbath."

At that the abbot and the rabbi began to weep together. Then they read from the Torah and spoke quietly of deep matters, trying to comfort each other. The time came for the abbot to return to the monastery, and the two embraced at the door. As he was about to walk away, the abbot turned and spoke: "It has been very good to be here with you. But I have failed in my expectation that you would have some words of wisdom. Is there nothing you can tell me to save the monastery—no advice?"

"No, I am sorry," answered the rabbi. "I have no words of wisdom. The only thing I can say is that the Messiah is one of you."

When the abbot returned to the monastery, the other monks rushed up to discover what he had learned from the rabbi. But the abbot shook his head. "He couldn't help," said the abbot. "All we did was weep together and read the Torah. The one thing he did say—and I don't understand what he meant—was that the Messiah is one of us."

In the days that followed the monks thought about this strange statement and wondered about it. How could it be possible that the Messiah might be one of us? We are the sorriest of creatures.

Could the rabbi have meant that the abbot is a great leader and just doesn't know it? He has been our leader for a very long time. . . . On the other hand, he might have meant Brother Timothy. After all, Brother Timothy is a man of great spiritual insight. . . . Surely, he didn't mean Brother Thomas. He's simply too quiet, even though he is the one who's there when you need him. . . . And it can't be Brother Joseph. He's too grumpy, although he is usually right. . . . That leaves only me. And I know I'm not the Messiah. After all, I'm just an ordinary fellow, with no special talents.

But suppose he did mean me? Suppose I am the Messiah. Oh, gee, I hope not. I don't have what it takes.

Yet all of the monks continued to think about the matter. And as they did they began treating each other differently—as though one of them might be the Messiah, deserving of great respect and assistance. As they treated each other like they might be the Messiah, they began to feel better about themselves.

Then one day some of the villagers went to the monastery to pray in the chapel. They were surprised by how different the place felt. They noticed, too, that the monks seemed to have a special regard for one another. The monastery had once again become a very spiritual place to be. So they went back to the village and told their neighbors.

Soon the villagers were coming to the monastery to help repair the buildings and to tend the garden, and one of them brought a goat, and another a couple of chickens. One of the villagers even asked if he might join the monastery. Then another. And another.

Before long the monastery was thriving. It became a center of hope and spiritual vitality. And it was not long before this goodwill and optimism had spread out to include the village. Even the rabbi was happier as his people began coming to the synagogue on the sabbath. It never occurred to him that the gift of respect and hope he had given the abbot had returned to include him, too.

15

The Spiritual Basis for Social Action

To change the world, I change myself first

There is a false doctrine abroad in the religious realm, one that has been outstanding for a very long time and which has caused much mischief. This false doctrine is the widely held notion that political activism and mysticism—social change and spirituality—have little in common and are even perhaps antagonistic.

I challenge that notion. In the strongest terms possible I will assert that social activism and mysticism are inextricably interwoven and that where they are not, the result is flawed and crippled.

I am reminded of Martin Luther King, Jr.'s warning: "Any religion that professes to be concerned with the souls of people and is not concerned with the slums that damn them and the social conditions that cripple them, is a dry-as-dust religion." Mahatma Gandhi said very much the same thing: "I cannot imagine better worship of God than that in His name I should labor for the poor." Thomas Merton, the Cistercian monk, wrote: "It is only in assuming full responsibility for our world, for our lives and for ourselves, that we can be said to live really for God." And from across the ages, Saint Teresa of Avila tells us poetically that "Martha and Mary must work together when they offer the Lord lodging."

Let us make no mistake about it—spiritual concern must include concern for the world. But then, just as there is the danger that a timid church will fall into irrelevance or worse when it ignores the social and political plights of the people, so there is a complementary peril for religious institutions that focus their full attention on "this world" to the neglect of the spiritual or mystical realm. My own religious movement found itself in this sort of predicament during the 1970s.

Beginning in the mid fifties, we religious liberals brought our social gospel to bear upon racial injustice, then the Vietnam War, and eventually upon other causes, including even the legalization of marijuana. Initially we were energized by our outreach, but when the civil rights movement turned militant and the Vietnam War dragged to its miserable finale, we became fatigued and discouraged. As our membership began dropping, we looked anxiously to our spiritual roots for guidance and inspiration and were dismayed to find that those roots had withered for lack of attention and nourishment.

It was a difficult time for us. Our nadir was signaled when, in desperation, our denomination actually conducted a contest in search of its own identity. Small wonder that we have since had a burgeoning interest in spirituality, feminist theology, and New Age thought, and that we have carefully rewritten our Statement of Principles and Purposes!

Hopefully we have learned that a vital religious movement which would live responsibly in the world must also attend to the needs of heart and spirit. As for the historic theological argument as to whether faith or works—spirituality or social concern—is the more important, let us remind ourselves regularly that this is no either/or duality. Not only are faith and works not separable in any authentic religion, but each is essential to the other. There is a critical both/and connection.

As a spiritual pilgrim—as a mystic—I believe that our supreme purpose is to discover who we really are. Our goal is to find out that we are indeed finite fragments of the Infinite—to learn, as the Buddhists put it, that we are already enlightened, we just don't know it. We must discover what Emerson knew: that we are "part and parcel of God."

Many contemporary persons don't understand what mysticism is. They have learned erroneously that mystics are people who have dropped out—either into their own inner depths or into the outer regions of esoterica. But, in truth, the authentic mystic is the most practical of persons, the most rigorous of realists. Indeed the traditional prayer of the mystic is "Lead me from the unreal to the real."

It's just that the mystic recognizes and honors the fact that reality as we perceive it is always partial. As one who has been a scientist, I know that this consideration applies even to science, which is nearly as dependent upon myths and models as theology is. The truth is ever beyond what we think it to be. And we must never give up our search for it.

I find it significant that all the major spiritual traditions recommend several paths as essential to spiritual growth: the path of discipline, the path of knowledge, the path of devotion, and the path of works. And although the mystic may periodically favor one path over the other, ultimately all the paths must be traveled.

For our purposes I wish to look at the fourth path, the path of works, the path of witness and action. This is the spiritual path taken by all the great reforming geniuses—Gandhi, Schweitzer, Dorothy Day, Edith Stein, Dag Hammarskjöld, Martin Luther King, Jr., Mother Teresa, and many others.

Among the Western religious sects, none has so thorough a reputation for combining spiritual concern and social service as the Friends, the Quakers, who are famous for their silent meetings. There is the story of a religiously unsophisticated man who happened into a Quaker gathering on a Sunday morning. Seeing all of the people sitting quietly, he took a seat and waited. When the people continued to sit there, saying and doing nothing, the visitor grew impatient and whispered to his nearest neighbor, "When does the service begin?" The neighbor replied, "As soon as the meeting is over."

The fact is, every religious tradition has its call for justice as a component of spiritual growth. In Buddhism, as in Vedanta (a Hindu school), and in all but the most recent forms of Christianity, right action is the means by which the mind prepares itself for mystical searching. Even in the Islamic Koran we read that "one hour of justice is worth seventy hours of prayer."

And so, as the historical and theoretical connection between spiritual growth and social action is widely recognized, so is the practical connection. I've long appreciated Emerson's dictum that the true preacher draws upon personal experience. Let me draw upon mine.

For three years during the mid 1980s, I was a leader in a citizens' nuclear watchdog group called HEAL, which stands for Hanford Education Action League. HEAL is concerned with bringing moral, political, and scientific accountability to the federal nuclear reservation at Hanford, Washington. Hanford is a nuclear weapons production facility operated by the United States Department of Energy, and like other such sites, it is a place of mystery, deceit, and worrisome impacts on human health and the environment. What HEAL discovered is that there is tremendous power in raising questions and ferreting out information on installations such as Hanford. In less than three years HEAL became something of a model among nuclear concern groups, with an impact all out of proportion to its members and resources.

But it was not easy. The most difficult part was not the size, complexity, and power of our scientific and bureaucratic adversary, but the difficulty of keeping ordinary human relationships straight and working. Often, in the midst of some internal organization conflict, I subliminally muttered a little prayer that went something like this: "Dear Lord, we can handle our opponents, but please help us with ourselves!"

Almost all social change organizations have similar experiences. Curiously, the reason has relatively little to do with lack of resources and volunteers, poor strategies, or even resistance by the political establishment. Rather, the problem is personal, spiritual.

In Buddhism reference is often made to the "five poisons," which are called "obscuring habits of the mind." The five poisons are ignorance, anger, desire, greed, and jealousy. And there is no way that we can make substantial progress toward spiritual maturity until we have come to terms with the presence of the five poisons in ourselves.

Ignorance, anger, desire, greed, and jealousy—these five, unacknowledged and unaddressed, will not only blight our own growth but will also distort and corrupt our projects in the world. I have seen more than one cause falter and fail because of the lack of spiritual wholeness in those who would promote the cause.

Or using different language: if we attempt to do good before having come to terms with our own egotism, brokenness, alienation, incompleteness, neediness, then these will tend to contaminate our motives and our actions. This is why spiritual leaders and other wise persons caution us over and over that, if we would change the world for the better, we must begin by changing ourselves.

This requirement, it seems to me, makes the task of those who would save the earth very clear. The world order, the prevailing cultural mythology or paradigm, is no longer serving the highest needs of humankind, if it ever did. And our fumbling attempts to dominate one another, to assure our own comfort at the expense of our fellows, to exploit the ecological systems of the planet, and to impose world peace by threatening nuclear annihilation are stark evidence of our failure.

We must become different people; otherwise we will go on making the same old mistakes. We must become persons who are more centered and whole in our own being, persons who relate more harmoniously with one another, who recognize and live in terms of the interconnections of the vast natural web of existence. We must become persons, finally, who know of their fundamental unity with that nourishing mystery—known by many names—in which we live and move and have our being.

In other words, if we are to overcome our current problems, it will require an evolutionary leap in the consciousness of enough of us to constitute a critical mass of creative change makers. Although Teilhard de Chardin was writing about such a shift decades ago, it still may sound like something so new, so mysterious, and so unlikely as to be impossible. But that is a misperception!

What I am talking about is an old, old story. It is the central theme of all the great religious traditions. It is the one sure goal that every living human being would appear to have. Some call it enlightenment; some call it satori; some call it salvation; some call if Self-discovery; some call it God-consciousness or Buddha-consciousness.

For the end point of this noble quest—this spiritual search—I return again to the way T. S. Eliot described it in his *Four Quartets:*

We shall not cease from exploration
And the end of all our exploring
Will be to arrive where we started
And know the place for the first time.

The beauty of good poetry is its expansive economy of words. Thus T. S. Eliot's four simple lines are both a summary and an initiation for the quintessential human task—finding out who we really are. It is our failure to recognize our inner divinity that both puts us out of touch with the spiritual realm and causes us to act destructively toward the material world.

Earlier I mentioned the five poisons referred to in Buddhism—ignorance, anger, desire, greed, and jealousy—as "obscuring habits of the mind," which both stand in the way of our spiritual maturity and corrupt even our best-intended projects in the world. The need for social and political change usually arises with the perception of injustice. And many of those who have this perception have been victims. They may be angry, fearful, vengeful, filled with righteous indignation, or in search of power. This is understandable, even excusable. But it is also a fundamental peril to the cause being pursued as well as to those pursuing it.

The civil rights movement and Martin Luther King, Jr. serve as fine examples.

When Dr. King came onto the national scene, our recognition of the depth and darkness of racism was just beginning. A centuries-long injustice both blatant and subtle was slowly and painfully revealed to both black and white. Anger, guilt, jealousy, greed, and the urge toward revenge all came bubbling to the surface of the average human consciousness and conscience. It was an environment in which outrages equal to or worse than those that had already occurred might readily have taken place, and sometimes did.

King saw the terrible danger of all this. Constantly he counseled forbearance, nonviolence, soul-force. Constantly he urged those who sat in with him, who marched with him, who went to jail with him, to search their own hearts and come to terms with the anger and hatred that was so understandably theirs. "Returning hate for hate multiplies hate," warned

King, "adding deeper darkness to a night already devoid of stars. Darkness cannot drive out darkness; only light can do that. Hate cannot drive out hate; only love can do that. Hate multiplies hate, violence multiplies violence, and toughness multiplies toughness in a descending spiral of destruction."

Such views and restrained behavior constitute the creative glory of the civil rights movement. The tragedy of the civil rights movement is that, especially following King's death, the cause increasingly fell into the hands of those who acted on their anger and hatred and who increasingly spoke more of power and less of love. The result was that progress was halted and many of the gains were lost in the reaction that followed.

Today it is clear that those causes most likely to succeed are those that give substantial attention to the spiritual training of their people. One of my favorite illustrations involves my stepdaughter, Kaky McTigue. In a family of social and political activists, Kaky is probably the busiest and certainly the most frequently incarcerated.

Several years ago Kaky belonged to a peace group that was concerned about the intercontinental ballistic missiles at Vandenberg Air Force Base in California. She and her fellows decided to register a nonviolent protest by going onto the base and hiking to one of the fenced-in missile silos where they intended to tie black ribbons on the fence and hold a silent vigil. But first they spent time forming and training what they called affinity groups. Besides the usual nonviolent resistance training, these affinity groups gave time to the discussion of ideals, concerns, and feelings. And they spent additional hours in spiritual practices, singing, and socializing.

When the time for the demonstration came, everything went as planned. In fact the demonstrators were able to march unobstructed all the way to the missile enclosure and hang their black ribbons on the fence. Only then did an Air Force jeep, accompanied by a military bus, come roaring across the hills to confront and arrest the intruders.

Kaky and her cohorts voluntarily entered the bus when ordered to do so. As they did, the military police insisted that they remove the black bands that they wore on their arms. Even though the demand was apparently part of a tactic to humiliate and depersonalize the demonstrators, they cooperated in such good humor that the police began to relax and act friendly. When it became Kaky's turn to surrender her arm band, she smiled at the young soldier before her and said, "I'll tell you what. I'll trade you my arm band for that medal you're wearing." And much to everyone's surprise and delight, he agreed.

The demonstrators went off routinely to jail and trial. But who can doubt that their impact on the military personnel they met that day was both significant and creative?

One of the things that happens when we get to know our opponents and act openly upon that knowing is that we become persons to each other. Even if we continue to disagree vehemently with what they stand for and do, still both they and we are changed, and the possibility for understanding and growth improves. Over and over I have found this to be true in my contact with Hanford people, particularly with the technical people who are not charged with defending government policies and actions.

Alexander Solzhenitsyn, the author of *The Gulag Archipelago*, wrote something that warns us against self-righteousness and polarized thinking. "If only it were so simple!" he cried. "If only there were evil people somewhere committing evil deeds and it were necessary only to separate them from the rest of us and destroy them. But the dividing line between good and evil cuts through the heart of every human being. And who is willing to destroy his own heart?"

In a peace-oriented church of my acquaintance, there was a bomber pilot who, if the nuclear holocaust should come, would be one of those likely to deliver it. When this man first arrived with his family at that church, there was much unease about his presence. The fact that he was an affable and humane fellow, and that his family was lovable, only served to intensify the ambiguity. There were church members who felt that "something" should be done, although they couldn't figure out what that might be. Finally, at a gathering of some church people one evening when the matter came up, a respected man rose to suggest that the pilot wasn't the sole cause for nuclear peril—that everyone present bore a share of the responsibility. The threat of nuclear war arose, he said, out of fears that all people had in varying degree; and if the bomb was ever dropped, the pilot would be that part of everyone that did it. Immediately the urge to harass the pilot decreased, and the net peacefulness of the world increased.

Is this, then, a model for creating social change? Shall we simply love our "enemies"? Well, it is a good place to start. And when we hear or use the word "love" in this context, we should pause to remind ourselves that it has little or nothing to do with ordinary liking. Rather, "love" as used in "love your enemies" needs to be translated to something like, "Know of your oneness with your enemies." And when we do that, we will be in a better position to decide what we need to do next.

But wait! I can hear the protest, "If love is sufficient, why the need for activism, why all that marching and noise?" And the answer is obvious: because activism properly done is an act of love.

One of my favorite illustrations of the need for activism in a religious context comes in an anecdote told by liberal theologian James Luther Adams. It seems that some years ago in a Chicago church there was a board member who had become notorious for his racism. Then one day this man announced, "The purpose of the liberal church is to get ahold of people like me and *change them!*"

Beyond the impact on others, however, there is the necessary reminder to ourselves that action always serves. I think of a variation, a sort of *midrash*, on a very old story:

A wise woman once went to preach righteousness in the wicked city of Nineveh, but without success. Then, someone asked her why she persevered in her efforts to change the people of Nineveh to be like her. And the wise woman replied, "Oh, I do not expect them to become like me, but I must continue my work so that I do not become like them."

Musings of a Pigherder

One of the skills I learned as a farmboy was how to herd critters—cows, sheep, pigs, chickens. It's not easy; the uninitiated can get into all sorts of trouble.

Pigs are usually the greatest challenge.

Most people think pigs are dirty and stupid. Both notions are false. Pigs do enjoy lying in nice, cool mud, especially on hot days. But they are really very clean in their personal habits. And they certainly aren't stupid.

As I said, herding pigs is a special challenge. They need to mill first. Anyone trying to move a batch of pigs without letting them stand about and shuffle and grunt first will encounter passive resistance.

The inexperienced or insensitive pigherder who fails to interpret this resistance properly will shortly be surprised. The pigs, heads slightly lowered, suddenly emit an explosive "Oink!" and take off at top speed in all directions. The time spent in getting them reassembled can be considerable.

When it comes to getting them moving in a certain direction, people aren't all that different from pigs. We need to mill first, especially if the intended direction is an unfamiliar one. Pushed too hard, we first resist and, second, bolt and run off in all directions. Getting us back together can be time-consuming or even impossible.

16

Holy Ground

Treading softly

Now Moses was keeping the flock of his father-in-law, Jethro, the priest of Midian; and he led his flock to the west side of the wilderness, and came to Horeb, the mountain of God. And the angel of the Lord appeared to him in a flame of fire out of the midst of a bush; and he looked, and lo, the bush was burning, yet it was not consumed. And Moses said, "I will turn aside and see this great sight, why the bush is not burnt." When the Lord saw that he turned aside to see, God called to him out of the bush, "Moses, Moses!" And he said, "Here am I." And he [the Lord] said, "Do not come near; put off your shoes from your feet, for the place on which you are standing is holy ground."

—Exodus 3:1-5

At a recent meeting of my ministerial colleagues, Dr. Phillip Hewett, senior minister of the Unitarian Church in Vancouver, British Columbia, shared a moving and memorable personal experience.

In the summer of 1987 Phillip and some friends went on a sailing cruise of western Canada's Queen Charlotte Islands. One of the places they stopped at was the deserted Indian village of Ninstints.

Ninstints is a haunting place. Abandoned by its native inhabitants more than a century ago because of a smallpox epidemic, the village is now mainly a scattered array of decaying totem poles, some standing, some leaning precariously, the rest fallen upon the beach. It is, Phillip reported, a powerfully significant place, and the experience of being there left him reflecting on the special aura that some locations seem to acquire and exude.

While preparing for the cruise Phillip read a book about Ninstints which had been written by George F. MacDonald, director of the Canadian National Museum in Ottawa. "If a visitor to Canada were to ask me where the holiest of holy places of this country were to be found," he wrote, "I would be quick to respond that there are but three. One is the line of silent stone figures marching along the ridges that mark ancient shorelines of Pleistocene seas at Eskimo Point in the Northwest Territories. A second is the sculpture in glowing yellow cedar of the Raven and The First Men by Bill Reid, the Haida master carver, at the Museum of Anthropology at the University of British Columbia. Last, but most impressive of all, is the Village of Ninstints at daybreak when the raven's cry once more brings the world into being."

I have seen only one of Dr. MacDonald's holiest of holy Canadian places—Bill Reid's totem carving in the museum at the University of British Columbia in Vancouver. Indeed, that massive sculpture is a breathtaking piece of artwork and metaphor: the coastal Indians' sacred bird is prying open a clam shell with its beak, so that the first human beings may walk onto the earth.

Almost all of us have been to places that we would call sacred or holy. Even though we may be intellectually dubious of the designation implied in these words, we have nonetheless had the emotional experience that says there is something special and powerful about a certain place. When we are there we instinctively fall into wonder, if not into a silence distinguished by reverence.

What is it that gives a place this unique and memorable quality?

Right at the onset, let me reveal to you that this is a subject about which I feel somewhat tentative. On the one hand I have no question whatever about the emotional reality of the matter. On the other hand the cognitive reality is slippery; language and logic do not work well in this realm. Nonetheless there is something significant, even awe-inspiring and life-changing here, and so it is a proper subject for exploration.

In talking about his own mystical experience at the abandoned village of Ninstints, Phillip, who is a careful and rational scholar, drew a distinction between holy places and sacred places. A student of languages, he suggested that a sacred place has been made so by human beings—either through long association or because of some special event that occurred there. He noted that the "–ed" ending of sacred is a perfect participle ending, so that it originally means "made holy." A holy place, on the other hand, would appear to have little or no human source. With its connotation of wholeness, a holy place simply seems to be that way; there is about it an almost palpable spirit which wells up and permeates the area.

Rudolph Otto, a German theologian, wrote a book titled *Das Heilige*. There is no exact translation; *das heilige* can mean either "holy" or "sacred." The translator of Otto's book elected as the English title *The Idea of the Holy*. He says he chose "holy" because that word is Biblical, meaning to be set apart, "characterized by perfection and transcendence." Curiously, while the word "holy" shows up in the Bible scores of times, the word "sacred" does not appear at all.

What makes something holy or sacred? When I ask that question, I'm not so much asking about the cause of holy places as about their particular qualities.

We may say that holy or sacred places have a "spiritual" dimension. But what does that mean? Spiritual to me is that which establishes a connection between the finite and the Infinite. In the Reverend Jacob Trapp's terminology, spiritual is where "the window of the moment open[s] to the sky of the eternal." Spiritual implies connectedness, a transcendence of the separated self. Spiritual may mean connection not only with the human community but also with the great chain of life—with what Albert Schweitzer meant when he said "one with all life that comes within one's reach."

But I think there is even more to the connectedness implied in spirituality than these, important though they are. Rudolph Otto referred to the *mysterium tremendum*—the tremendous and fascinating mystery at the heart of things, what traditionalists have typically called God. And here we begin to get into territory where the feeling senses begin to overwhelm the ability of words to communicate.

This emotional reality stretches around the globe and across the centuries. Confucius, the great Chinese prophet who lived five centuries before Jesus, is often discounted by religious scholars because he refused to conceive of an anthropomorphic deity. But he did acknowledge a pervasive spiritual presence—what he called "the power of spiritual forces in the universe." That this presence was palpable to those who paid attention is shown by his statement: "Like the rush of mighty waters, the presence of unseen Powers is felt, sometimes above us, sometimes around us."

I have known places which I think are sacred or holy. And I generally agree with Phillip's suggestion that sacred places are somehow made, created through human experience, while holy places seem to have their special quality apart from human activity. But it is also inevitable, I think, that the words "sacred" and " holy" will get used interchangeably.

Sacred places I have known are the Lincoln Memorial in Washington, D.C., the great meeting room in Independence Hall in Philadelphia, a dark kiva in a ruin at Mesa Verde National Park, and King's Chapel in Boston. I would mention, too, the Arizona Memorial in Pearl Harbor and several different Civil War battlefields—the Peach Orchard at Shiloh, the Dunkard Church at Antietam, the Jackson Monument at Chancellorsville, and the High Water Mark at Gettysburg—awesomely ambiguous though they all are. I would name finally half a dozen sublimely beautiful Japanese gardens that I have visited in the United States and Canada.

When we come to holy places, designation becomes more difficult because of the inevitable intersection of the human and the nonhuman. Either by experience or report, I know of several mountainous locations that I would risk calling holy. I think of the high mountain lake called Evolution Lake in California's Sierra Nevada, which I have twice visited. On each occasion it was the scene of a powerful experience that left me fixed and transformed. Image Lake in the North Cascades is a site where I once gazed in wonder across the Suiattle River Valley toward ice-clad Glacier Peak, iridescent with the rising sun. I remember, too, an unnamed mountaintop in Alaska's Brooks Range upon which I sat and looked out over hundreds of square miles of spruce forests, tundra, and waterways—all of it, so far as I knew, devoid of living human beings but filled with the ghosts of those who, one hundred years ago, had flocked into that vast region in search of elusive gold fortunes. Finally I would mention Mount Constitution on Orcas Island in Puget Sound's Strait of Juan de Fuca, which one evening at sunset seemed to show me the whole world at the dawn of creation.

In terms of ancient tradition, the spot on Mount Horeb where Moses encountered the angel of the Lord in the burning bush was, as the text in Exodus says, holy ground. So, too, the volcanic mountain called Sinai, from which Moses descended with the Ten Commandments, is designated as holy by millions. Finally Tai Shan, the peak where Confucius had his inspiration, was called by poet Eunice Tietjens "the beautiful, the most holy."

Indeed such mountains seem to have a special attraction to those who locate temples and monasteries. Mount Sinai has a monastery. Tai Shan has a sanctuary. And we are all acquainted with the sacred city of Kyoto in Japan which sits upon the flanks of a mountain dotted with countless temples, shrines, and monasteries. In this country Mount Shasta, the spectacular volcanic peak in northern California, has been a spiritual magnet to people both ancient and modern, and it is covered with myriad spiritual centers.

Second only to mountains in their power to evoke a sense of the holy are forests. In ancient Israel groves of trees were frequently the sites of places of worship, so much so that a favorite way of attacking an enemy's religion was to cut down the sacred groves. Today there is a certain spot among the

towering redwoods in California's Muir Woods where the sunlight slant-
ing through the trees creates a cathedral that rivals—perhaps surpasses—
all of those erected by human hands.

Beyond mountains and forests the ocean itself is capable of evoking
holy awe. Many beaches and headlands on the Pacific Coast, at different
times of day and night, have the power to relate us to something larger,
more powerful, and more enduring than ourselves. The ocean reminds us
of an ancient lineage, perhaps stretching back to the time when our nonhuman forebears left their original watery home and laid tenuous claim to
the dry land.

Mountains, forests, and the ocean—all of these are nearly universally
acknowledged by those who take the idea of the holy seriously. But a mountain or a forest and certainly the ocean are all huge. Perhaps their size
qualifies them. What about less expansive locations?

When Phillip Hewett talked with his colleagues about holy places, he
shared with us a moving letter he had received from a trusted member of
his congregation in Vancouver:

> There is one place near here which I think may be a holy place. It
> is in the meadow in Jericho Park. Someone told me early this year
> that there was a holy place there a long time venerated by Indians.
> My informant had been told about it by an Indian but was not sure
> where it was.
>
> One day when I was walking . . . I noticed some people standing
> around in the middle of a meadow. So the next time I was there I
> investigated. A path through the grass led me to a circle of stones
> some three feet across. In the middle were various offerings—
> flowers, a feather, forked sticks. Standing there just at that spot
> looking across the water to distant mountains, I was overcome with
> such a beautiful feeling of deep peace and wholeness—one of those
> times you feel related to and in touch with the whole world and
> universe.
>
> Now, I know the mind plays interesting tricks. And yet, and yet,
> each time I stand there I experience something similar, as if, just
> there, there is really a holiness. I have since shared my knowledge
> of this place with several friends. One of them told me that the pal-
> liative care unit of, I think, the General Hospital regularly brings
> patients to the Jericho Beach or Park area because there is some-
> thing healing there.

Phillip's reading of this letter took my own thoughts to a holy place I
know about but which relatively few people have seen.

At my Pend Oreille County farm there is a small clearing in the woods which is special. I was struck by this open spot from the very first time I saw it. Unlike the house site and the pasture, this clearing has no view. In fact part of its uniqueness is that, except for several trails leading into it, it is totally enclosed. Neither are the trees remarkable in themselves—some quite ordinary firs, pines, larches, and vine maples reaching up all around with the usual brush growing at their trunks. What is remarkable is the clearing itself. Except for native grass which seems to be self-regulating in its height, there isn't anything else to speak of—no stumps, no brush, no thistles or other weeds common to the area. Just a clearing.

From the very first time I walked into that clearing, I have felt a presence there. New Agers might call it a power point, but I wouldn't use that term. It's just special. My natural impulse there is to be quiet and attentive. I often go into that part of the woods for no purpose beyond sitting there to listen or meditate. Sometimes the feeling evoked is quiet and pensive; other times it is deeply moving and joyful. Most of the friends I've taken there immediately notice something unusual about the place without being prompted. Once in a rain shower I took a ministerial colleague there, and after a moment of slack-jawed looking, she burst into tears.

I call this place "the still point" after T. S. Eliot's famous poetic reference in his *Four Quartets* which begins: "At the still point of the turning world," and, after several lines of provocative description, ends, "Except for the point, the still point/There would be no dance, and there is only the dance."

Down by the road there is an engraved wooden sign denoting our whole farm as "The Still Point," but relatively few people, certainly none of the neighbors, know that the real Still Point is a small clearing in the woods which is self-tending and which causes human beings who pay attention to feel a profound peace and joy, and a sense of connection to something greater than they are.

Just as some natural settings appear to attract shrines and temples, suggesting some innate holiness in the sites, so other places, by virtue of what happened there, become sacred and even holy.

Psychologist and author Lawrence LeShan is a skeptical investigator of what some would call supernatural events and places. He described, for example, the convergence of ancient mysticism and modern physics some years before Fritjof Capra wrote his best-selling *The Tao of Physics*. And he is one of our most credible researchers on humanistic psychic healing techniques. LeShan is, however, somewhat leery of any suggestion that supernatural forces may be at work in the world. He continues to be a staunch supporter of the scientific method. Still, his work has led him to the conviction that there are human experiences that simply do not fit into the usual scientific parameters. So he has evolved a systematic theory suggesting that reality may vary depending upon the perception or state of consciousness of the observer, a postulation that is similar to the notion in physics that the consciousness of the scientist may affect the outcome of an experiment.

Though some would conclude that LeShan has taken leave of his senses, he dares to propose that there are "ways of being in the world" other than the usual linear way, where only that which can be seen, touched, heard, tasted, and smelled is considered real. But he is careful in his hypotheses. He avoids suggesting that laws of science may be abrogated in some situations or settings. And he invites learned critics to pass judgment on his conclusions.

Shortly after LeShan completed his initial work on reality theory, he sent his manuscript out to several people whose thinking he respected. They liked the general direction of his theory but were disturbed that he may have stopped short. One of LeShan's correspondents was Edgar Jackson, a Christian faith healer who also respects rational thinking and the scientific method. After reading one of LeShan's manuscripts Jackson wrote back emphatically that it was time that he and LeShan go to visit the Gothic cathedrals of northern France.

LeShan accepted the invitation and, as they traveled, learned what had bothered his critic. In "his gentle, loving voice" Jackson sternly pointed out that LeShan was not dealing truthfully with the relevance of his data—that he was avoiding its disconcerting but more pertinent implications. Still, understanding came slowly. Only as the two men began touring some of the great European cathedrals did the psychologist commence apprehending what his companion wanted him to see and feel.

It was within the immense cathedral at Metz that LeShan stood transfixed and silent. Awestruck by the mystical aura of the place, he later described the scene before him: "The vaulted roofs appear to tumble endlessly upward, inviting and urging you to an experience if you are ready for it."

Even though LeShan's descriptions continue to be carefully linear and logical, it becomes clear that he's talking about a sacred sense—about what he called at one point "the All." And while his awakening awareness did not in the least appear to diminish his devotion to scientific accountability, it left him with the humbling conviction that there is more than ratiocinative language can manage to tell about—that science, as conventionally defined, does not and cannot take all human experience into account.

LeShan ended by concluding that there is another state of consciousness or reality—what he analytically calls "transpsychic reality"—during which the interconnectedness of everything is palpably clear. Without using the term, LeShan knew he had discovered "the holy." He related it to an experience described by mystic Bernard Berenson: "It was a morning in early summer. A silver haze shimmered and trembled over the lime trees. The air was laden with their fragrance. The temperature was like a caress. I remember—I need not recall—that I climbed up a tree stump and felt suddenly immersed in Itness. I did not call it by that name. I had no need for words. It and I were one."

Whether such an experience of "the holy" is innate to a place or is the result of an interaction between that place and the human participant, I am not prepared to say. It's rather like the old question: "If a tree falls in the forest and there's no one present to hear it, does it make a sound?" Of one thing I am sure: the experience itself is real and valid. And for those who are sensitive, it occasionally changes lives.

Something else seems clear to me. Whatever their initial qualities, holy places somehow acquire more mythic power as human beings come to them to share in, and add their own experience to, the existing essence. When Thomas Merton visited the reclining Buddhas of Polonnaruwa, Sri Lanka, he was powerfully moved by the holiness of the site—a quality due in part, he thought, to the millions who had made pilgrimages to the shrine and paid homage.

Note that Merton, a devout Roman Catholic, had no problem relating to a Buddhist holy place. Theological orientation does not matter at such sites. While the theology represented in Catholic churches is not my theology, I've found many of the sanctuaries to be spiritually powerful places. I am quite sure that, because of the memories and hopes, the prayers and meditations, the profound comings and goings of such places, they become "generically" holy.

So it is with all such places. The theology used to explain them is quite irrelevant to the feelings generated. Anyone who has visited a primitive holy place such as Ninstints might conclude as much. Canadian artist and writer Emily Carr did so when she visited a similarly abandoned Indian village not far away: "It was so still and solemn on the beach. It would have seemed irreverent to speak aloud. It was as if everything were waiting, holding its breath. The dog felt it, too. He stood with cocked ears trembling."

A great many of us accept—that is, we "enjoy"—sacred and holy places for their emotional impact, whether such places be a mountaintop, a cathedral, or some national historical shrine. Far fewer of us would think of actually creating such a place.

Most Japanese homes still have shrines, set aside places, where prayers and offerings, values and commitments, continuity between past, present and future, natural objects, and works of art come together in some acknowledgement of the interconnection between the finite and the Infinite. A poem written during the Chinese Ming Dynasty (which makes it at least three hundred years old) speaks of such created sacred places:

On the low wall of my garden
There stands a tiny shrine
Half hidden in the shadow of the trees.
When I am weary of this sad world and of human toil and strife,
I steal off to my shrine among the trees.
There, with silent prayer and incense,
I find my soul again
And thank heaven for my shrine among the trees.

We all need such sacred or holy places. And we should, I would say, dare to create them, preserve them, and use them. As I mentioned earlier, in both of my residences, in town and at the farm, there are Buddhist shrines—a Buddha, a vase of flowers, a candle holder, an offering dish, and an incense burner. I don't claim to be a Buddhist, although I do admire much of what Buddhism stands for. But the purpose of my Buddhist shrines is to serve as spiritual prompters. They tell me to pay attention, to practice devotion, and to avoid attachment. Most of all, they speak to the essential oneness of all things. During some periods I sit in meditation before my shrines; at other times they're just there reminding me that my life would be more complete if I slowed down and listened. They serve as stabilizing points in my often topsy-turvy life.

I happen to believe that a spiritually vital church is a holy place, a place to which we come in order to get in touch with a deeper spiritual center within ourselves, to be reminded of lasting values and of the interconnectedness of this universe. There we may be gently reminded of what I call "the nourishing mystery in which we live and move and have our being."

In such a place we preserve our memories and cherish our hopes. There we are reminded that growth is the lifelong task of us all.

There we celebrate our comings and our goings, the transitions and passages of our lives. There we pause to remember that, as members of one organic body, we are indebted to each other and responsible for each other. As John Donne wrote, none of us is an island.

There we learn the truth of Marcus Aurelius's words: "People are prone to look for places into which to retreat. But there is no place to which you can withdraw more quietly than into your own soul." There we discover, paradoxically, that withdrawal has purpose and meaning only as we are able to return to the world and respond to its opportunities and duties.

Finally, in any temple of spiritual treasures and yearnings, we should be nudged toward the wisdom of the aphorism: "Tread softly; all the earth is holy ground."

Worship

To worship is to stand in awe
under a heaven of stars,
before a flower, a leaf in the sunlight,
or a grain of sand.
To worship is to work
with dedication and skill;
it is to pause from work
and listen to a strain of music.
Worship is loneliness
seeking communion.
It is a thirsty land
crying out for rain.
Worship is kindred fire in our hearts;
it moves through deeds of kindness
and acts of love.
Worship is the mystery within us
reaching out to the mystery beyond.
It is an inarticulate silence
yearning to speak;
It is the window of the moment
open to the sky of the eternal.

—Reverend Jacob Trapp

17

From the Sublime to the Ridiculous

The saga of the dung beetle

Beware of the man [or woman] who will not laugh, for he takes himself seriously, and therefore there is no health in him. A sense of humor is a sense of proportion, of balance, of relative values, and the wise man [woman] knows that few things matter much in life and most don't matter at all. . . .

Away, then, with solemnity, for life is fun, an ever-renewed beginning, and all our suffering, our own, our neighbours' and our friends', is only the tragic element in a show which without it would be very dull.

—Christmas Humphreys

And so, what's it all about? After countless decades of speculation, we still don't know. Nor, perhaps, shall we ever know in this realm. As a matter of fact such an impasse may be inevitable when the finite attempts to understand the Infinite.

A main point of German philosopher Ludwig Wittgenstein's thought is that we cannot make any ultimately valid statement about the whole of reality because there is no place outside of reality from which we can compose such a description. As Krishnamurti put it, "Water can never find out what water is."

Possible responses to the mystery of existence can range from Sören Kierkegaard's fear and trembling before an angry God to Alan Watts's guffaws of delight at religious pomposity. In general, I side with Watts. I also resonate to Robert Frost's irreverent little poem:

> Forgive, Oh Lord, my little jokes on Thee,
> And I'll forgive Thy great big one on me.

Some years ago I attended a ministers' meeting where we had ventured far into the swamps of some murky metaphysical question, and someone presumed to suggest what was going on in the mind of God. Suddenly I found myself being swept by the silliness that I sometimes experience when tedium weighs upon me. I blurted out, "Look! It's a joke; it's all a cosmic joke. Whatever we conclude will be in error and, in the great scheme of things, it won't matter."

From across the room came a gasp as one of my colleagues stared insistently and demanded, "But if it's all a joke, Bill, how come you look so serious?"

My response came automatically. "Because it is serious! That's what makes it so funny. What else can one do but laugh?"

How often it hits me, seemingly at the most inappropriate times: the tragedy of the human comedy. Or is it the other way around: the comedy of the human tragedy?

In my work as a clergyman I often spend time with people when their lives are at their worst. I feel anguish with them over the pain and disappointment and injustice of life. Like Jacob wrestling with the angel of the Lord, I struggle alongside them as they search for a perspective or a possibility that will make it bearable to go on. The saving grace in this work is that occasionally I am able to be with the same people in their moments of release, triumph, and joy. But when they are in pain, how much I would like to remind them that, while they will never forget their suffering, the day will likely come when they will look back upon this particular time of trouble and it will appear almost quaint. It will, anyway, if they can develop that special insight called a sense of humor.

I think of the time perhaps twenty years ago when Sam Wright and I were sitting by a campfire along Kibby Creek in the Sierra Nevada. It had been a busy church year for both of us, and we were fed up with all the details of our mutual profession. So we were taking turns doing some heavy griping. The disgust and righteous indignation were rising to monumental proportions. We were building up to an international episode.

Abruptly, one of us—I can no longer remember which—said, "Let's stop it! For God's sake, let's stop! This has gone on long enough. What we need to do is walk up to that little knoll over there and sit down where we can see most of the stars in the sky. Next, when we're real still inside and can feel the whole cosmos opening up to us, let's tell our troubles to whomever is up there. Let's do it with feeling! Cuss a little so they'll take us seriously! Then, listen! Listen real carefully! And, if we do that, and do it right, we'll hear a great big voice laughing and laughing."

There followed a moment of the most penetrating silence. And then the laughter came—our own laughter—rip-roaring, leg-slapping, and glorious. It was a miracle, and we were healed of our "dis-ease."

The British essayist G. K. Chesterton once said, "Angels can fly because they take themselves lightly." It's good advice to anyone who would live with some equanimity and grow spiritually.

Woody Allen is one of my favorite gurus. Every serious spiritual pilgrim should have some of his books in her or his library. Woody addresses the large questions as readily as the small ones, and usually without indicating which is which. "More than any other time in history," he observes, "Mankind faces a crossroads. One path leads to despair and utter hopelessness. The other, to total extinction. Let us pray we have the wisdom to choose correctly."

And then without drawing a breath he rushes on to say, "I will speak with a panicky conviction of the absolute meaninglessness of existence which could easily be misinterpreted as pessimism. It is not. It is merely a healthy concern for the predicament of modern man."

Concluding that, "The universe is merely a fleeting idea in God's mind," Woody admits that it's "a pretty uncomfortable thought, particularly if you've just made a down payment on a house."

I don't recommend Woody Allen's wisdom to those who are in the depths of despair, any more than I actually retort, "Why not you!?" to the victim of misfortune or injustice who cries, "Why me?" The timing is wrong.

But the person who can appreciate the gallows humor of Woody Allen may be more capable of creating the psychic space or emotional reserve that preserves sanity. As I reflect soberly on the nature of reality and pile up circumstantial evidence that the cosmos is knowable, I delight in Woody Allen's sign-off conclusion: "My God, it's hard enough finding your way around Chinatown."

Of course I still ask the questions. But now they are more in the spirit of the advice that Rainer Maria Rilke offered in his *Letters to a Young Poet*: "I want to beg you, as much as I can . . . to be patient toward all that is unsolved in your heart and to try to love the questions themselves. . . . Do not seek the answers, which cannot be given you because you would not be able to live them. And the point is, to live everything. Live the questions now. Perhaps you will then gradually, without noticing it, live along some distant day into the answer."

Our human failure to live in our questions, to treat our questions gently, is graphically evident at every level of existence. Even in the funny papers.

One of my favorite comic strips is "Calvin and Hobbes." Calvin is a precocious little boy about five years old, and Hobbes is a stuffed toy tiger who, in Calvin's active imagination, is alive, playful and wise.

One profound episode appeared on a Good Friday: Calvin is sitting against a tree thinking cosmic thoughts. "Why do you suppose we're here?" he asks the laid-back tiger. The nonchalant answer comes, "Because we walked here." "No, no . . . I mean here on Earth," insists Calvin. To which Hobbes responds, "Because Earth can support life." "No," says Calvin, his irritation rising, "I mean why are we anywhere? Why do we exist?" By now Hobbes is looking a little perplexed, too. "Because we were born." "Forget it," says Calvin, sulking. And the tiger answers quickly, "I will, thank you."

Appearing as it did just before Easter, this sequence felt only slightly short of prophetic. For Easter—by long tradition, a tradition longer than history itself—celebrates the season of new beginnings. And what beginning could be a more appropriate Easter topic than the one that put us here, the beginning of the universe itself?

Now that's either a scientific question or a theological question, but seldom both. Either way it's serious business. Often too serious! And the only prudent response may be a chuckle.

So let's ask: "How did the universe begin?" Singularities and Big Bangs and universes exploding out of nothing come to mind. One can compare them with the creation myths that pop up in most religions. But I ask you, which boggles the mind more?

Recently I read about a maverick scientist named Edward Fredkin who claims that the universe is a computer and was built for a purpose. And since the primary stuff of computers is information rather than matter or energy, he postulates that information is actually the primary stuff of the universe. Fredkin is serious. He's not speaking metaphorically.

Naturally he gets into all sorts of verbal wrangles with scientists who are more accustomed to thinking of matter and energy as the primary stuff. They ask him questions like, "What's it all for?" With nary a blink, Fredkin answers, "We won't know until it's over." He says he doesn't believe in God, but that if there were a God, even God wouldn't know what the outcome of existence is, because if God knew, then there'd be no point in starting the universe in the first place.

And so it goes. Any time we ask big questions like, "Who created the universe?" the scientists step back and the metaphysicians rush in. "Why, God did!" comes the self-assured answer. If the discussion is truly open, someone will then say, "Is that so! Then who created God?" And there we have the start of what is called an "infinite regression"—a rhetorical marathon in which every answer yields another question. It's the same process that left Calvin and Hobbes breathless and fed up with each other.

This is what happens whenever we finite beings start getting pushy in the questions we ask about the Infinite. We're in for a lively time of it. And that's where a sense of humor comes in. The next time you find yourself up against an infinite regress of cosmic questions and answers, you might want to recall The Turtle Story. Or check with Woody Allen. Or consult Douglas Adams's four-volume *The Hitchhiker's Trilogy*.

We all know how, when our answers don't fit, we're either pushing the river or asking the wrong questions. And what we need to do then is relax and approach again from an unexpected direction. One of the funniest and most sobering moments in *The Hitchhiker's Trilogy* is where it becomes apparent that human beings (who think they are dolphin-trainers) are really an experiment being conducted by dolphins. In the end, the dolphins sign off with the words: "So long, and thanks for all the fish."

Such offbeat humor can be redemptive, if we let it! And it can save us from the deadliest of the Seven Deadly Sins: pride.

Even though I can claim no convincing answer to our initial question, "What's it all about?", intuitively I sense that the fundamental reality is profoundly simple. Perhaps it is the spiritual counterpart of the singularity that astrophysicists say preceded the Big Bang. And I have a lurking suspicion that the complexity that we observe in the finite realm may be born of our inability to comprehend the fundamental simplicity.

It intrigues me, for example, how the physicists, in their search for the fundamental particle, the "building block of the universe," keep finding more and more exotic entities. Along with some physicists, I wonder whether the very act of searching may somehow create the very particles that are found. We know from quantum mechanics that particles appear and disappear. Could the expectations of the researcher have something to do with that? In other words, just as the Cosmic Consciousness may have "created" the universe as we know it, does the consciousness of the scientist do something similar at a subatomic level?

Some years ago cartoonist Bill Steinberg produced one of his typical line drawings of a human face in profile. Out of the mouth of the face came an intricate and endless paisley pattern. Is that what we humans are all about? Is the evolution of paisley patterns our primary function? Do we endlessly spin complexity in our search for the fundamental simplicity? And is the awe-inspiring sense of simplicity that comes with peak experiences a momentary parting of the veil of our contrived complexity?

I don't know. But the possibility comforts me and causes me to smile. It also helps me to cope with the exigencies of everyday life. There is a secondary Hindu scripture called *The Ramayana* in which it is written:

There are three things that are real:
    Brahman, human folly, and laughter.
The first two are beyond comprehension,
So we must do what we can with the third.

I've twice mentioned a nuclear concern group named the Hanford Education Action League (HEAL) that was in the center of my life for three years, displacing even the writing of this book. A grassroots organization of concerned citizens, HEAL began with the classic liberal thesis that truth is powerful and will prevail if held up to public view.

HEAL's mission was to bring the powerful, deceitful, and environmentally suspect United States Department of Energy nuclear weapons facility at Hanford, Washington, to public accountability. It was an ambitious, even presumptuous, undertaking. Especially at the outset, it seemed like a grossly uneven David-and-Goliath contest. The likelihood that a poorly financed citizens' group one hundred miles away could wage an effective contest with Hanford's one-billion-dollar annual economic power appeared unlikely and even foolish. Yet that was exactly what HEAL set out to do. And it succeeded in ways unimagined in the beginning. But not without occasional reminders to maintain a sense of humor.

As an example, in the fall of 1984 we summoned the audacity to ask the Energy Department boss at Hanford to come to Spokane and defend his facility at a HEAL public forum. He agreed and arrived exuding confidence. In fact, as an apologist and public relations expert, he was so skilled that, by the end of the well-attended meeting, we HEAL members were awed and depressed by his effectiveness. We knew that he had given the facts a fast shuffle, but he was so good at it! How could a band of ordinary citizens hope to counter such facile and well-funded propaganda?

Later, after the audience had gone home, Larry Shook, another HEAL founder, and I were commiserating about the evening. Mostly we were taking turns exchanging outbursts of righteous indignation. No doubt we were searching desperately for some reassurance that the truth HEAL planned to tell would have a prayer of a chance against a chronic and obstinate government policy of secrecy and deception.

And then, as we struggled together to find direction and hope in the evening's events, I had one of those irreverent flashbacks that arrive unbidden and which sometimes radically transform a situation. This one was so unlikely and ludicrous that I might easily have dismissed it. Fortunately, I didn't.

In my recollection I was a farm boy again—tarrying on my way to bring the cows in for milking. Before me on the path of the pasture were two three-quarter-inch black beetles struggling together to roll a large one-inch sphere of what was obviously cow manure through the dust. One was pushing, the other was on the opposite side pulling. And they were making slow progress indeed as the erratically rolling ball repeatedly dumped them onto their backs. I had never seen anything like it, and I was both dumbfounded and delighted.

Later I learned that the local grownups called these insects doodlebugs; in that priggish culture, the nature of their work was a source of both embarrassment and humor. Fascinated, I started going for the cows early so as to continue my observations of these strange creatures that apparently made it their life work to fashion cattle dung into nearly perfect spheres.

Especially I recalled how superior I felt to creatures with such a lowly calling. "Cow manure? Ugh! Imagine spending your life as a doodlebug! How much better to be a human being and engage in such lofty pursuits as going to school, playing baseball, planning jungle expeditions, damming rivers, making great historical speeches, and waging war!"

By then Larry's eyes, sparkling with anticipation, were urging me to get to the point of my narration.

"What I know now is that those bugs are called dung beetles. Did you know that the sacred scarab of the ancient Egyptians was a dung beetle? And that the scarab symbolized immortality and resurrection? And that the manure ball was regarded as a symbol of the world?

"Sometimes, Larry, when the importance of my work starts to get the better of me, I think about the dung beetles and the work they do. Is what we humans do substantially more important in the cosmic scheme of things? The dung beetles roll their manure spheres around their world of the cow pasture; we roll ours around the cow pasture of the cosmos. But on an infinite scale, and whether sacred or profane, it's all cow shit! Maybe we'd be happier and more effective if we didn't take ourselves so seriously."

Instantly the twinkle of curiosity in Larry's eyes gave way to chuckles. What a healing recognition it was for both of us! Roaring with laughter, we exchanged hugs and went to our homes, relaxed, more balanced, and buoyant with resolve.

Later I recalled something profound from Martin Buber: "Every man [woman] should have two pockets. In one pocket he [she] should carry the words, 'I am ashes and dust.' And in the other pocket he [she] should carry the words, 'For me the universe was created.' "

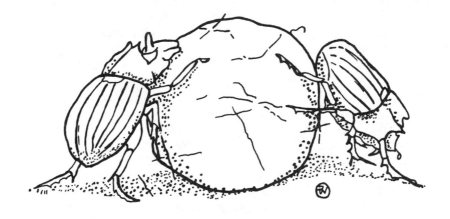

Asked, "What is the Path?", the Master replied, "Walk on!"
—Christmas Humphreys

18

Nature As a Source of Spirit

Where the finite and the Infinite most naturally come together

---

The convergence of nature and spirit is a theme scattered throughout this book, especially in Chapter 16, "Holy Ground." Recalling Schleiermacher's definition of religion as "some intuition of the infinite in the finite," it is an inescapable fact that such an intuition is likely to happen in a place where the basic facts of existence are the most immediate. I think it both logical and grounded in human experience that, when we are most firmly interconnected with the finite (and surely the natural order is a fundamental aspect of the finite!), then we are most likely to find the strength and courage to reach toward the Infinite.

My memory stretches back one quarter of a century. Two dozen high-school-age people, three other adults, and I had backpacked into Evolution Valley—the sublime locale in California's High Sierra where Sam Wright and I had had a life-changing encounter with our own mortality two years before.

It was early August. The trek to our camping spot on McGee Creek covered 28 miles and took two and one-half days. We established a base camp by pitching our tents at the edge of an alpine meadow abloom with paintbrush, lupin, western anemones, and other wildflowers. The southern sky was filled by a great, ragged, granite mountain called The Hermit. Off to the east, Mts. Darwin, Huxley, and Wallace maintained a vigil over the verdant valley called Evolution.

The kids were tired but exultant. For most, this was their first in-depth wilderness experience, and they were caught up in both the novelty of the event and their accomplishment of it. Curiously, I noticed that few of them realized they were in the very center of the Sierra Nevada's most spectacular scenery.

After a day's rest in camp, the majority of us set off on a 12-mile day hike that covered a circular route. It was a fabulous blue-sky day of the sort that mountain-lovers know. We headed up McGee Creek toward the chain of lakes bearing the same name. At first, the young people were playful and noisy, a sign of their pleasure in being free of their heavy packs. Then, as we passed the last lake and began a steep scramble up a boulder-strewn slope perhaps 500 feet high, they became quiet and fell into single file behind me.

This was familiar terrain to me, but I had not told them the real destination of our hike. Topping a grassy ridge, we all paused to marvel at the silent, jagged escarpment—John Muir's fabled "range of light"—that swept the horizon from north to south. Saying nothing, but knowing of one more wonder to come, I led them another two hundred yards to where the ridge plunged out of sight.

Chattering softly about the view and scattering about like puppies, the kids followed. One by one, they arrived at the edge to peer down 700 feet at Turquoise Lake. The flashing water contained within its rock-rimmed basin was an unbelievable blue. And the mountainous setting surrounding it would have done justice to the finest gem.

The amazement that laid hold of my companions was palpable. Spellbound, they stood for a full minute, not speaking or stirring. And then a 15-year-old girl said softly, "I'll never be able to go to summer camp again." There were tears running down her cheeks.

Whether or not she ever did go to summer camp again, I do not know. But twelve years later, I received a folded note from her, the front of which bore a photographic view of another Sierra Nevada wonder. The handwritten message inside said, "I've just returned from Rae Lakes—one of many backpacks I've made into your favorite mountains. And every one of them reminds me of that first hike you took us on. It changed my life, and I'll always be grateful."

This young woman's original experience is perhaps more easily described than understood. The scenery she saw was breathtaking. Had she somehow arrived by automobile and come upon the same view of Turquoise Lake from a roadside pull-out, she would have, no doubt, been thrilled. But she would not, I'm sure, have had an experience that "changed" her life.

The struggle of getting there was crucial to her experience. The preceding days of effort, of fatigue, of sleeping on the ground under skies starry and stormy, of eating trail food she wouldn't have touched at home—all of these conspired to prepare her for that which she probably could not have gained in any other way.

Curiously enough, most of us have yearnings within that prime us for this kind of possibility. How else do we account for a millenia-old fascination with wild places all over the earth? Mountain ranges, deserts, isolated shorelines, and deep forests on six continents are noted for their sacred places and their centers of retreat and self-searching. They are central to the visions of most of the saints and prophets who are key figures in the world's great religions.

Moses, while tending his father-in-law's sheep, had his momentous conversation with a burning bush on the slopes of Mt. Horeb and then, during the flight from Egypt, ascended another (or the same?) volcanic mountain to receive the Ten Commandments and various other laws. Zoroaster, in preparation for his transforming revelation, spent seven years in a mountain cave subsisting on cheese. Jesus, before setting forth on his whirlwind and brief career of preaching and miracle-making, took himself into the desert for forty days. Mohammed, sick at heart over bloody tribal wars, wandered into the hills near Mecca to brood and had an epiphany that included the archangel Gabriel. Buddha, after six years of wandering and self-denial, sat down to meditate under a bo tree where he resisted three fierce challenges before experiencing a blissful awakening that immobilized him for forty-nine days. Confucius had his revelatory experience on the holy mountain of Tai Shan and, throughout his life, made nostalgic references to a boyhood spent in fishing and hunting. Chuang-Tzu so stressed the wisdom found in observing nature that, for centuries thereafter, Chinese artists, painters, and poets alike, sought to express the eternal Way *within* nature.

(Morikage Painting, ca. 1700)

Indicative though they are, the legendary and supernatural feats of the immortal sages do not necessarily translate into experiences accessible to more ordinary human beings. And yet, as with the young girl whose life was "changed" by a single encounter with a glacial lake ten thousand feet above sea level, human lives are radically altered by wilderness experiences. Sometimes the transformation is sudden, other times it is more gradual.

For millions who take their nature experiences vicariously, Henry David Thoreau and the journal he kept while living in a crude hut on the shore of Walden Pond are repeatedly cited.

Thoreau, you'll recall, went to the woods because he "wished to live deliberately, to front only the essential facts of life." "There at last," he wrote in 1857, "my nerves are steadied, my senses and my mind do their office." Thoreau, a transcendentalist and colleague of Emerson, believed he found in the wilderness, "some grand, serene, immortal, infinitely encouraging, though invisible, companion, and walked with him."

Emerson, although he did not share his younger friend's enthusiasm for prolonged solitude and austerity, did nonetheless believe that "the whole of nature is a metaphor of the human mind." Late in life, he traveled west to befriend the great naturalist John Muir. Their meeting took place in Yosemite Valley. Muir was so excited by the arrival of the transcendentalist sage that he tried to persuade Emerson to accompany him on "a month's worship with Nature in the high temples of the great Sierra Crown beyond our holy Yosemite." Emerson was saved by his traveling companions and took lodging at the hotel instead.

Compared to others who are less famous, Henry David Thoreau was hardly the wilderness recluse some of his admirers imagine. While at Walden, he often walked into the town of Concord for a free meal at Emerson's table. And on one of his three treks into the wilds of northern Maine, he was shocked that it was "even more grim and wild than . . . anticipated, a deep and intricate wilderness." He described the view from Mt. Katahdin as "savage and dreary" and himself as "more lone than you can imagine." And yet, those who think that Thoreau was wholly negative to his Maine experience are probably wrong. Some years earlier, Thoreau had asked, "What shall we do with a man who is afraid of the woods, their solitude and darkness? What salvation is there for him?"

In Maine, Thoreau found his answer, an answer that almost anyone who spends considerable time in the wilderness discovers. It is the very darkness and desolation of such places which may fill us with an awe verging on terror, but also connect us to an inner darkness and desolation that becomes somehow more easily accommodated. By having a nearly overwhelming wilderness experience, we see ourselves as though in a mirror and come closer to a creative inner resolution.

Who can doubt, for example, when Robert Frost stopped by some woods on a snowy evening and observed that the woods were lovely, dark, and deep, but he had miles to go before he slept that he was also acknowledging some lovely, dark, and deep places inside himself . . . and resolving to go on?

Thoreau left Walden after twenty-two months. When queried about that, he replied, "I left the woods for as good a reason as I went there. I found I had several more lives to live." And indeed he did, including getting himself arrested for refusing to pay his poll tax to support the Mexican War.

Actually, Thoreau never did recommend the wholesale desertion of civilization. He felt he lived a "sort of border life." He sought the wilds for spiritual nourishment, for an opportunity to commune with himself and his "maker" and even to experience savage instincts. But he firmly believed that an optimum existence required alternating between wilderness and civilization.

So, too, have innumerable others. As Lorraine Anderson wrote in the preface to *Sisters of the Earth*, her shimmering collection of women's nature writings: "Nature has been for me, for as long as I can remember, a source of solace, inspiration, adventure, and delight; a home, a teacher, a companion."

It can even be a matter of life and death. One of the writers featured in Anderson's book is Laura Lee Davidson, a Baltimore schoolteacher who, in 1914, chose to live alone for a year on an island in Canada's Lake of Many Islands. "I am tired to death," explained Davidson to her concerned family and friends. "I need rest for at least one year. I want to watch the procession of the seasons in some place not all paved streets, city smells and noise. Instead of the clang of car bells and the honk of automobile horns, I want to hear the winds sing across the ice fields; instead of the smell of asphalt and hot gasoline, I want the odor of wet earth in boggy places. I have loved the woods all my life; I long to see the year go round there just once before I die."

And so, as autumn was about to begin, Laura Lee Davidson was left with her modest assortment of belongings on a tiny island where she made ready to live in a one-room shack. It was an adventure easily the equal of Thoreau's at Walden. And, when it was over, she told her story in *A Winter of Content*.

> It has given me health. I have forgotten all about jerking nerves and aching muscles. I sleep all night like a stone; I eat plain food with relish; I walk and row mile after mile; I work rejoicing in my strength and glad to be alive.

> There has been also the renewing of my mind, for my standards of

values are changed. Things that once were of supreme importance seem now the veriest trifles. Things that once I took for granted, believing them the common due of mankind—like air and sunshine, warm fires and the kind faces of friends—are now the most valuable things in the world. . . . And I shall carry away a gallery of mind-pictures to be a solace and refreshment through all the years to come.

As I read Davidson's description of what she had seen and learned, my thoughts shifted to a parallel experience of my own where a wilderness adventure (more brief than hers) restored my tattered spirit and brought me back to equilibrium.

It was in the mid-1960s. The Vietnam War was well along in the dreary escalation that led to the tragedy so many of us feared. I was living in Redwood City, California, ministering to my first congregation. The city government decided to lease some public land to a firm that proposed to manufacture napalm bombs. This demanded a protest, and protest we did! Over the ensuing months, the cause burgeoned via public meetings, letters to the editor, a referendum, lawsuits, silent vigils, civil disobedience, and eventually, a mass demonstration that attracted thousands, including one of two U.S. Senators who originally had voted against escalating the war.

The popular outcry against the Vietnam War had not yet reached a crescendo. And for those of us leading the crusade against the napalm bomb plant, it was a lonely, frantic, fatiguing, and, at times, fearsome experience, especially when the mail brought unsigned letters of outrageous charges and threats of bodily harm. I was nearly exhausted and thoroughly dispirited by all that had been happening. I felt possessed by a great void of despair when a wise and faithful friend came to my rescue.

Calling from his home in Berkeley, California, Sam Wright practically ordered me to assemble my gear for a four-day trek into the Thousand Island Lake region of the northern Sierra. After only a modicum of resistance from me, off we went in his old Jeep. As we crossed the range at Toulumne Pass and the medicine of vast natural spaces began its work, I finally realized just how much I needed to do what we were doing.

Within an hour, we had our packs on our backs and were beginning the long slog up the precipitous eastern slope of the Sierra into another region fabled for its beauty and isolation. It was early October and the area was deserted. Gaining elevation with every step, we walked more and more into autumn. Winter was imminent. It would snow any time; we knew that. But, for now, the whole territory was ours. A sublime and awesome aura of waiting was in the air. The birds were gone; the marmots were underground; even the insects had been frosted out.

When we topped the last pass and saw the view of Thousand Island Lake with Mt. Ritter and Banner Peak soaring behind, I was swept by the most ecstatic feeling. How far away was Redwood City and its napalm plant (already spewing out jellied death) and its nearly slanderous newspaper and its antagonized and confused citizens! How nearly incidental was my own fury at it all! How much easier it was to summon some compassion for all of those persons suffering on both sides of that fateful issue!

For three sub-freezing nights, we camped by the lake with its scores of granite boulders thrusting out of the water. The days were brilliantly sunny and relaxing. On one of those days, we took our lunch and hiked over the shoulder of Mt. Ritter, from which we could see 150 miles westward to where a dense, yellow smog obscured the horizon. Beneath that noxious pall lay San Francisco and its associated cities, including the one torn apart by a monstrous decision and activity. And yet, from that promontory, I could feel calm and even forgiveness. That which had been tearing apart my spirit became somehow more bearable, and I was able to return to my work, renewed, pacified, and more whole.

"In wildness is the preservation of the world." Never before had Henry David Thoreau's famous utterance made so much sense to me. Wildness, as Thoreau means it, can also be the preservation of one's self.

Wyoming author Gretel Ehrlich first moved to that state to be with a dying man whom she loved. Perhaps borrowing Thoreau's term, she wrote: "We use the word 'wilderness,' but perhaps we mean wildness. Isn't that why I've come here? In wilderness, I seek the wildness in myself—and in so doing, come on the wildness everywhere around me because, after all being part of nature, I'm cut from the same cloth."

Actually, as wild places bring healing to the spirit, they can also minister to the body. Former Supreme Court Justice William O. Douglas, himself a wilderness lover, wrote of "a man who was told by the doctors he had only six months to live. Where would he like to spend that time? He chose the North Minam Meadows in the [Oregon] Wallowas. . . . This man was so ill he sent the camp in ahead of him and had it all in readiness for his arrival. He came by horseback; he lay weakly for days listening to the murmur of the North Minam and the music of Englemann spruce. In four months he was fishing. In six months—when he was supposed to die—he was building trails with pick and shovel."

A happy coincidence, you say, not statistically significant? Perhaps not in the allopathic medical sense, but even had this man died at the end of six months, his dying would have been more victory than defeat.

Indeed, the wild places and those spots where one can get closer to the solace and healing medicine of nature *are* nearly magical in their impact upon us. Without them, we actually risk our well-being. At the Ninth

Biennial Wilderness Conference, Dr. William C. Gibson said, "The parklands of America are the greatest mental health guardians we have." And Dr. Karl Menninger offered confirmation by adding that he regarded "a proximity to larger non-urban areas of farm or wilderness . . . as essential to the mental health of both child and adult."

Novelist and naturalist Wallace Stegner believed that wild places are valuable simply because they exist—even for those who never visit them. They serve as a reservoir; they hold out the possibility of new beginnings. As this is true spiritually, so it is also true genetically. Stegner was probably more of a prophet than he knew when he called the world's remaining wilderness "part of the geography of hope."

Justice Douglas understood Stegner's "geography of hope" when he said, "The wilderness somehow gives [us] a sense of unity that [we] get nowhere else—a feeling of belonging to the earth and being an important part of existence."

Obviously, for every wilderness-loving hiker or backpacker, there are hundreds of city dwellers like humorist Fran Lebowitz: "Now, nature as I am only too well aware, has her enthusiasts, but on the whole, I am not to be counted among them. To put it rather bluntly, I am not the type who wants to go back to the land—I am the type who wants to go back to the hotel."

Other than replying that nature is important because of its "useful" resources, we are wise to heed the sentiments of naturalist Aldo Leopold. It was Leopold who used the term "ecology" long before it became a buzzword. Leopold warned against thinking of the natural order in terms of its "use" to human beings. A utilitarian attitude, he argued, almost inevitably leads to "using up"—to the destruction of the very thing we claim to love.

Near the end of his life, Aldo Leopold described how his awareness of the interconnectedness of all living beings had grown to include the idea of all existence as one great vital whole. After an experience in Mexico's expansive and primitive Sierra Madre wilderness, he wrote: "It was here that I first clearly realized that the land is an organism," and he coined the term "ecological conscience" to recommend care and respect for the living planet. Thus, he understood the principle that we know today as the Gaia Hypothesis.

The vital interconnectedness that Aldo Leopold learned in the woods and mountains, Hildegard of Bingen learned in the "wilderness" of the cloister.

I am the one whose praise echoes on high.
I adorn all the earth. I am the breeze that nurtures all things
    green.

I encourage blossoms to flourish with ripening fruits.
I am led by the spirit to feed the purest streams.
I am the rain coming from the dew
that causes the grasses to laugh with the joy of life.
I am the yearning for good.

One of the most satisfying lessons to be gained from this sense of wholeness which comes with the wilderness experience is that, for those who can come into harmony with the natural order, the cosmos is indeed a nurturing place—one that can be trusted to sustain us and entertain us, trusted even as it inflicts us with suffering and death.

As in all matters spiritual, we finally come to the wisdom and sanctity of our own personal experience. In his poem, "The Peace of Wild Things," essayist, novelist, and poet Wendell Berry goes into the woods when he feels despair for the world. There, he can "come into the peace of wild things," and as he lies there for a time, he can "rest in the grace of the world, and [is] free."

The Sacred Web of Life

Every part of this earth is sacred to my people. Every shining pine needle, every sandy shore, every mist in the dark woods, every meadow, every humming insect. All are holy in the memory and experience of my people.

We know the sap which courses through the trees as we know the blood that courses through our veins. We are part of the earth and it is part of us. The perfumed flowers are our sisters. The bear, the deer, the great eagle, these are our brothers. The rocky crests, the juices in the meadow, the body heat of the pony, and humans, all belong to the same family.

Teach your children what we have taught our children—that the earth is our mother. What befalls the earth befalls the sons and daughters of the earth.

This we know: the earth does not belong to us, we belong to the earth. All things are connected like the blood that unites us all. We did not weave the web of life; we are merely a strand in it. Whatever we do to the web, we do to ourselves.

—as attributed to Chief Seattle, 1854

19

Living With Death

Like a swallow in the night

The fact is that we must die. Our awareness of that sobering fact is said by many sages to be the impetus for all spiritual striving. According to Arthur Schopenhauer, "all philosophy is a muse on death."

Whether or not death is the primary stimulus for the human quest for meaning, we may debate. But it seems clear to me that death does confront us with the most serious spiritual problem we have. No other aspect of life asks so insistently that we deal with who we really are. At no other time in life are we so earnestly required to come to terms with attachment and loss.

Unfortunately, our materialistic and hedonistic culture distorts the finite reality of death and effectively thwarts what it has to teach us! We spend billions every year to disguise the evidence that aging and dying are as integral (and necessary!) to living as birth is. We seldom speak personally of death, except in religion where we tend to deny our mortality via fanciful theologies. We hide the experience of death within our medical and funeral practices. And then, midst all the denial, we burlesque death through our media and entertainment.

Notice how much attention we give to violent death and to mortality as it affects the rich and famous. But the obituaries of ordinary people are published in small print in the advertisement pages. We exclaim in horror when a bomb in London or Beirut kills twenty, or when a tornado leaves a hundred corpses in its wake. But the statistic that over 70 million people die annually is scarcely noticed by anyone.

Ironically and tragically, none of our avoidance strategies work long-term. As Emily Dickinson so eloquently put it: "Because I could not stop for Death, He kindly stopped for me; . . ." And yet, for most of us, Dylan Thomas seems the braver and wiser poet because of his fierce counsel to not go gently into the night, but to "rage, rage against the dying of the light."

We look on hopefully, yet with doubt at author and photographer Dame Freya Stark's adamant pronouncement: "An absolute condition of all successful living, whether for an individual or a nation, is the acceptance of death."

But we find little to smile about in writer and activist Charlotte Perkins Gilman's impertinent question: "Death? Why this fuss about death? Use your imagination, try to visualize a world *without* death!"

By growing up on a farm and having a maternal grandfather who was a village undertaker in the Shenandoah Valley of Virginia, I gained a somewhat greater familiarity with death than did most children my age. I often stayed with my grandparents in the summer, and it never seemed odd to me when someone made reference to there being "a new body in the shop." I remember especially the funerals—the preaching, the wailing, the fervent shouts of "Amen." Most of all, I recall the singing. No country funeral service was complete without a profoundly poignant rendition of "Abide With Me."

> Abide with me! Fast falls the eventide;
> The darkness deepens: Lord, with me abide!
> When other helpers fail, and comforts flee,
> Help of the helpless, Oh abide with me!

Even now, I can feel the power and ambiguity of that old hymn—a certain fear and loneliness on the one hand, and a tenuous reaching for reassurance on the other.

The threat of non-being—that's what Protestant theologian Paul Tillich called the fear of death. However, isn't it intriguing how seldom we ask the question, non-being for what?

Because it seems to threaten us with the loss of everything that is "us," death *is* the most fundamental human fear. Humans through the eons have tried to escape it. Most religions have attempted to mitigate the fear of death by negating the non-being, by promising some sort of afterlife, usually with two options—one rewarding, the other punishing.

From Christianity to Judaism to Islam and stretching back to the ancient Norse, Aztec, and Zoroastrian religions, the virtuous survived and the evil suffered. And still the ambiguity toward death endured! Death became a dark and fearful journey to be delayed at all costs even though notions of heaven and hell became widespread as promises of an afterlife.

These are disquieting notions to the believer and the freethinker alike.

We are all familiar with the fearsome images of the Christian evangelists—the epitome of such being Jonathan Edward's sermonic depiction of the sinner's soul being dangled by an angry God over the leaping fires of the Inferno.

The faithful Christian listens to such vivid horrors with a quavering hope for salvation. The religious freethinker rejects such images as unworthy of human rationality and dignity. But the freethinker's rejection seldom saves him or her from struggling mightily and not very successfully with the mystery of death.

Most religious liberals would, I suspect, put themselves into the freethinker's or humanist's camp. We don't have much patience with ideas of heaven and hell. Especially, if we come out of the Universalist tradition, we are revolted by the suggestion that an all-wise, all-loving, all-merciful God would create fallible human beings and then roast them for all time in Hell for acting fallibly.

Still, the problem of death does not go away and must be dealt with. The humanists among us either deny the possibility of answering such questions, or resort to the reductionistic position in which humans are produced by evolutionary accident from a mechanical universe and return just as indifferently to it at death.

This is not a very comforting proposition, and many humanists, even as they reject the usual notions of immortality, continue to reach for rationalistic approximations. We hear promises that we will "live on" in our children . . . or in the lives of those whom we touch . . . or in our deeds. Some attempt to find meaning and comfort by seeing themselves as a link in the great and unbroken chain of life. These attempts at a rational immortality often reach a peak at Easter when, in response to the acclaimed resurrection of Jesus, liberals become lyrical about the vital resurrection represented in the leafing of trees and blooming of flowers.

More recently, many religious liberals have taken a special interest in the near-death studies of thanatologists Elizabeth Kubler-Ross and Raymond Moody, in the rather remarkable talents of various psychics, and in the past-life regression activities of certain New Age therapists and hypnotists. These studies are viewed as quasi-scientific evidence that humans do individually survive the demise of their physical bodies. They are also viewed as a positive affirmation of the cycles of reincarnation that are espoused by certain Eastern religions, such as Hinduism.

I find the near-death studies especially interesting, but, beyond their suggestion that dying is neither fearsome nor painful, I don't know how to interpret them. I am tentative about drawing conclusions because I see no *necessary* connection between *almost* dying and death itself.

As for the psychics and their channelings from the spiritual realm, I have had enough contact with several psychics that I believe at least some of them to be honest persons of unusual talent reporting authentic experiences. I don't know, however, what to make of their reports. It may well be that, in all innocence, their language is more metaphorical or poetic than factual. I don't say this to belittle their experiences, but to guard against leaping to mundane conclusions when more mystical interpretations may be closer to the truth.

Finally, on reincarnation, I have never been much of a believer, except, as I have already discussed, in the idea that each of us is an incarnation of the divine principle. Ordinary reincarnation, serial reincarnation, the repeated reincarnation of a single personality in a series of bodies—these theories have all sorts of problems, including the question of which self— younger or older—is reborn. And what, I always wonder, happens to the soul who was born mentally retarded or who died of Alzheimers? Does the limited self carry on to the next life? I can't imagine it!

Of one thing I am quite certain: the isolated reality of my own life is an illusion. I simply cannot conceive of a person as coming into existence at one time and going out of existence at another time. I think it's more of a continuum than that. Let me illustrate by telling a story.

During the seventh century, the Anglo-Saxon King Edwin was importuned by an emissary of the Pope to convert to Christianity. Later, while trying to sort out the merits of such a conversion, Edwin consulted his advisors.

One of the advisors replied: "It has often seemed to me that our life on earth is like a swallow that suddenly darts into a brightly lighted banquet hall on a stormy night, lingers a moment, and then darts out a window on the other side. It comes from the wintry darkness into the warmth and light, and for a moment we see it clearly. Then it disappears into the darkness outside. . . . That is how my life appears to me. I do not know from where I came into this world or where I am going; all I know is the brief span of light which I fly through all too swiftly."

What a potent image! A swallow flashing out of the night into the lighted room and then, after a brief sojourn, disappearing just as quickly into the darkness. Indeed, on a factual basis, this is how life seems to us, the living. All the rest is speculation and commentary. And yet, one of the crucial aspects of this imagery is the point from which it is viewed. Except for those with rather mystical insights, the darkness from which the bird flies and into which it returns is a mystery. We don't really know, in any cognitive way, how we came or how we will go. So, we are stuck with a complex mixture of inference, intuition, and yearning.

Let us imagine, however, that we are standing outside the banquet hall where our eyes would be more accustomed to the darkness. Out there we might be able to see the swallow against the night sky and hear the beat of its wings. From that perspective, we would experience not only its brief tenure in the bright life of the hall, but also the wider world out of which it flew and into which it is returned. A fanciful speculation? Perhaps! But it does, I think, lift the corner of the concealing curtain. It makes the unknown less mysterious and more acceptable.

It also reminds me of another story. This one is called a midrash. A midrash is a story that is meant to enlarge upon a scriptural passage and is told by a rabbi or teacher. This particular midrash begins thus.

I am standing upon the seashore: a ship at my side spreads her white sails to the morning breeze and starts for the blue ocean. She is an object of beauty and strength, and I stand and watch her until at length she hangs like a speck of white cloud just where the sea and sky come down to mingle with each other. Then someone at my side says, "There! She's gone!" Gone where? Gone from my sight— that is all. She is just as large in mast and hull and spar as she was when she left my side and is just as able to bear her load of living freight to the place of destination. Her diminished size is in me, not in her; and just at the moment when someone at my side says, "There! She's gone!", there may be other eyes watching her coming and other voices ready to take up the glad shout, "There she comes!" And that is dying.

Now, it's not my intention in sharing this midrash with you to move you toward some literal interpretation that there are "others"—"those who have gone before"—on "the other side" waiting to welcome the newly dead. I don't know about that and have no indisputable basis on which to discuss it. But this story does have enormous significance because it reminds us that our understanding of any mystery depends on the place from which we view it.

So it is, I'm sure, with death. Whatever death is, I have no doubt that it is other than what we see from the perspective of the living. Death may be much more complex than we imagine, or it may be much simpler. I'm inclined toward simplicity, but I have no doubt that it *is* different.

In the Taoist tradition with its principle of rhythmic complementarity, there is a story about Chuang-Tzu which brings us close to harmonizing the seeming contradiction of life and death. Chuang-Tzu's wife has died and his friend, Hui-Tzu, has come to offer his condolences. Expecting to find the sage in mourning, Hui-Tzu is astounded to find him sitting on the ground, drumming away on an overturned wooden bowl and singing at the top of his voice.

"What is this?" demands Hui-Tzu. "Your wife of many years, the mother of your children, and the woman who has stuck with you through your quest for understanding has died. Had you shed no tears over her remains that would have been bad enough, but for you to sit singing and beating on a bowl—this is too much!"

You misjudge me!" protests Chuang-Tzu. "When she died, I grieved as deeply as any husband. But then I realized that before she was born she had no body, and that the same process that brought her to birth has, in the fullness of time, brought her to death If someone is tired and goes to lie down, we do not pursue them howling and bawling. She whom I have lost has taken off her body and left it asleep in the space between heaven and earth. To moan and groan while my wife is sleeping would be to deny the wisdom of nature's sovereign law. So I refrain and celebrate instead that Tao is working as it is supposed to."

Stories such as this delight my spirit, and often do more to relieve my puzzlement concerning some mystery than can many pages of well-reasoned prose. But, as a scientist with a pronounced fondness for theories and models, I also enjoy diagrams. And so, I have evolved a cosmological paradigm that has proved useful to me on many occasions, where I am face to face with the mysteries of existence and need to communicate what is more intuited than known.

Cosmic Paradigm

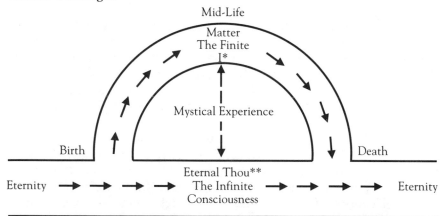

* Within "I" there is "I-It ⟷ I-Thou"
** "Eternal Thou" is always "Thou" and never "It"

Like all theories and paradigms, this one has little literal truth. Its "truth" rests in its usefulness, in the fact that it helps to make sense of our experience and assists us in communicating with one another. Just as verbal images of mysteries fall short of the reality, so do visual images. (A picture of God, such as Michelangelo painted on the ceiling of the Sistine Chapel, is just as limited as a Christian fundamentalist's imaginary picture of Jehovah sitting on a golden throne in heaven!)

This cosmological diagram is obviously inadequate because it takes what can only be a holographic entity and breaks it down into parts. Furthermore, as it is spatially limited, so it is temporally limited. Time, as many philosophers and most quantum physicists will tell you, is a construct. My diagram, by implying that time flows in one direction, is inaccurate. Nevertheless, with these limitations in mind, the diagram is still useful.

As I have stated before, the Infinite is everything, existing and potential. It is Huxley's "one, divine Reality substantial to the manifold of things and lives and minds," but through history and in various spiritual traditions, it has been called God, Yahweh, Brahman, Tao, Allah, the Cosmic Consciousness, Divine Mind, the Eternal Thou, the Ground of Being, and innumerable other names. And of course, it has often been described in terms that fall far short of the mystical whole toward which it points.

The Infinite, as such, is a seamless whole—"not two, not two." But aspects of the Infinite, which by definition are finite, can seem to separate from the whole and acquire a kind of separate existence. In the diagram, this possibility is shown by the loop flowing out of the Infinite, and it represents the entire existing universe.

In the case of human beings, birth (or perhaps better, conception) occurs, and a separate being is born, which quickly forgets where it came from and almost immediately becomes preoccupied with surviving as a separated entity. This struggle for survival requires the creation of an individual identity—an ego, a sense of self that comes to recognize everything beyond the body as not-self. The not-self is both a challenge and an opportunity; to the degree possible, it must be managed, controlled, and accommodated. In Buberian terms, what was once a relationship described as I-Thou becomes predominately I-It. The Eternal Thou has been forgotten and is but faintly heard.

But there are intimations. Through various intuitions, peak experiences, and sacred teachings, attention is called to the Infinite. These intimations become stronger as mid-life is reached and, depending on how attached the individual person has become to the finite, may or may not augment the search for an increased spiritual awareness.

To the degree that the individual is successful in recognizing the divine identity that has lain largely dormant within (and this recognition can be encouraged by all of the techniques that have been the subject of this book), he or she moves toward what has been variously called enlightenment, satori, salvation, etc.

To the degree that the spiritual quest is successful, the individual becomes more comfortable with both the finite and the Infinite. Death or the return to the Infinite is accepted as both necessary and appropriate. These are the deaths most likely to be recognized and experienced as "a peaceful death," what is described by Elizabeth Kubler-Ross as watching a falling star disappearing into "the endless night forever."

It is through understandings such as this that I have become certain that the fear with which we ordinarily regard death is unnecessary, and is born of a mistaken notion as to who we really are—a finite aspect of the Infinite which has "forgotten" its eternal identity.

Going back to the story of King Edwin and his advisor, we are like the swallow that flies into the window. In our unnecessary fear of death, we are so bedazzled by the glitter and commotion of the banquet hall that we forget what we are, and forget especially what is outside the hall and come to fear the outside because it is the unknown. Chuang Tzu once asked a question that touches upon all of this. "How do I know that the love of life is not a delusion, and that the dislike of death is not like a child that is lost and does not know the way home?"

Since our response to death is so heavily dependent upon who we really are, the reader's attention is particularly directed to Chapter Eleven, "Self-Discovery."

As death insistently asks us who we really are, so it also requires us to come to terms with attachment. Obviously, the two requirements are intricately related, but in western society, attachment is an even greater challenge than self-identity.

In western spiritual literature, the Buddha's primary teaching is commonly translated: "The cause of all suffering is desire." In my experience the teaching is seldom persuasive to westerners. Having "desires" is so central a feature of our everyday life that being asked to give them up sounds like ceasing to exist, or living a life of indifference.

In Buddhism, the First Noble Truth states that life is *dukkha. Dukkha* is not easy to translate. Literally it means suffering, but the feeling is impermanence. Because human beings are not able to deal with the impermanence of all things, they suffer. The path to peace of mind is the acceptance of *dukkha* to the point where we no longer struggle against it. That, taught the Buddha, is the way beyond suffering. Death, of course, tends to yield the greatest suffering because death seemingly threatens us with the loss of everything we have, of all that is truly real.

One of the essential aspects of spiritual growth is that the successful pilgrim becomes less and less attached to temporal and material things This does not mean, however, that the spiritually mature person loses all interest in such things, but that such a person does not allow these attachments to dominate his or her life. Recall Chuang Tzu's warning: "When one tries to expand his power over objects, those objects gain power over him."

So it is with a frantic attempt to maintain ordinary life and hold away death. This is an attachment that not only turns death into a fearful inevitability, but also inhibits spiritual growth. It is here that Jesus' enigmatic pronouncement, "Those who would keep their lives shall lose them, and those who would give up their lives shall find them," begins to make some sense.

What does all of this mean when we experience feelings of grief when someone we love dies! Well, grief is the work we do in accommodating any significant change in our lives. Death, as loss, *is* a change. And it is not wrong that we grieve. What is wrong is if we do not grow because of our grief, if we make no progress in overcoming our attachment.

No one is so spiritually advanced as to be beyond all attachment and beyond all grieving when great loss comes. I have cited before the example of St. Ignatius of Loyola, who gave his whole life to the founding of the Jesuit order and who was once asked what he would do if the Pope commanded him to dissolve the order. "A quarter of an hour of prayer," replied St. Ignatius, "and then I should think no more about it."

This is an amazing response which, at first, seems harsh and uncaring. But St. Ignatius obviously cared a great deal about his lifework. His devotion was enormous, but his attachment was miniscule. Hence, after fifteen minutes of prayerful mourning, he would go on to new duties and responsibilities.

All of this shows, I hope, how we, in our mortal attachment, may be nervous about death and even mourn deeply its impact, but not fear death. Thus, as we grow in spiritual understanding, we may more and more appreciate something that Nathaniel Hawthorne said: "We sometimes congratulate ourselves at the moment of waking from a troubled dream; it may be so at the moment of death."

A few years ago, I spent many hours with a man whose final year was an enormously ambiguous one—a year marked by heroic determination and dismal failure, and then by heroism again. Although he was not able to sustain a temporary recovery from a relentless illness, he still managed to die as magnificently and purposefully as anyone I've ever known. And I tell his story, not because it is so unique, but because it illustrates so graphically what Kubler-Ross meant when she called death "the last stage of growth."

This man's profession was healing. At first he sought desperately for a way to heal his body. Then he turned his attention to healing his spirit. Taking up the discipline of meditation, reading voraciously from a wide range of spiritual writings, and spending many hours with others discussing what he read and thought and felt, he gradually came to understand how his childhood abuse and adult obsession with comfort and competence had delayed his own spiritual development. All of the five delusory Ps— possessions, power, prestige, profit, and pleasure—had been pursued as symbols proving that he was a worthwhile human being. Bursting through occasional panics at letting go, he worked one by one through these attachments.

In the process, he began to learn who he really was. The small self that had been his essential identity for most of his life was more and more subsumed into the large Self that he had always been, but hadn't recognized.

The man did not consider himself Christian, nor did he expect any kind of personal survival to follow his death. Yet, the famous prayer attributed to St. Francis became his mantra, and I sometimes found him repeating it quietly when I came to visit.

> Lord, make me an instrument of thy peace.
> Where there is hatred, let me sow love;
> Where there is injury, pardon;
> Where there is doubt, faith;
> Where there is despair, hope;
> Where there is darkness, light;
> Where there is sadness, joy.
>
> Grant, Oh Divine Master, that I may not so much seek
> To be consoled, as to console,
> To be understood, as to understand,
> To be loved, as to love.
> For it is in giving that we receive;
> It is in pardoning that we are pardoned;
> It is in dying that we are born to eternal life.

And, indeed, he did become a transforming instrument of peace for himself and others. Because he was such an inspiring example and so uplifting to be with, people sought to spend time with him. One by one he opened himself to his friends and loved ones to share what he had learned in the course of his struggle and to assure them of their place in his affections. And he spent many hours with his children similarly involved. In his last days, he wrote each of them a personal letter, to be opened after his death, telling them why he loved them.

Meanwhile, even as the ravages of his disease inexorably reduced his body to a fraction of its former vigor, there came into his eyes a soft glow of acceptance, and from his lips came many a chuckle at the irony of his plight. "My last adventure," he whimsically called his mortal condition, "I wonder how it will turn out." Guided by the faith of Claire Morris's heroic verse, which he kept written on a small card by his bed, he finally walked through the valley of the shadow of death as though he were taking a stroll through a park on a sunny afternoon.

When we walk to the edge of all the light we have and take a step into the darkness of the unknown, we must believe one of two things will happen—there will be something solid for us to stand upon, or we will be taught to fly.

Works Consulted

Aurobindo, Sri, *The Life Divine*, Pomoma: Auromere, 1983.

Adams, Douglas, *The Hitchhiker's Trilogy*, New York: Crown, 1984.

Adler, Margot, *Drawing Down The Moon*, Boston: Beacon, 1979.

Allen, Woody, *Getting Even*, New York: Vintage, 1978.

____, *Side Effects*, New York: Ballantine, 1975.

____, *Without Feathers*, New York: Warner, 1972.

Anderson, Lorraine, *Sisters of The Earth*, New York: Vintage, 1991.

Bailey, Raymond, *Thomas Merton on Mysticism*, Garden City: Image, 1907.

Ballou, Robert O. (editor), *The Bible of The World*, New York: Viking, 1939.

Barry, William A. and William J. Connolly, *The Practice of Spiritual Direction*, San Francisco: HarperCollins, 1991.

Bartlett, Lael, *Psi Trek*, New York: McGraw-Hill, 1981.

Bateson, Gregory, *Steps Toward An Ecology of Mind*, New York: Ballantine, 1972.

Bateson, Gregory and Mary Catherine Bateson, *Angels Fear: Towards an Epistomology of the Sacred*, New York: Bantam Books, 1988.

Berry, Thomas, *The Dream of The Earth*, San Francisco: Sierra Club Books, 1988.

Berry, Wendell, *Openings*, New York: Harcourt, 1968.

Blackney, R.B. (translator), *Meister Eckhart*, New York: Harper & Row, 1941.

____, *The Way of Life: Lao Tzu (Tao-Te-Ching)*, New York: Mentor, 1955.

Brand, George, *The Religious Experience* (two volumes), New York: Braziller, 1964.

Bratton, Fred Gladstone, *A History of The Bible*, Boston: Beacon, 1959.

Briggs, John and F. David Peat, *Turbulent Mirror*, New York: Harper & Row, 1989.

Buber, Martin, *I and Thou*, New York: Scribner's, 1958.

____, *Good and Evil*, New York: Scribner's, 1952.

Burkan, Tolly, and Peggy Burkan, *Building Yourself into A Spiritual Reality*, Twain Harte: Reunion, 1983.

Cameron, Anne, *Daughters of Copper Woman*, Vancouver: Press Gang, 1981.

Campbell, Joseph, *Myths to Live By*, New York: Bantam, 1973.

____, *The Masks of God* (three volumes), New York: Viking, 1958-64.

Capra, Fritjof, *The Tao of Physics*, New York: Bantam, 1977.

Capra, Fritjof and David Steindl-Rast, *Belonging to the Universe*, San Francisco: HarperCollins, 1991.

Carrington, Patricia, *Freedom in Meditation*, New York: Anchor, 1978.

Christ, Carol, *Diving Deep and Surfacing*, Boston: Beacon, 1980.

Christ, Carol, and Judith Plaskow, *Womanspirit Rising*, San Francisco: Harper & Row, 1979.

Ch'u Ta-Kao (translator), *Tao-Te-Ching*, Winchester: Allen Unwin, 1982.

Clissold, Stephen, *The Wisdom of St. Francis*, New York: New Directions, 1978.

Cohen, J W., and J.F. Phipps, *The Common Experience*, Los Angeles: Tarcher, 1979.

Conze, Edward (editor), *Buddhist Texts*, New York: Philosophical Library, 1954. Coomaraswamy, Ananda, *Hinduism and Buddhism*, Westport: Greenwood, 1943.

Cragg, Kenneth, *The Wisdom of The Sufis*, New York: New Directions, 1976.

Csikszentmihalyi, Mihaly, *Flow*, New York: Harper & Row, 1990.

Dass, Ram, *Journey of Awakening*, New York: Bantam, 1978.

Davidson, Laura Lee, *A Winter of Content*, Nashville: Abingdon-Cokesbury, 1922.

Day, Dorothy, *Therese*, Springfield: Templegate, 1960.

deChardin, Teilhard, *The Phenomenon of Man*, New York: Harper, 1961.

Deikman, Arthur, *The Observing Self*, Boston: Beacon, 1982.

Dooling, D.M. and Paul Jordon-Smith, *I Become Part of It*, New York: Parabola Books, 1989.

Dossey, Larry, *Recovering The Soul*, New York: Bantam, 1989.

Easwaran, Eknath, *Meditation*, Petaluma: Nilgiri, 1978.

——, *The Compassionate Universe*, Petaluma: Nilgiri, 1989.

——, *The Supreme Ambition*, Petaluma: Nilgiri, 1982.

Edwards, Tilden, *Spiritual Friend*, New York: Paulist, 1980.

Eliade, Mircea, *Yoga, Immortality and Freedom*, Princeton: Princeton University, 1969.

——, *Patanjali and Yoga*, New York: Schocken, 1975.

——, *Shamanism*, Princeton: Princeton University Press, 1972.

Eliot, T.S., *Collected Poems, 1909-1962*, New York: Harcourt, 1963.

——, *Four Quartets*, New York: Harcourt, 1943.

Emerson, Ralph Waldo, *Collected Works*, Brooklyn: McKibbin, n.d.

Faraday, Ann, *Dream Game*, New York: Harper & Row, 1974.

——, *Dream Power*, New York: Coward McCann, 1972.

Ferguson, Marilyn, *The Aquarian Conspiracy*, Los Angeles: Tarcher, 1980.

Fields, Rick, et al, *Chop Wood, Carry Water*, Los Angeles: Tarcher, 1984.

Fowler, James, *Stages of Faith*, New York: Harper & Row, 1981.

Fox, Matthew, *Compassion*, Oak Grove: Winston, 1979.

——, *Musical Mystical Bear*, Ramsey: Paulist, 1976.

——, *Original Blessings*, Santa Fe: Bear, 1983.

____, *Western Spirituality*, Santa Fe: Bear, 1981.

Frazer, Sir James, *The Golden Bough*, New York: MacMillan, 1960.

Freemantle, Anne (editor), *The Protestant Mystics*, New York: Mentor, 1964.

Friedan, Betty, *The Second Stage*, New York: Summit, 1982.

Friedman, Lenore, *Meetings With Remarkable Women*, Boston: Shambhala, 1987.

Frost, Robert, *Complete Poems of Robert Frost, 1949*, New York: Holt, 1949.

Furlong, Monica, *Merton*, San Francisco: Harper & Row, 1980.

Gendlin, Eugene, *Focusing*, New York: Everest, 1978.

Ghose, Sisirkumar, *Mystics as a Force for Change*, Wheaton: Quest, 1981.

Giles, Herbert (translator), *Chuang Tzu, Mystic, Moralist and Social Reformer*, New York: AMS Press, 1926.

Gilligan, Carol, *In a Different Voice*, Cambridge: Harvard, 1982.

Goldenberg, Naomi, *Changing of The Gods*, Boston: Beacon, 1979.

Goldstein, Joseph, *The Experience of Insight*, Boulder: Shambhala, 1983.

Goleman, Daniel, *Varieties of Meditative Experience*, New York: Irvingron, 1977.

Govinda, Lama, *The Way of the White Clouds*, Boulder: Shambhala, 1966.

Gray, Elizabeth Dodson, *Green Paradise Lost*, Wellesley: Roundtable, 1981.

____, *Patriarchy as a Conceptual Trap*, Wellesley: Roundtable, 1982.

Griffiths, Bede, *Return to The Center*, Springfield: Templegate, 1976.

Grof, Stanislav, *Ancient Wisdom and Modern Science*, Albany: SUNY, 1984.

Harmon, Willis, *Global Mind Change*, Indianapolis: Knowledge Systems, 1988.

Harner, Michael, *The Way of the Shaman*, New York: Harper & Row, 1980.

Hawken, Paul, *The Magic of Findhorn*, New York: Bantam, 1976.

Hayward, Jeremy, *Perceiving Ordinary Magic*, Boston: New Science, 1984.

Herrigel, Eugen, *Zen in The Art of Archery*, New York: Vintage, 1971.

Hixon, Lex, *Coming Home*, Garden City: Anchor, 1978.

Houston, Jean, *Life Force*, New York: Delacorte, 1980.

Howard, Vernon, *Mystic Path to Cosmic Power*, West Nyack: Parker Publishing, 1967.

Hume, R.E. (translator), *Upanishads*, New York: Oxford U., 1931.

Humphreys, Christmas, *Walk On!*, Wheaton: Quest, 1977.

____, *A Western Approach to Zen*, Wheaton: Quest, 1971.

Huxley, Aldous, *The Perennial Philosophy*, New York: Harper Colophon, 1970.

Jahn, Robert G. and Brenda J. Dunne, *Margins of Reality*, San Diego: Harcourt, 1987.

James, William, *Varieties of Religious Experience*, New York: MacMillan, 1961.

Jantsch, Erich, *The Self-Organizing Universe*, New York: Pergamon, 1980.

Jeffers, Robinson, *The Beginning and The End and Other Poems*, New York: Random House, 1963.

Johnson, Raynor, *Imprisoned Splendor*, New York: Harper, 1953.

____, *Watcher on The Hills*, New York: Harper, 1959.

Johnson, Willard, *Riding The Ox Home*, Boston: Beacon, 1986.

Johnston, William, *The Inner Eye of Love*, New York: Harper & Row, 1978.

____, *Silent Music*, New York: Harper & Row, 1976.

Kataguri, Dainin, *Returning to Silence*, Boston: Shambhala, 1988.

King, Martin Luther, Jr., *I Have A Dream* (compiled by Lotte Hoskins), New York: Grosset & Dunlap, 1982.

King, Ursula, *Towards a New Mysticism*, New York: Seabury, 1981.

Koestler, Arthur, *The Act of Creation*, New York: MacMillan, 1964.

____, *The Roots of Coincidence*, New York: Vintage, 1972.

Krieger, Delores, *Therapeutic Touch*, Englewood Cliffs: Prentice-Hall, 1979.

Krippner, Stanley, and Alberto Villoldo, *The Realms of Healing*, Millbrae: Celestial Arts, 1976.

Krishnamurti, Jiddu, *Krishnamurti's Journal*, San Francisco: Harper & Row, 1982.

____, *Krishnamurti's Notebook*, New York: Harper & Row, 1976.

____, *Krishnamurti to Himself*, New York: Harper & Row, 1987.

____, *Think on These Things*, New York: Harper & Row, 1964.

Kubler-Ross, Elizabeth, *Death: The Last Stage of Growth*, New York: Simon & Schuster, 1986.

Kuhn, Thomas, *The Structure of Scientific Revolutions*, Chicago: Phoenix, 1962.

Kushner, Harold, *When Bad Things Happen to Good People*, New York: Avon, 1981.

Latourette, Kenneth, *A History of Christianity*, New York: Harper, 1953.

Lemkov, Anna F., *The Wholeness Principle*, Wheaton: Quest, 1990.

Leonard, George, *The Silent Pulse*, New York: Dutton, 1978.

____, *The Transformation*, New York: Dell, 1972.

LeShan, Lawrence, *Alternate Realities*, New York: Ballantine, 1976.

____, *How to Meditate*, New York: Bantam, 1974.

____, *The Medium, The Mystic and The Physicist*, New York: Ballantine, 1973.

____, *The Science of The Paranormal*, Wellingborough: Aquarian Press, 1987.

Lessing, Doris, *The Children of Violence*, New York: Penguin, 1970.

Levine, Stephen, *A Gradual Awakening*, Garden City: Anchor, 1979.
____, *Who Dies?*, Garden City: Anchor, 1981.
Lewis, C.S., *Mere Christianity*, New York: MacMillan, 1943.
Lifshin, Lyn, *Ariadne's Thread*, New York: Harper Colophon, 1982.
Loori, John Daido, *Mountain Record of Zen Talks*, Boston: Shambhala, 1988.
MacDonald, George F., *Ninstints*, Chicago: University of Chicago, 1985.
Man-ch'ing, Cheng and Robert W. Smith, *T'ai-Chi*, Rutland: Tuttle, 1967.
Margenau, Henry, *The Miracle of Existence*, Boston: New Science, 1987.
Maslow, Abraham, *Religions, Values, and Peak Experiences*, Columbus: Ohio State, 1964.
May, Rollo, *The Courage To Create*, New York: Norton, 1975.
McArthur, Tom, *Beyond Logic & Mysticism*, Wheaton: Quest, 1990.
McKibben, Bill, *The End of Nature*, New York: Random House, 1989.
Merton, Thomas, *Asian Journal*, New York: New Directions, 1973.
____, *Mystics and Zen Masters*, New York: Dell, 1967.
____, *New Seeds of Contemplation*, New York: New Directions, 1972.
____, *The Seven Storey Mountain*, New York: Harcourt Brace, 1948.
____, *The Way of Chuang Tzu*, New York: New Directions, 1965.
Miller, Ronald S., *As Above So Below*, Los Angeles: Tarcher, 1992.
Miners, Scott, *A Spiritual Approach to Male/Female Relations*, Wheaton: Quest, 1984.
Miura, Isshu, and Ruth Sasaki, *The Zen Koan*, New York: Harcourt, 1965.
Naranjo, Claudio, *How To Be*, Los Angeles: Tarcher, 1989.
Needleman, Jacob, *A Sense of The Cosmos*, New York: Dutton, 1976.
Nhat Hanh, Thich, *Being Peace*, Berkeley: Parallax, 1987.
____, *The Miracle of Mindfulness*, Boston: Beacon, 1976.
Otto, Rudolph, *The Idea of The Holy*, New York: Galaxy, 1958.
____, *Mysticism East and West*, New York: MacMillan, 1932.
Overbye, Dennis, *Lonely Hearts of The Cosmos*, San Francisco: Harper Perennial, 1992.
Oyle, Irving, *The Healing Mind*, Millbrae: Celestial Arts, 1975.
____, *The New American Medicine Show*, Santa Cruz: Unity, 1979.
____, *Time, Space and the Mind*, Millbrae: Celestial Arts, 1976.
Pearce, Joseph Chilton, *The Bond of Power*, New York: Dutton, 1981.
Peck, M. Scott, *The Different Drum*, New York: Simon & Schuster, 1987.
____, *People of the Lie*, New York: Simon & Schuster, 1983.
____, *The Road Less Traveled*, New York: Simon & Schuster, 1978.
Pelletier, Kenneth, *Mind as Healer, Mind as Slayer*, New York: Delta, 1977.
____, *Towards a Science of Consciousness*, New York: Delta, 1977.
Polkinghorne, John, *Science and Creation*, Boston: New Science Library, 1989.

Po-Tuan, Chang, *The Inner Teachings of Taoism*, Boston: Shambhala, 1986.

Prabhavananda, Swami, and Christopher Isherwood (translators), *Bhagavad-Gita*, New York: Mentor, 1944.

Progoff, Ira, *At A Journal Workshop*, New York: Dialogue House, 1975.

_____, *The Practice of Process Meditation*, New York: Dialogue House, 1980.

Rainer, Tristine, *The New Diary*, Los Angeles: Tarcher, 1978.

Rama, Swami, *Choosing A Path*, Honesdale: Himalayan, 1982.

_____, *Lectures on Yoga*, Honesdale: Himalayan, 1979.

Reps, Paul, *Zen Flesh, Zen Bones*, New York: Anchor, 1961.

Revised Standard Version, *The Bible*, New York: Nelson, 1952.

Roberts, Bernadette, *The Experience of No-Self*, Boulder: Shambhala, 1984.

_____, *The Path of No Self*, Boulder: Shambhala, 1985.

Roberts, Elizabeth and Elias Amidon, *Earth Prayers*, San Francisco: HarperCollins, 1991.

Russell, Peter, *The Global Brain*, Los Angeles: Tarcher, 1983.

Sahtouris, Elisabet, *Gaia: The Human Journey From Chaos to Cosmos*, New York: Pocketbooks, 1989.

Satprem, Sri, *Aurobindo, or The Adventure of Consciousness*, New York: Inst. Evolutionary, 1984.

Schleiermacher, Friedrich, *Speeches*, New York: Harper, 1958.

Schumacher, E.F., *A Guide for The Perplexed*, New York: Harper & Row, 1977.

Schloegl, Irmgard, *The Wisdom of The Zen Masters*, New York: New Directions, 1976.

Schuon, Frithjof, *The Transcendent Unity of Religions*, Wheaton: Quest, 1984.

Shah, Idries, *Nasrudin*, New York: Dutton, 1971.

_____, *The Sufis*, Garden City: Doubleday, 1964.

Sheldrake, Rupert, *A New Science of Life*, Los Angeles, Tarcher, 1981.

Slater, Philip, *The Wayward Gate*, Boston: Beacon, 1977.

Smith, Adam, *Powers of Mind*, New York: Ballantine, 1976.

Smith, Bradford, *Meditation: The Inward Art*, Philadelphia: Lippincott, 1963.

Smith, D. Howard, *The Wisdom of The Taoists*, New York: New Directions, 1980.

Smith, E. Lester, *Intelligence Came First*, Wheaton: Quest, 1975.

Smith, Huston, *Forgotten Truth*, New York: Harper & Row, 1977.

Spangler, David, *Revelation*, San Francisco: Rainbow Bridge, 1976.

Starhawk, *Dreaming The Dark*, Boston: Beacon, 1982.

_____, *The Spiral Dance*, San Francisco: Harper & Row, 1979.

_____, *Truth or Dare*, New York: Harper & Row, 1987.

Steindl-Rast, David, *Gratefulness, The Heart of Prayer*, Ramsey: Paulist, 1984.

____, *A Listening Heart*, New York: Crossroads, 1983.

Steltenkamp, Michael F., *The Sacred Vision*, Boston: Shambhala, 1988.

Strauch, Ralph, *The Reality Illusion*, Wheaton: Quest, 1983.

Suzuki, D.T., *An Introduction to Zen Buddhism*, New York: Grove, 1964.

____, *Mysticism: Christian and Buddhist*, New York: Harper, 1957.

____, *Zen Mind, Beginner's Mind*, New York: Weatherhill, 1970.

Swimme, Barry, *The Universe Is A Green Dragon*, Santa Fe: Bear, 1984.

Tagore, Rabindranath, *Collected Poems and Plays*, New York: MacMillan, 1964.

____, *The Religion of Man*, New York: MacMillan, 1931.

Talbot, Michael, *Mysticism and The New Physics*, New York: Bantam, 1980.

____, *The Holographic Universe*, New York: HarperCollins, 1991.

Targ, Russel, and Harold Puthoff, *Mind-Reach*, New York: Delta, 1977.

Taylor, Jeremy, *Dream Work*, New York: Paulist, 1983.

Thompson, William Irwin, *Darkness and Scattered Light*, Garden City: Anchor, 1978.

Trefil, James, *The Dark Side of the Universe*, New York: Doubleday, 1988.

Turnbull, Colin, *The Human Cycle*, New York: Simon & Schuster, 1983.

Underhill, Evelyn, *Mysticism*, New York: Meridian, 1955.

____, *Practical Mysticism*, New York: Dutton, 1915.

Watson, Lyall, *Supernature*, Garden City: Doubleday, 1973.

Watts, Alan, *Beyond Theology*, New York: Vintage, 1973.

____, *Om—Creative Meditations*, Millbrae: Celestial Arts, 1980.

____, *The Supreme Identity*, New York: Vintage, 1972.

____, *Tao: The Watercourse Way*, New York: Pantheon, 1975.

____, *Way of Zen*, New York: Pantheon, 1957.

Watzlawick, Paul, *How Real Is Real?*, New York: Vintage, 1976.

____, *Change*, New York: Norton, 1974.

____, *The Invented Reality*, New York: Norton, 1984.

Weil, Simone, *Waiting for God*, New York: Harper & Row, 1973.

Welch, Holmes, *Taoism—The Parting of The Way*, Boston: Beacon, 1957.

White, John, *What Is Enlightenment?*, Los Angeles: Tarcher, 1984.

____, *The Meeting of Science and Spirit*, New York: Paragon House, 1990.

Wilber, Ken, *The Atman Project*, Wheaton: Quest, 1980.

____, *No Boundary*, Los Angeles: Center, 1979.

____, *Quantam Questions*, Boulder: Shambhala, 1984.

____, *The Spectrum of Consciousness*, Wheaton: Quest, 1977.

Woods, Richard, *Understanding Mysticism*, Garden City: Doubleday, 1980.

Wright, Sam, *Koviashuvik: A Time and Place of Joy*, San Francisco: Sierra Club Books, 1989.

Yutang, Lin, *The Wisdom of China and India,* New York: Modern Library, 1942.

Zukav, Gary, *The Dancing Wu Li Masters,* New York: Morrow, 1979.

Index